1.00

D0982435

STORY
of
STORIES

STORY *of* STORIES

A Guided Tour
from Genesis to Revelation

KAREN LEE-THORP

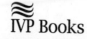
IVP Books

An imprint of InterVarsity Press
Downers Grove, Illinois

InterVarsity Press
P.O. Box 1400, Downers Grove, IL 60515-1426

InterVarsity Press® is the book-publishing division of InterVarsity Christian Fellowship/USA®, a movement of
students and faculty active on campus at hundreds of universities, colleges and schools of nursing in the United
States of America, and a member movement of the International Fellowship of Evangelical Students.

All Scripture quotations, unless otherwise indicated, are taken from THE HOLY BIBLE, NEW
INTERNATIONAL VERSION®, NIV® Copyright © 1973, 1978, 1984, 2011 by Biblica, Inc.™ Used by
permission. All rights reserved worldwide. With permission, Old Testament references to "the LORD" have been
replaced with "Yahweh."

Cover design: Cindy Kiple
Images: Welsh Bible title page: Bridgeman Art Library
        Starfield: Pleio/iStockphoto

Interior design: Beth Hagenberg

ISBN 978-1-62490-523-0

Printed in the United States of America

CONTENTS

INTRODUCTION

Why I Want to
Tell You This Story

*A*t the age of twenty-five I was hit by a truck. A large industrial truck loaded with gravel. The driver hit my little car because of someone else's error, and the results for me included permanent injuries and brain damage. Two years after that accident, when I was still coming to grips with how those few minutes were changing my life, I began to write this book.

It's not the story of my hardships, nor the story of how I've grown amid hardships, as important as that tale is (to me, anyway). Instead it's the vast story of God at work in the world, the Lover who has pursued his wayward beloved across millennia despite hardships I can scarcely imagine. I tell this story because I don't think I'm the only person who needs to know that I'm part of a tale much bigger than the one that started on my birthday. My life is not an indie film in which I'm the director and the star. I'm a small but valued player in an epic masterpiece in which God is the Director and the Star. So are you.

God has an annoying habit of not telling me why my scenes go the way they do. However, he has given me an overview of the whole story and has explained some of the past scenes. The Bible is the definitive account of how God's epic unfolded from the creation of the world through about A.D. 100. It closes with a glimpse of the glorious finale that has not yet taken place. It's a huge help when I have to decide how to play a scene, or when I'm frustrated and want to quit. It's also a ripping good yarn.

Yet lots and lots of people who revere the Bible don't get around to reading more than a few famous lines here and there. They don't know what to do with stories and poetry and letters written twenty or thirty centuries ago in Hebrew or Greek. I was trained how to read something written long ago and hear it speaking afresh to my generation, how to research an ancient culture to fill in the background the original readers already knew. I've written several dozen study guides on books of the Bible, so my head is deep into the ancient world. But not everyone has the time or aptitude for that. I've read the Bible with heroin addicts and engineers, survivors of child sexual abuse and parents with toddlers. All of these people have needed to know that God is not an abstract doctrine, but a Person, and that they are part of a great story that is good and beautiful and true.

So I decided to write a guided tour of the great story that doesn't make it seem boring. *Story of Stories* isn't fiction—I haven't invented any scenes, and if you see dialogue in quotation marks, it's word-for-word from the New International Version (NIV) translation of the Bible. Yet I've tried to show how gripping, sometimes funny, sometimes heartbreaking the story is if you know what's going on. I've included background information that's not found in the Bible itself but that will help you understand what's happening and why.

Did I mention funny? It turns out that God has a sense of humor, especially about the gap between what people think they know and what they really know. If you don't like irony, this may not be the book for you. After all, I'm the person God hit with a truck.

There are many different ways to use this book. You can read *Story of Stories* cover to cover like a novel, or you can sample what it says about a specific section or book of the Bible. You may wish to read a chapter, or part of a chapter, each day in your personal or family devotions. If you're just about to read through a particular part of the Bible, you might find it helpful to get the background here first. The table of contents in the front and the index in the back can help you find particular passages.

For the past five hundred years or so, passages in the Bible have been referenced by book, chapter and verse. The name of the book comes first, then the chapter number(s) and then, after a colon (:), the verse number(s), if any. For example, Genesis 1–3 means the first three chapters of the book of Genesis. Genesis 1:1 means the book of Genesis, chapter one, verse one. In books with only one chapter, just the verse number is used, for example, Obadiah 12. The chapter and verse divisions were added many centuries after the Bible was written, and they often don't provide an accurate indication of the natural divisions within the biblical books. However, they do help us find particular places in the Bible easily, so I use them throughout this volume.

I have left out many, many details from the story—not because they're unimportant, but for several reasons. First, I want to give you the big picture. Second, I want to give the most help with the parts of the story that are hardest for readers today. It kills me to cover Jesus' Galilean ministry with his disciples in one chapter, but for readers today the Gospels are much easier than, say, the Prophets.

Third, this is not a scholarly reference book. It is, however, thoroughly researched. The technical work and theological reflections of many scholars—more than could possibly be listed—have gone into it. Biblical scholars differ on many important points of interpretation and continue to debate them actively. But every position taken in this book has significant support within these scholars' debates, particularly among those who honor the Bible as the inspired and authoritative Word of God.

There are plenty of good reference texts available, but they often deal with debates that leave ordinary readers in the dust. So I've chosen to tell the story of God reaching down to mortals—which is truly the story of all stories—as if we were talking in my living room, yet with the deepest respect for God and his Book. I hope this telling motivates you to read the Bible itself with a sense of its flow, its drama and, above all, its main character, who invites you to join him in scenes that I look forward to hearing retold at the end of days.

Karen Lee-Thorp

Part One

A Promise of Deliverance

1

BEGINNINGS

Genesis 1–3

*I*nside most of us is a nagging feeling that things aren't going the way they were meant to go. We're not the people we were meant to be. And there's more to life than meets the eye. So we start asking questions:

What's going on?

Is there any point to this exercise?

Does anybody care?

How did we get into this mess, anyway?

Genesis is a Greek word meaning "beginning." The book of Genesis is the first book of the Bible, so it is (not surprisingly) about beginnings—of the earth, the human race, marriage, languages—and also of how we got into this mess. It launches the tale of the making, breaking and restoring of the friendship between God and humans.

"God" is the name Genesis uses in its first sentence to name a Being with personality and aliveness, a Being who is communicating to us from beyond our world. Genesis doesn't argue for this Being's existence; it assumes it. After all, according to tradition the book was written by a man named

> *The book of Genesis . . . launches the tale of the making, breaking and restoring of the friendship between God and humans.*

Moses who had an intimate friendship with this God. To the writer of Genesis, God's existence seemed obvious.

The events of Genesis occurred long before Moses was born. Many of them were passed down orally from generation to generation among his people, the Hebrews. Some were probably written family records. And Moses got the straight story from God when God assigned him to write the book. Imagine penning a book by discussing the material with a Being you could not see but whose presence and personality you were constantly aware of. To Moses, this was not spooky stuff—God was his Boss and Comrade.

Moses was the leader of a motley rabble of fugitive slaves who wanted to know just what we want to know: How did we get into this situation? What's going on? And who is this God? So Moses wrote, "In the beginning . . . "

CREATION

"In the beginning God created the heavens and the earth" (Genesis 1:1). God has always existed. He is perfectly, exuberantly content in himself, but he enjoys expressing his personality in making things. He is not a force like electricity, or a concept, but a Being with character and creativity and life. In fact, he is the very essence of those things.

Moses wrote in Hebrew, and in Genesis his word for God is *Elohim*. In Hebrew, *el* means "god" and *elohim* means "gods." But God is one God, not a group of distinct gods. Moses used the plural to convey God's majesty, his endless potential. It's like spelling his name with capitals.

God's way of creating is to speak things into existence. His word is so powerful that he simply uttered, "Light!" and the whole spectrum of electromagnetic energy with all its intricate properties came into being.

God took six "days" to create the physical universe. (It's unclear what a "day" was before the earth rotated and revolved around the sun.) He started with a formless, empty void. On the first three days he gave form to what was formless by organizing atoms into energy and matter, air and water and land. On the second three days he filled what was empty: the universe with stars, moons and planets; the skies and seas with birds and fish; and the earth with animals and a special creature called *adam* in Hebrew.

The word *adam* has traditionally been translated as "man," but today many people feel this term excludes women. That's not the intention here. Genesis 1 is clear that "man" has two sexes, male and female, and together they reflect the glory of their Creator. We'll use "man" here so that later in the biblical story, when we get to the important phrase "Son of Man," you can hear the story echoing Genesis.

To manage all of his earthly creation, God made this creature called "man" in his own image. Not in his physical image (God isn't a material being), but with abilities to reason, to create, to make moral choices and to love. Genesis says that God made man "from the dust of the ground" (the Hebrew word *adam* is related to the word for "ground," *adamah*), but this dust creature was something with which God could relate person to person. Man would be his friend and the resident manager of his earth.

God looked at the ordered and life-filled world he had made, and he pronounced it "very good" (Genesis 1:31). It was so splendid that he took another whole day and rested to enjoy it. (God is a dedicated artist, but he's no workaholic.)

Focus on Man

Genesis describes the creation from the perspective of our earth. The rest of the universe is not the point of the story, even though it is just as precious to its Creator. Likewise, after Genesis 1, the Bible zeros in on humans and pays little attention to the rest of the earth. Geology and botany are very important to the God who invented rocks and plants, but they are not what the Bible is about.

The invention of man was a risk, the consequences of which the all-knowing God could already foresee. Sun, ocean, tree and fish wouldn't give God any trouble; they would do what he desired them to do according to the laws he had built into them. But a creature free to choose to obey and love could equally choose to betray and reject. And God had given that creature authority over the whole earthly creation. The one who uttered neutrons into existence was yielding much control over his masterpiece and exposing himself to the pain of jilted love. Pain! He could have existed into eternity without pain, but he risked anguish in order to have something outside himself to love that could love him back.

This was the genius of God's invention. He had previously made creatures who were pure spirit: they could reason, make moral choices and perceive qualities in God like his majesty. "Holy, holy, holy!" they cried as they worshiped him unceasingly for his greatness and perfection. But could they love? We don't know. Perhaps angels love in a high, clear way, like a galaxy swirling its love for its maker. But perhaps a being needs feelings—even passion—to offer oneself to another vulnerably, to share something of God's love that an angel can never know. God was a passionate, self-giving Being, and his angels were unable to appreciate this side of him. On the other side, animals had feelings but could not reason and make moral choices; their love lacked consciousness and maturity. Man was God's ingenious hybrid—spirit and embodied soul, reason and passion, the finest reflection of himself that God could produce.

> *A creature free to choose to obey and love could equally choose to betray and reject.*

So God put his first man in a garden where a mighty river and warm mist provided water for a lush array of fruit trees. To practice his Godlike qualities of creativity and authority, Adam (the first individual had the same name as the whole race) was to begin with gardening and naming the animals. To practice his ability to make moral choices, he received one restriction, so that he could choose whether to obey his Parent. In the middle of the garden grew "the tree of life" and "the tree of the knowledge of good and evil." Adam could eat from any tree except the tree of the knowledge of good and evil. Of the tree of life God said nothing.

When Genesis focuses on man, it uses a personal name for Elohim, YHWH. English Bibles render this word as "the LORD" with capital letters, or as "Jehovah" or "Yahweh." Modern scholars think "Yahweh" is the most probable original pronunciation, so we will use it (substituting "Yahweh" for "the LORD" in Scripture quotes). Yahweh had made Adam need relationship the way he needed food and water. Most of all he needed relationship with Yahweh, but he also needed it with someone physical like himself. None of the animals would suffice because they didn't bear Yahweh's image. Adam needed a partner who could share his noble work. So Yahweh took part of Adam and made a second dust creature like him. The two became man and woman, husband and wife. He would call her Eve, because she would become "the mother of all the living" (the name Eve is similar to the Hebrew word for "life"). They were completely open to each other, emotionally and physically. They were an inseparable unity: "one flesh." Adam may have been the leader, but there was no dominating or manipulating.

TREASON

Earth and its inhabitants were "very good." All but one—an invader from outside the physical universe, a spirit who camouflaged himself as a snake. He had been the highest of God's angelic servants until he rebelled. According to tradition, his name had been "morning star" (in Latin translation, Lucifer or "light bearer"), but it became Satan ("the adversary") and Abaddon ("the destroyer"). He simply did not care to spend eternity loving and acknowledging his dependence on his Creator. He considered that boring and beneath him. So he declared his independence and set up a rival kingdom.

That meant war. A number of spirit beings joined with the rebel while the rest fought for God. When his direct attack failed, Satan resolved to strike at God indirectly by corrupting his physical creation. He would smash the hopes of this foolish God who tied his own hands by giving choice to dust creatures. He would claim earth for his own kingdom, reduce its inhabitants to slavery and make them an eternal grief to their spurned Creator. (Note that Satan's so-called freedom made others slaves.)

Most of this information is inferred from comments scattered later in the Bible (such as Isaiah 14:12-15; Ezekiel 28:11-19; Revelation 12:1-9). In Genesis we see only the snake appearing to the woman as one of her harmless and loyal subjects. She was queen of her garden and feared nothing.

First the serpent politely dropped a question: Did God really ban you from eating fruit from these fine trees? (How unreasonable! Tyrannical!)

No, said the woman, "we may eat fruit from the trees in the garden, but God did say, 'You must not eat fruit from the tree that is in the middle of the garden, and you must not touch it, or you will die.'" Now God had said nothing about touching the tree. Already his instructions and character were blurring in her mind.

Into this tiny crack of doubt the viper thrust a wedge. "You will not certainly die," he declared. (God is a liar!) "For God knows that when you eat from it your eyes will be opened, and you will be like God, knowing good and evil." (God doesn't love you. He wants to keep you in slavery and ignorance. Rebellion is the only rational course to protect yourself.)

Everything the woman knew about God's loving care, his desire for her and Adam to rule the earth, his wisdom and gentleness—all was forgotten as she considered the snake's charges. The fruit's scent and color enticed her senses. And its deeper properties—its capacity to give her wisdom beyond what God had yet seen fit to grant—tantalized something else welling up within her. The serpent knew its name, though she did not. The name belonged to the knowledge of evil she had not yet tasted. It was pride.

So this woman—who lived in unimaginable luxury as queen of virtually all she surveyed—chose to grab for yet more status and sensual pleasure. Had she waited, would God have given her the sweet fruit with the joy of knowledge in his own time? We can't say, for she elected what the Bible calls sin—falling short of God's best, rejecting his instructions, seeking to take by force what he would give by grace.

> *She elected what the Bible calls sin . . . seeking to take by force what he would give by grace.*

But the snake hadn't won yet. The man was the senior partner in this marriage, and he might still have run to his Lord and begged pardon for his bride. We don't know what might have happened if the man had done that.

Because he didn't. The story tells us that Eve was deceived (maybe Adam didn't explain Yahweh's command to her properly), but Adam made a clear-eyed choice. Understanding the implications, he chose pride and sensuality over patience and trust. And when both of them had eaten the fruit, they understood evil from the inside. They felt guilty, exposed, shameful. They tried to cover their naked bodies. When Yahweh came to enjoy their company, what had before been delight was now sheer terror. Something in their minds had been twisted so that their perceptions of reality were distorted. They were paranoid—their beloved Friend seemed a grim enemy. They hid.

Yahweh knew what had happened. But in order to give every chance for a change of heart, he called out from a distance, "Where are you?" Are there any shreds of sanity that I can reach?

Instead of a gentle probe, the deluded man heard a harsh demand. Instead of crying out for forgiveness, he made excuses and blamed the woman—"the woman you put here with me"—for the trouble. She blamed the snake. The diagnosis was clear: acute paranoid psychosis. No signs of remission.

Heaven wept. The ache of rejection touched the Infinite One, and he embraced it. A spurned Lover, a betrayed Parent, he could have battered these rebels back into submission.

But Yahweh had foreseen this tragedy long before he formed these choosing creatures. He already had a plan to deal with their loss of mental and moral health, a plan that would astonish not only the fallen spirits who thought him mad, but also the loyal ones who knew only the cool obedience of pure reason. When God wooed these renegades back with love instead of power, the cosmos would marvel and understand.

Yahweh's first step was to curse the snake. It would eat dust for the rest of its existence—a hint of degradation, but also an ominous sign because man was made of dust. Furthermore, the battle for the earth was not over. There would be permanent war between the descendants of the woman who served Yahweh and the descendants of the

> *When God wooed these renegades back with love instead of power, the cosmos would marvel and understand.*

serpent who served him. And one day a descendant of this woman would finally crush the snake, even though he would be bitten in the contest.

Next Yahweh turned to the woman. The price of choosing pride and delusion was the warping of womanhood: childbearing would be agony and marital partnership would degenerate into lust, futile craving for intimacy and fearful domination.

The man's cost was a curse on his beloved earth. He would still have the dignity of tending it, but his labor would be bitter toil ending in the futility of death and dust.

There was no cruelty in these judgments. The joys of marriage and childbearing and fruitful labor were not wholly taken away, and Yahweh was merely declaring the natural consequences of the humans' choice. He had warned that stealing the fruit would bring death, and so it had: moral death, the death of friendship with God and intimacy between man and wife, the death of clear thinking and feeling—with a scent of corruption permeating every aspect of life.

Physical death would come too. Yahweh banished the humans from the garden so that they would not also steal from the tree of life. For as much as it grieved him to see his beloved ones decay and die, it would be far worse for them to live forever physically in moral and relational death. He planned to use physical death to restore real life.

As a sign of this, he killed an animal for the first time and used its skin to clothe his humans. Innocent blood was shed to cover their shame. It would not be the last time.

Questions for Reflection and Discussion

1. Yahweh is the main character of this story. What can we learn about him from this beginning? How would you describe him?

2. Where do you see in your own life, or the lives of those around you, these aspects of humanness:
   - We are made by someone else, not self-made.
   - We are made in God's image.

- We have the inclination to take by force what God would give by grace.
- We hide from God.
- We need relationships, but we handle them badly.
- Our labor is often bitter toil, ending in dust.

3. As bad as things are at the end of Genesis 3, there is a glimmer of hope: a promise. What is that promise?

2

THE SPREAD
OF CORRUPTION

Genesis 5–11

*I*n one day Adam and Eve fell from being lords of a garden paradise to being subsistence farmers struggling to eke out a crop using stone tools and sweat. They could no longer chat with Yahweh familiarly but had to learn formal rites through which to worship him. They were helpless to shake off the serpentine smog that had infected their minds, hearts and wills. Their one hope was the promise that a child of Eve would break the viper's corrupting power.

That promise was on the snake-spirit's mind, too, no doubt. When Eve bore her first two sons, he conceived a plan to foil God's intent. He easily seduced the older son, Cain, into pride, jealousy of his brother's favor with God and eventually murder. That got rid of the younger son, who might have become the devil's foe.

Yahweh might have killed Cain for his crime, but he didn't. In mercy he only banished Cain from his presence and predicted that he would pass his life as a restless, dissatisfied wanderer. Yahweh even marked Cain in some way to protect him from vengeance by any of Adam's future children. Cain married someone (a sister?) and had children, and his children had children. But it was always like father, like son. Cain's great-great-great-grandson was Lamech, a wanton prince who boasted that he would kill a man even for injuring him. He raised some ingenious sons dedicated to mastering nature and raising a civilization. (One son invented nomadic shepherding, a second musical instruments and a third metalsmithing.) They were making it without God and proud of it. Fortunately, Cain was not the only son of Adam left.

Adam fathered a herd of children, but the Bible focuses on just one— Seth. Seth's descendants were a bit better than Cain's; they did their best to humbly acknowledge their dependence on God. But none became the promised Deliverer. Each one fell in the end to death. The one exception, Enoch, lived such an exemplary life of love for God that he was taken to God without dying. It was a whisper of hope in a weary age.

For the serpent was still at work behind the scenes. The Bible doesn't mention him, but his fingerprints are all over the data. The line of Seth was pure; these were the true sons of the woman. But the line of Cain became more and more a viper's brood with every generation. What if the two were blended? When you mix water and poison, which overcomes the other? If the only pure line of humans were tainted, then perhaps the Deliverer could never be born. Snakish reasoning.

By this time the devil knew that even the noble sons of Seth were vulnerable to sexual seduction, and the brazen daughters of Cain knew how to seduce. The Bible says with its usual understatement, "The sons of God saw that the daughters of humans were beautiful, and they married any of them they chose" (Genesis 6:2). Thus the line in which the character of God still shone mixed with the one whose traits were mere debased humanness. The result was a race whom people considered "heroes . . . men of renown," but whom God named the Nephilim, "the fallen ones."

He mourned. "Yahweh saw how great the wickedness of the human race had become on the earth, and that every inclination of the thoughts of the human heart was only evil all the time" (Genesis 6:5). Pride, lust, violence, exploitation—it was disgusting. Yahweh decided to wipe out the human race. (Did the devil chuckle when he heard this?)

The Flood

But Satan hadn't won yet. There remained one descendant of the pure line of Seth. Noah was not the promised Deliverer, but he did honor

Yahweh and try to live his way as much as possible.

He probably prayed to Yahweh regularly for guidance, and one day he got more than he bargained for. Yahweh informed Noah that he planned to destroy all human and animal life on the earth with a massive flood. When Noah recovered from the shock, Yahweh gave him detailed instructions for building a wooden ship the size of an ocean liner. He was to bring two of every kind of animal (plus extras of certain species) with him and his family into the vessel so that the earth could be repopulated afterward.

In a landlocked region hundreds of miles from the sea, Noah built his ocean vessel. His wife must have spent weeks trying not to notice the neighbors whispering. Imagine pairs of animals beginning to line up in your backyard. Then hauling them and their fodder into the dark wooden box shaped alarmingly like a casket. These people had some gutsy trust in their God. It was vindicated when the rain began to fall and fall and fall.

For forty days eight humans and a lot of animals listened to rain pelt the ceiling of their ship. For another 110 days they floated aimlessly. Maybe they wondered as the months passed whether God had forgotten them, "but God remembered" (Genesis 8:1).

The waters receded, and at last the ship landed on a mountaintop in what is now Turkey. Seven months later the waters were low enough for the whole crowd to emerge into the sunlight. After more than a year in a floating box, solid ground must have felt like heaven.

THE RAINBOW COVENANT

Upon landing, almost the first thing Noah did was to sacrifice some of the extra animals as a gesture of thanks to Yahweh. It seems like a grisly thing to do, but Yahweh had commanded the practice to sear a lesson into his people's minds: Human selfishness is ugly. Not only is it treason against the rightful King, but it smashes every relationship and stains the whole creation. It therefore merits the death penalty, and somebody has to pay the price. In his mercy, Yahweh accepted the blood of animals in exchange for that of humans. It was not a permanent solution.

In response to Noah's obedience, Yahweh made a covenant with him in the sunlight of a freshly scrubbed world never again to deal with human evil through annihilation. A covenant is an agreement between two parties: a marriage, a business contract, a political treaty, a friendship pact. Many covenants are two-sided agreements between equals. But the Bible records a series of covenants that God freely bestowed on people as acts of love and grace. These covenants tied God and people together like a marriage bond, a legal adoption into a family or a king's agreement to rule a group of people with justice. The covenants were solemnly sealed with legal ceremonies.

The covenant Yahweh made with Noah was his first with a member of the human race. The sign of his commitment never to destroy the earth again was light refracting through rain clouds into the full spectrum of the first rainbow. Sheer force had failed to achieve Yahweh's goal: freely chosen love from his people. He had a better plan.

Furthermore, Yahweh granted humans the right to eat meat (before this they presumably ate little or no meat) as long as they didn't drink blood. To humans blood symbolized the mysterious power of life and they had devised

> *Sheer force had failed to achieve Yahweh's goal: freely chosen love from his people. He had a better plan.*

magical rituals of drinking blood to try to preserve or increase their life force. However, life was Yahweh's gift, and it was rebellion for people to try to take it against God's will. Magic was the epitome of Adam's sin: humans' attempt to control power so they need not depend on Yahweh's generosity.

THE NATIONS

Yahweh sent the humans and animals off to repopulate the earth. It was just as well that he had sworn not to engulf the world again, for it didn't take long for human perversity to reassert itself. Noah grew grapes and got drunk on wine. His youngest son, Ham, invited his brothers to mock the sot lying unconscious and mostly naked in his tent. Noah was livid when he awoke, and in his rage he prophesied the fates of all his descendants.

He cursed the line of Ham's son Canaan to be the slaves of his other sons' offspring. The Canaanites became a wicked Caucasian people who lived in Palestine. (We'll see what happened to them in chapter 9.) The rest of Ham's descendants filled southwestern Asia and northeastern Africa. God chose not to include them in their father's curse. One of them, Nimrod, founded the first "kingdom"—a state in which someone ruled not just a clan but a group of unrelated people—in Mesopotamia (modern Iraq). He did this by being the first to conquer subjects by force of arms. Nimrod was the first military dictator.

Unlike Ham, Noah's son Shem loved Yahweh. To him Noah passed on the ancient hope of fathering the Deliverer. To his third son, Japheth, Noah prophesied that his territory would be great and that one day his offspring would share Shem's blessing of being God's chosen ones. The Japhethites became Europeans and Asians. The Shemites became the people we call Semitic: Arabs, some Mesopotamians and Jews.

Babel

The descendants of Shem, Ham and Japheth bred prolifically. By 4000 B.C. (archaeologists tell us) there were a lot of little farming communities with stone-walled cities and rock-hewn wells. Many communities developed their own cults and dedicated themselves to their cultic gods. In rituals timed to the cycle of seasons, the people worshiped gods of rain, sun and fertility. The community's chief was usually its priest.

Eventually communities began to unite under one cult with one priest-king and one temple. The cult ran the kingdom. Those early religious states invented arithmetic to record economic transactions and astrological observations, and they invented writing for legends, songs, poems, laws and ethics.

Naturally, the descendants of Noah all spoke the same language. This made the gathering of communities into kingdoms easier. The people of Nimrod's kingdom believed they could control human destiny by reading the movement of the stars. To this end they invented the zodiac and horoscope. Their gods were the sun, moon and the five planets known to them. They decided to build an immense temple-tower as a staircase from earth to the heavens.

On the same site we can still see the ruins of a tower called Birs Nimroud, perhaps a later attempted reconstruction. The base was built of mud bricks and tar in seven stages, like a staircase-hill. Each stage was painted a color that corresponded to one of the gods—black for Saturn, orange for Jupiter and so on. On top was a tower painted with the signs of the zodiac, in which the priests sought to reach the heavens by magical rites. This tower was 153 feet high and covered nearly four acres.

The goal of the enormous tower was to win fame for its builders. They hated the idea that one day they would die and be forgotten, so they assuaged their wounded pride by striving for an immortal reputation (Genesis 11:4).

Now, Yahweh intended to one day unite all humankind in love of each other and of him. But here they were uniting in honor of human pride and false gods (behind whom he saw spirit beings allied with Satan). Through their star magic, aided by their demon gods, they hoped to wrest control of human destiny from Yahweh. This was clearly another plan of that snake to rule the world through evil people.

Yahweh had no intention of allowing a united world government on those terms. Unruffled, he simply touched the people's minds so that they could no longer understand each other. That put a stop to this project. The builders had called their city Babel (Babylon), which meant "gateway to a god," but Yahweh punned that it was really *balal* (translated "confused" in Genesis 11:9). A divine chuckle. Then Yahweh scattered the people over the earth. They carried with them their false worship and their pride, but they were no longer powerful enough to hinder Yahweh's plan. It was an intricate strategy that set up his next critical move.

Questions for Reflection and Discussion

1. How might each of these situations have derailed the promise of the Deliverer?

   - The tension between Cain and his brother
   - The corruption in the time of Noah
   - The attempt to build the Tower of Babel

3

GOD CHOOSES
A FAMILY

Genesis 11:10–50:26

As Noah predicted, the line of Shem was the focus of Yahweh's plan. Generations passed into centuries, wars flared here and there, the Babel debacle was dealt with, and inconspicuously a Shemite named Terah fathered three sons: Abram, Nahor and Haran.

Terah was a herdsman near the prosperous and sophisticated city of Ur. It was a splendid site in Terah's youth, until a horde of barbarians called Guti conquered the region. They squandered Ur's wealth, let commerce and culture decline and exploited the local population. Still, Terah managed to raise his three sons and get all of them married.

But eventually Terah decided he'd had enough of Ur and the Guti. (See map, page 348.) So he set off with his family for the land of Canaan, a thousand miles away. However, after covering six hundred miles, Terah called a halt in the town of Haran. Perhaps he'd heard that beyond Haran travel was a thirsty, risky business, and both the customs and climate of Canaan would be hard for an old man to adjust to. Haran, though, was more or less like Ur. Both towns were watered by the Euphrates River so they didn't have to worry about rainfall, and in both towns the people worshiped the moon god Nannar and other astral deities. Terah's family were probably moon worshipers as well. But there was also a family memory of a god named Yahweh.

Back in Ur, before the family set out for Canaan, Abram had had a strange encounter with Yahweh. Was it a dream? A vision? An audible voice? It was a sevenfold promise out of the blue:

- "I will make you into a great nation."

- "I will bless you."

- "I will make your name great."

- "You will be a blessing [to others]."

- "I will bless those who bless you."

- "Whoever curses you I will curse."

- "All peoples on earth will be blessed through you." (Genesis 12:2-3)

All peoples. Even now, as Yahweh focused on a single family, he had all earth's families on his heart. Most of them, from Peru to China, had forgotten he existed and went on with their lives as though no world-shattering promise had come to a herdsman in Iraq. But the snake knew. From this one would come the son of Eve.

Greatness! Fame! Protection! And all Yahweh told Abram to do (at this point) was go to Canaan.

To Canaan

Abram didn't actually manage to obey this instruction until Terah had died in Haran. By that time Abram was seventy-five years old—but better late than never.

So after burying Terah, Abram set out on the four-hundred-mile trek. With him went his wife, Sarai, his nephew Lot and all of the animals and hired or purchased workers Terah had acquired in Haran. They would have had to find a caravan driver who knew the ropes, for between Haran and Egypt water was available only at closely guarded wells and springs. The driver had to know where those wells were, what route would assure that the animals could reach a well every evening, and how to negotiate payment for the water according to the local customs. At fifteen miles a day on foot, the trip would have taken about a month.

Eventually the family arrived at Shechem in the very center of Canaan. From one of the two hills nearby, Abram could have looked over the whole country. There Yahweh appeared to him and added an eighth promise: "To your offspring I will give this land" (Genesis 12:7). This must have been the most staggering promise yet from Abram's point of view, especially since the land was already teeming with thousands of Canaanites.

And the Canaanites were a proud and unruly bunch. Each city was independent, and the communities constantly feuded among themselves over land and trading rights. Strangers planning to settle down among them were not always safe. So Abram led his caravan of family, servants, retainers, sheep, goats and donkeys south to the rugged land near the semi-desert Negev. This region sufficed for grazing but not for growing crops, so only a few herdsmen used it. Their life included watching for lions, jackals and bears, calling wandering sheep, carrying young lambs and kids, milking and shearing, mending tents and searching endlessly for grass and water.

FAITH AND OBEDIENCE

Yahweh's great plan focused on a ragged nomad in the middle of nowhere. Not even an especially honest nomad: early on Abram fled Canaan during a drought and actually told his wife to say she was his sister so that Egypt's ruler wouldn't kill him to take her for his harem. And anyway, Abram reasoned, it wasn't exactly a lie—Sarai was his half-sister.

But Abram was strong raw material: perhaps he was fed up with the ritualized appeasement of vague and arbitrary gods, and was ready for a forthright give-and-take with a God with moral fiber. With a little coaching he could become the progenitor of a prime family through which he would bless the nations.

So Abram lived a hundred years after he left Haran, and Yahweh spent the first forty leading him through a course designed to teach him one basic lesson: Trust and obey me, no matter what the situation looks like. The course went like this. On the one hand, Yahweh repeatedly got Abram out of messes and turned everything he touched to gold. But on the other hand he kept dangling that promise before Abram's nose— "Your offspring will be countless and will possess this land"—and never so much as let Sarai get pregnant or allowed Abram to own a bucketful of real estate. Three decades of this drove Abram crazy. But when he tried to handle matters himself by seeking a surrogate mother in Sarai's handmaid, he only ended up with a domestic nightmare. Slowly he learned that the only thing worse than waiting on Yahweh was not waiting on Yahweh. And in his better moments, even though he ranted about the raw deal he was getting, Abram was convinced deep down that he could trust Yahweh. The evidence of his Friend's character outweighed that of the laws of nature. After all, who made the laws? This quality of faith was what Yahweh was striving for, the one criterion for the kind of friendship he longed to have with his human inventions.

So Yahweh let Abram and Sarai endure thirty years of silence with only rare promises to hang onto. Why wasn't he quicker? Because love trusts. Love waits because it knows the beloved's character. Yahweh didn't want to be loved because he always showed up on cue to grant wishes. He wanted to be trusted in the dark.

> *Yahweh didn't want to be loved because he always showed up on cue to grant wishes. He wanted to be trusted in the dark.*

Then suddenly, after a thirteen-year silence, Yahweh appeared in some kind of physical form on Abram's doorstep. Over lunch, as though the two were old buddies who hadn't seen each other for awhile, the visitor announced that Sarai would have a son the following year. He put a letter from his own name (the Hebrew "h") into Abram's and renamed him Abraham, "father of many." He renamed Sarai as Sarah—"princess"—mother of nations and kings. (Renaming was an ancient way of claiming authority over someone as well as a way of declaring something essential about the person.) To Abraham's male descendants he gave an unforgettable mark of loyalty: circumcision. It symbolized a self-cursing oath: "If I am not faithful to Yahweh, may he cut off me and my offspring as I have cut off my foreskin." And to top it all off, Yahweh named the long-promised son Isaac ("he laughs"). Giving sons to ninety-year-old women in answer to thirty years of prayer was Yahweh's idea of a joke—albeit a happy joke for Abraham and Sarah.

FINAL EXAM

Abraham's final test came when Isaac had grown to adolescence. One day Yahweh ordered Abraham to take Isaac to a certain mountain, slit his throat and burn the body. What? But "trust me" had been engraved into Abraham's gut. The one nonnegotiable fact on which he had bet his life was that Yahweh would keep his promises, even if it meant raising Isaac from the dead. So Abraham didn't have to lie awake at night worrying or try to put the ugly order out of his mind. He simply obeyed. When Isaac asked him why they weren't bringing an animal to sacrifice, Abraham was able to reply that God himself would provide it. He didn't know how, but he knew his Friend.

And Isaac trusted his father and his God. He didn't resist when Abraham tied him and laid him on the altar. And at the last instant, when Abraham was about to plunge the knife into his son's throat, an angel stopped him. Abraham had demonstrated that nothing—not even his beloved son or his dreams of greatness—meant more to him than Yahweh. So because they were not idols, he could keep both son and dreams.

Abraham lived long enough to see Isaac married with two sons, but he owned nothing but a field for a family burial plot (for which he paid an exorbitant sum). Yet he died content that just as Yahweh had fulfilled his promise of descendants, so he would someday fulfill his promise of land.

ISAAC

Considering all the agony Abraham went through to get Isaac, you might think the Bible would say a lot about him. But it doesn't. Isaac's role in Yahweh's plan was to raise his sons to be like his dad.

Isaac and Rebekah more or less relived Abraham and Sarah's life. Isaac became extremely rich; Rebekah was barren; Isaac even lied to a powerful prince that Rebekah was his sister for fear that the man might kill him to take her. Where have we heard that one before?

JACOB'S TRANSFORMATION

When at last Rebekah became pregnant with twins, they were rivals from the start. They even came out of the womb competing to see who would be born first. Because the younger appeared grasping the older one's heel, he was named Jacob, "heel-grasper."

Yahweh selected the younger twin to carry on the plan. It was not out of cruelty that Yahweh kept setting aside whole populations and choosing others who were in no way superior. On the contrary, by grooming the chosen branch in each generation (Abraham, then Isaac instead of Ishmael, then Jacob instead of his older brother Esau), Yahweh planned ultimately to bring blessing and deliverance to all the other peoples. To make the point that the non-chosen branches of the family were not forgotten, Genesis always includes short genealogies for them. Yahweh was also underscoring the fact that he had the right to choose whomever he wished and that he thought little of human criteria. He had selected an insignificant nomadic family—not sophisticated aristocrats or philosophers—out of all the families of the earth. He had closed Sarah's womb and then opened it when she was ninety. And now he selected Isaac's younger son when the human custom was to honor the firstborn.

Jacob's name suggested a man who would hold fast to his goals and duties, but it also implied "deceiver," "supplanter." Jacob was the true son and grandson of men who had lied more than once to save their own necks.

So while Abraham's training in trust was a matter of endless waiting, Yahweh had to put Jacob through an obstacle course to fairly beat out of him his bent to use guile to get what Yahweh would give by grace.

Jacob was barely a teenager when he had to flee from home to escape his brother Esau's wrath. He had swindled Esau out of the firstborn's rights (a double portion of the inheritance, leadership of the family and the father's blessing). He was scared as he began hiking northward five hundred miles from Isaac's camp in Beersheba to his relatives' place in Haran. In those days, a person was a fool to travel without a caravan of food, water and companions to discourage robbers. Jacob had neither a map nor a guide. And like most people of his day, he probably believed that his father's God had power only in a particular locality—in this case, Canaan. Jacob had great confidence in his wits, but he was out of his depth.

On Jacob's first night out, Yahweh appeared to him at a spot called

Bethel and repeated the covenant promises he had made to Abraham and Isaac. Land and descendants meant little to teenage Jacob, but he clung to one assurance: "I am with you and will watch over you wherever you go, and I will bring you back to this land. I will not leave you until I have done what I have promised you" (Genesis 28:15). Here was a God who claimed power anywhere in the world! Jacob made a deal with Yahweh: You take care of me and I'll worship you. It was not quite the arrangement Yahweh had with Abraham, but it would do as a beginning.

THE WRESTLER

It took Yahweh twenty years to break Jacob. It took an uncle who was a worse cheater than Jacob was and two wives who treated him like a stud stallion to fuel their childbearing competition. It took twenty years of backbreaking work and endless bickering in his burgeoning tents. He became as rich as his dad and supported two wives, two concubines (slave semi-wives), thirteen children and a lot of servants. He thought he owed his success to his own cleverness, even though Yahweh really deserved the credit. Yet in the end Jacob's uncle was mad enough at his good fortune to seize his family, so he tried to run again.

But this time his uncle caught up with him, and even Jacob could see that only divine intervention, not his own cunning, saved his skin. He also finally faced the fact that running from broken relationships was futile. So although he was heading to Bethel and would pass nowhere near Esau's land southeast of Canaan, Jacob sent a message to his brother that he was returning and wanted to be reconciled.

Jacob spent the night before their meeting alone, having it out with Yahweh. He wasn't so much concerned that Esau was coming with four hundred armed men who might slaughter his family. For the first time, he didn't want something from God, he wanted God. In the night a man appeared to him and wrestled with him until dawn. In the morning, his hip was injured so that he limped, and he had a new name: Israel, "he struggles with God." Like a proud stallion, Jacob had been broken to God's hand over twenty years of wrestling. Though he limped from the struggle, he was transformed. No more "Jacob the deceiver," cunning as a serpent; he was now a true son of the promise.

SIBLING RIVALRY

So Jacob-Israel settled down in Canaan and became a responsible patriarch over a large household and thriving livestock business. Everything was going smoothly except that his twelve sons were a delinquent gang capable of inflicting revenge on a whole town when one citizen raped their sister. Yahweh had slated Jacob's sons to father the twelve tribes of Israel, the bearers of his plan, and they needed more of Yahweh's discipline than Abraham, Isaac and Jacob put together.

To mold the brothers for this role, Yahweh selected for special treatment number eleven, the adolescent Joseph, whose ten older siblings detested him for two reasons. First, he was Jacob's pet. Second, he dreamed about his family bowing down to him as their master. So one day, the ten brothers sold Joseph as a slave to some merchants traveling to Egypt, then went home weeping and telling their father that a wild animal had eaten him.

As Joseph's dreams attested, Yahweh had grand intentions for him, but the road to greatness in Yahweh's service is rarely without its potholes. As a slave Joseph rose to become the household manager for the captain of the Egyptian pharaoh's guard. But the captain's wife became insulted when he resisted her sexual advances, so she accused him of attempted rape. Joseph found himself in Pharaoh's dungeon.

By contrast, consider Joseph's brothers back in Canaan. Reuben, the eldest, was disinherited for seducing one of his dad's concubines. Son number four, Judah, had two of his sons killed by Yahweh for their depravity, but Judah blamed their widow, Tamar. He refused to marry his one remaining son to her, even though custom demanded it, and condemned her to childless widowhood. Desperate, she disguised herself as a prostitute and waited along a road she knew Judah was traveling. He hired her services and in pledge of payment gave her his staff and signature seal. When he got home, he tried to send payment, but no one had ever heard of this prostitute. Three months later, Tamar turned up pregnant, and when she was brought out to be executed for adultery, she practically threw the staff and seal in Judah's face. Ashamed, he took her back into his house and took responsibility for her. She bore twin sons, Perez and Zerah, who became Judah's sole heirs.

While Reuben and Judah dallied, Joseph languished in Pharaoh's jail until word reached Pharaoh that a certain Hebrew rotting in his prison was a master of dream interpretation. In the time it took Yahweh to give Joseph the meaning of Pharaoh's latest dream and a strategy for handling the agricultural disaster it portended, Joseph went from dungeon rat to prime minister.

Seven years later famine hit the whole Middle East. But news spread that Egypt had grain because the prime minister had been stockpiling it. People began to stream from everywhere to buy food.

Jacob dispatched his ten older sons, but inexplicably the prime minister had them jailed as spies. (Joseph had recognized them immediately, but it never dawned on them that this thirty-eight-year-old, clean-shaven Egyptian lord might be the obnoxious teenager they had sold some twenty years earlier.) After three days he released all but one and declared that until they brought to Egypt the youngest brother they claimed to have, brother Simeon would sit in Pharaoh's jail.

The nine were aghast. They knew their God well enough to recognize his hand somewhere in all of this, punishing their cruelty to Joseph. And Jacob was beside himself when they returned without yet another of his sons. He wouldn't hear of sending his youngest, Benjamin, to Egypt. But when the grain ran out and the children began to cry, he gave in. Reuben and Judah pledged their lives if they didn't bring both Simeon and Benjamin home safely.

Upon their return Joseph played some more mind games with them until they were convinced that Yahweh was destroying them for betraying their brother. When it was obvious that all of them had cracked under pressure, Joseph burst into tears and told them the whole story. It took several reassurances before they grasped that he was not about to execute them for their past malice. But Joseph had come to see that although they were responsible for their freely chosen crime, Yahweh had used it to save the whole Middle East from a desolating famine and especially to protect his chosen family from extinction.

Out of gratitude to Joseph, Pharaoh invited his whole family to come and live in some of Egypt's best land. Yahweh told Jacob to go. It so happened that the Egyptians considered herdsmen disgusting, so Pharaoh selected the fertile but out-of-the-way region of Goshen for Jacob's clan to settle in. There would be no temptation to intermingle with the Egyptians and lose their family traditions.

INTO THE FUTURE

On his deathbed, Jacob's mind was on the all-important divine promises. He made Joseph promise to bury him with Abraham and Isaac in Canaan as a sign of faith that the land would one day be theirs. He also pronounced prophetic fatherly blessings on each of his sons, as well as on Joseph's two sons. In these blessings he declared how the family inheritance would be distributed and foresaw what would happen in future centuries as his sons' families became tribes of the great nation God had promised.

First was the matter of the firstborn. Reuben had forfeited the eldest son's rights. His tribe, therefore, would never fulfill its hope of greatness, and Reuben himself would inherit neither the headship of the family nor the double portion of property.

Simeon and Levi, the next two eldest, had instigated the massacre to avenge their raped sister. Therefore, Jacob passed them over for the firstborn's rights and said their tribes would be scattered among their brothers' tribes.

The fourth eldest was Judah. Despite his own failings he had not forfeited the right of headship, so Jacob declared that Judah would be the ruling tribe of Israel "until he to whom it [the scepter of kingship] belongs shall come" (Genesis 49:10). Whatever that meant. Did Jacob and sons think of the son of Eve? Surely the serpent did.

The next six sons received their blessings in their turns—all double-edged, foreseeing both their greatness and their weakness. Then came Joseph, the eldest son of Jacob's favorite wife. To him Jacob bequeathed the firstborn's double portion. He adopted Joseph's two sons, Ephraim and Manasseh, and gave each a full inheritance equal to that of Joseph's brothers. Ironically, Ephraim was the younger of the two, but Jacob said that he would be the greater one. He recognized that Yahweh was giving to Ephraim, with no need for human scheming, what he himself had stolen from Esau.

Joseph ruled in Egypt about another sixty years after Jacob's death, raised his grandchildren and kept his heart on the covenant between his father and God. His last words to his family reassured them that Yahweh would one day bring them home to Canaan to take possession of it. Trusting in that conviction, he asked to be put in a coffin but not buried until the family could return to bury him with his ancestors in their promised home.

∞∞∞

Questions for Reflection and Discussion

1. What do you learn about Yahweh from the way he deals with Abraham and Sarah? With Isaac? With Jacob? With Joseph?

2. How does the story of the promise develop in Genesis 11–50?

3. Tamar plays a key role in the lineage of the promise. What do you think of her? Why?

4

LIBERATION

Exodus 1:1–15:21

*F*or two centuries the family of Jacob-Israel herded sheep and goats in the fertile Nile delta. After the arid pastures of southern Canaan, this was sheep heaven. The flocks were prolific, and so were the humans.

The Egyptians left the filthy Hebrew shepherds alone with their animals and their strange uncivilized customs. In two hundred years the children of Israel picked up very little from the art, literature, religion, science and social life of the culture only miles away. They simply milked their goats, sheared their sheep, clung stubbornly to their one God and multiplied. Soon there were thousands of them.

Meanwhile the Egyptian court forgot about Joseph. The dynasties of the Middle Kingdom were overrun by Hyksos, a Semitic people who regarded their fellow Semites as rivals. And the Egyptian lords who finally rooted the Hyksos out of their country were in no mood to be harboring huge enclaves of Semitic foreigners. After all (reasoned Pharaoh Ahmose, the founder of the eighteenth Egyptian dynasty and the man who finally expelled the Hyksos), if war broke out, these Israelites might side with our enemies and then leave when we are overwhelmed again.

Ahmose was not about to let that happen. And since he wanted to build some fine cities for his glorious new dynasty, he enslaved all the Israelites, appointed slave masters to keep them in line and assigned them to forced labor in his fields and brickworks. But the more the Egyptians drove the Israelites, the more they seemed to breed like rabbits. Exasperated, the pharaoh decreed that all Hebrew boys must be killed at birth.

A Savior Is Born?

But Jochebed, a descendant of Jacob's son Levi, resolved to protect her son from the slave masters. When he was three months old she put him in a basket and floated it in the Nile. Pharaoh's daughter came down to bathe, found the baby and decided to raise him for reasons the Bible doesn't explain. Not even Ahmose could dissuade his daughter, so a Hebrew joined the royal family. The princess named him Moses, which meant "is born" in Egyptian (her father's name meant "[the god] Ah is born") but also happened to sound like the Hebrew for "to draw out."

Moses was raised as an Egyptian noble, studying astronomy and astrology, music, history, literature and the practical wisdom of a sophisticated society. But while on the outside he was a smooth-chinned Egyptian aristocrat, on the inside he became a Hebrew hothead. He would go out to the fields and construction sites to watch his kinsmen and grind his teeth when a slave driver abused one of them.

One day when Moses was about forty, he lost his temper and killed an Egyptian who was brutalizing an Israelite. The next day he saw two Hebrews fighting and intervened. One of the men shot back, "Who made you ruler and judge over us? Are you thinking of killing me as you killed the Egyptian?"

His crime was known! Soon the current pharaoh (probably Thutmose III) was out to arrest and execute him. Moses fled to Midian, in southeastern Sinai. (See map, page 348.) The semi-desert and its tribes of wandering shepherds were a sharp change for a man raised in the luxurious Egyptian court, but Moses was safe from retribution. He married the daughter of a pagan priest and she bore him a son. For forty years he followed his father-in-law's flocks from summer to winter pasture and back again.

The Emissary Commissioned

Meanwhile, Thutmose died and another pharaoh took the throne. The

Israelites began to cry out to their God for freedom. That was what he was waiting for. He had not forgotten his covenant with Abraham, Isaac and Jacob. He had told Abraham that the chosen family would become slaves in a foreign land. The whole thing was a scheme to get the Israelites out of Canaan and off by themselves for a few hundred years. There they could multiply numerically without attracting hostile attention in Canaan. At the same time the Canaanites could become thoroughly depraved and deserving of judgment. And the Israelites could get enough of a taste of bondage to make them sick of authoritarian rule and desperate for a strong and merciful God.

For as long as they were sleek and happy in Goshen, the Israelites were not desperate. They remembered the God of Jacob, but they forgot both his awesome majesty and his desire for the kind of friendship he'd had with Abraham. They rarely, if ever, used his name, Yahweh. He was just their tribal god.

> *The Israelites began to cry out to their God for freedom. That was what he was waiting for. He had not forgotten his covenant with Abraham, Isaac and Jacob.*

That attitude was going to end. Yahweh grieved to put his children through the anguish of bondage, but they had needed the discipline. And now he was about to liberate them.

His grand plan centered around a certain broken-down, eighty-year-old shepherd in the wastes of Sinai. Moses was a long way from the refined gentleman he had been. Wind-burned and sun-darkened, his beard long and his hair wild, he was typecast to play the desert prophet marching into the Egyptian court. But Moses didn't see it that way at all.

One dusty day in the shadow of Mount Sinai, the shepherd caught sight of a bush on fire but not being consumed. As he drew near, a voice from within the flames called his name. "Do not come any closer," said the voice. "Take off your sandals, for the place where you are standing is holy ground. I am the God of your father, the God of Abraham, the God of Isaac and the God of Jacob." Moses was terrified.

"I have indeed seen the misery of my people in Egypt," God went on. "So I have come down to rescue them. So now, go. I am sending you to Pharaoh to bring my people the Israelites out of Egypt."

"Who am I?" Moses asked. Do you know me? I'm the murderer who ran for his life forty years ago. I tried to help my people then, and look where it got me.

"I will be with you," God replied. So it doesn't matter who you are.

Moses was thinking fast. Not having been raised among his Hebrew kin, he knew little about the God of Abraham. What if the Israelites ask your name? What should I say?

"I AM WHO I AM" declared the voice in the flame. I am Yahweh, the God of Abraham.

I AM. The Hebrew verb means not just "I exist," but "I am actively present." I am with you. The name Yahweh comes from this same verb, and now the significance of the name becomes clearer. Unlike the gods of Mesopotamia, Canaan and Egypt, this God intended to be intimately present in the affairs of his people, no matter where they sojourned and what they suffered. He had been actively with childless Abraham, with Jacob fleeing alone to an unknown land and with Joseph in the dungeon. And he was "I will be with you" to Moses facing Pharaoh and to the Israelites journeying back to Canaan.

Trust me, the wind whispered. But as Yahweh unfolded his plan—the elders of Israel will listen to you, but Pharaoh will laugh in your face until I do works of supernatural power to convince him—Moses grew more and more alarmed.

"What if they do not believe me?" I could lose my neck! Yahweh gave him a couple of minor supernatural feats to impress his audience, but Moses was not comforted. I'm a lousy speaker, he protested. I'm definitely not your man for addressing the Egyptian court.

Yahweh was losing his temper. I made you with your mouth and your brains, didn't I? Do you think I don't know what I'm doing? Cutting the argument short, Yahweh said Moses' brother Aaron was a fine speaker and would be Moses' mouthpiece to Pharaoh. The debate was over. Moses was left speechless before the smoldering bush wishing he had never been born.

YAHWEH VERSUS EGYPT

The elders of Israel were delighted when Moses told them Yahweh was about to liberate them and turned his staff into a snake to prove it. But the meeting with Pharaoh fulfilled Moses' worst fears. The lord of Egypt sat haughtily on his throne, flanked by his counselors and sorcerers, wearing his high royal headdress with its golden cobra on the front. The king was a veritable serpent himself. Not only did he deny Israel the right to go to the desert for a three-day worship festival (he regarded it as a flimsy ruse), but he decreed that since the Hebrews had time to sit around fomenting rebellion, they had time to gather their own straw to make bricks for the city they were building. That was the end of the interview. And later, when the Hebrews failed to meet their brick quota because they were out gathering straw, they were flogged. The Israelite foremen vented their fury at Moses and Aaron, who had caused this impossible situation.

Moses, in turn, let Yahweh have it: "Why, Lord, why have you brought trouble on this people? Is this why you sent me? Ever since I went to Pharaoh to speak in your name, he has brought trouble on this people, and you have not rescued your people at all."

Yahweh told Moses to relax. I have a covenant with Abraham, he said. I am He Who Is With You, and when I get through with Pharaoh, you and all Egypt and Israel will know what that means.

Reluctantly, Moses went back to Pharaoh. The staff-into-snake stunt did not impress him; his own magicians were able to do the same thing by the power of the Egyptian gods (who were really servants of the snake himself). So the next morning, Yahweh sent Moses to meet Pharaoh by the Nile after his bath and tell him, "By this you will know that I am [Yahweh, He Who Is Present]: With the staff that is in my hand I will strike the water of the Nile, and it will be changed into blood. The fish in the Nile will die, and the river will stink; the Egyptians will not be able to drink its water."

That failed to move Pharaoh, so the next week Yahweh caused the Nile's frogs to multiply rapidly and infest Egypt's houses, the beds, even the ovens and kneading troughs. Frogs everywhere! It was revolting. Pharaoh's sorcerers were helpless to get rid of the critters.

Yahweh was ridiculing two of Egypt's chief gods. Ha'pi, the Nile god, was supposed to make sure that the river stayed life-giving and not destructive. The frog goddess Heqit supposedly governed human fertility and assisted women in childbirth. But Yahweh mocked, So you like frogs in your beds, ladies? Okay, I'll give you frogs!

Pharaoh gave in to Moses just long enough for the frogs to die, then reneged. This business of repent and unrepent became a pattern as Yahweh sent in turn gnats, biting flies, a livestock disease carried by the flies, a related human skin disease and the worst hailstorm in Egyptian history. The Egyptian gods in charge of animals, crops and health did nothing. Pharaoh's officials (financially ruined in the loss of herds and crops) urged him to give in before the eighth plague hit. But Pharaoh just could not bring himself to lose so many excellent slaves.

Yahweh had selected this particular man to be king of Egypt at this time because he knew this pharaoh would harden his heart against Moses' pleas. Indeed, the Bible goes so far as to also say that Yahweh himself hardened Pharaoh's heart. To people trained in Western logic, these two statements may seem to contradict each other. But the biblical writers were Eastern, and to them it was not only possible but necessary to hold certain apparent opposites in tension. "Both-and," not "either-or," was their approach in these cases. Yahweh had chosen and formed this pharaoh in order that his "name might be proclaimed in all the earth" (Exodus 9:16). It was all part of Yahweh's plan to reveal himself to the nations who had turned their back on him and no longer knew anything about him. Yet Pharaoh was still free to choose—he was not Yahweh's puppet—so he remained morally responsible for his choices. Yahweh was able to turn even his enemies' choices to serve his plans.

So the wheat, spelt and fruit trees that had survived the hail were devoured by locusts in plague number eight. When that didn't move Pharaoh, a plague of darkness (possibly a sandstorm) afflicted the whole land, except Goshen, for three days. This was an insult to Egypt's greatest god: Ra, the sun.

By now Pharaoh was ready to bargain, but Moses' position remained all or nothing. "Just as you say," Moses retorted as he walked out. But he promised that tomorrow Pharaoh would beg the Israelites to leave Egypt, because at midnight every firstborn son of man and beast in the country would die.

ESCAPE

Moses left Pharaoh and his officials to chew on that one and returned to prepare the Israelites for the final plague. It was spring; the goats and sheep were giving birth. Yahweh had decreed that from now on, this month (Abib) would be the first month of the year. And this night, and each year on the fourteenth of Abib, each Israelite household must slaughter a year-old, flawless male lamb at twilight. They must smear some of its blood on the doorframes of their houses, then roast the meat and eat it with bitter herbs and unleavened bread while being dressed and ready to leave home. For tonight Yahweh would pass through Egypt, and in every home not marked with lamb's blood he would strike the firstborn dead. The blood would warn death to pass over the house that believed in Yahweh, so the annual commemoration would be called Passover. Once again, the blood of a substitute stood between Yahweh's people and death.

> *Once again, the blood of a substitute stood between Yahweh's people and death.*

At midnight, wailing could be heard from every non-Israelite home in Egypt. From Pharaoh to the least slave to the cattle—every family lost its firstborn. Pharaoh ordered Moses and Aaron to get out of Egypt, they and their people. The Egyptians, who by this time held Moses and Israel in high respect, were glad to give the Israelites their silver, gold and fine clothing if only they would leave immediately. Thousands of Israelites set out east, and not a few Egyptians joined them, having been convinced that Yahweh was greater than the gods of Egypt. Many of the joiners were probably slaves and laborers hoping for a better life with these impressive Hebrews.

Moses led the throng, carrying with him the bones of Joseph. Leading the fugitives was a glowing cloud that shaded them from the intense sun during the day and lit their way by night. The cloud was called the "glory" of Yahweh, a physical manifestation of his presence.

ACROSS THE REED SEA

Following Yahweh's instructions, Moses led the people by the desert road to the "Sea of Reeds" (Exodus 13:18, Hebrew). Moses told the crowd to camp by the sea. For Pharaoh had changed his mind yet again and was in hot pursuit with his whole army in chariots. Yahweh wanted Pharaoh to think he had Israel helplessly pinned against the sea.

The Israelites were certainly convinced. "Was it because there were no graves in Egypt that you brought us to the desert to die?" they wailed at Moses. This was not the last time they would wail at Moses. But Moses told them that if they would just shut up, Yahweh would fight for them. Yahweh wanted Egypt to remember that he was the God Who Is Present. So all night long a strong east wind blew back the waters of the sea. Toward morning, the whole throng of Israelites was able to walk across the deep lake bed. When the Egyptians pursued, Yahweh jammed their chariot wheels in the mud. As horses reared and men cursed, the water swept back into the sea bed and swallowed all of them up. The Israelites stood wide-eyed on the opposite side watching the bodies wash up onto the shore. They were starting to take Yahweh and his envoy Moses seriously. For a while the crowd was silent as the cries of the dying faded into the breeze. Then Moses led the people in a song of praise:

> Who among the gods
> > is like you, Yahweh?
> Who is like you—
> > majestic in holiness,
> awesome in glory,
> > working wonders?
> You stretch out your right hand,
> > and the earth swallows your enemies. (Exodus 15:11-12)

Moses' sister Miriam was a prophetess. She began to lead the women in a dance. They shook their tambourines, sang and shouted their thanks to Yahweh:

> Sing to the Lord,
> > for he is highly exalted.

Both horse and driver
    he has hurled into the sea. (Exodus 15:21)

Questions for Reflection and Discussion

1. How would you describe Moses as a young man? How had he changed by the time he was ready to be Yahweh's messenger? Why was this change necessary?

2. What does "I AM WHO I AM" tell you about Yahweh?

3. The deliverance from Egypt set the pattern for the deliverance that was to come. What did the plagues signify? What was the point of smearing lamb's blood on the Israelites' doorframes? What was Israel supposed to learn from this experience?

5

A TREATY
WITH YAHWEH

Exodus 15:22–23:33

The next day, Moses led the still-exultant mob eastward into the desert. But for three days they traveled without finding water. They were used to hard work and poor rations, but not this grinding thirst and endless walking in the heat and glare. Moses' formerly awed fans began to grumble. When at last they found water but it proved to be undrinkable, the crowd's mood grew ugly.

In desperation, Moses cried to Yahweh for help. Yahweh showed him a piece of wood and told him that if he threw it into the water, the water would become safe to drink. That seemed ridiculous, but no more so than anything else that had happened during the last couple of months. So Moses obeyed, and it worked. While the people were drinking and watering their fainting herds, Yahweh gave Moses another message:

> If you listen carefully to Yahweh your God and do what is right in his eyes, if you pay attention to his commands and keep all his decrees, I will not bring on you any of the diseases I brought on the Egyptians, for I am Yahweh, who heals you. (Exodus 15:26)

Trust me, obey me, and I will take care of your physical needs. Ignore me, and you are at the mercy of the climate, the food supply and of things called "germs" that you know nothing about. Yahweh must have felt like the parent of two million two-year-olds, with only one eighty-year-old nurse to commiserate with.

WHAT IS IT?

The travelers recouped at a large oasis beyond which lay the foreboding Desert of Sin. Two weeks had passed since the Reed Sea, and the people were getting tired of hiking. The kids were crying, everybody had sore feet, and there was little to drink and less to eat. They were forgetting how bad it had been to make bricks for the Egyptians; all they could remember were the stews they had cooked. A riot was brewing. Once again Moses and Aaron faced the rabble and said, "You're not grumbling against us, but against Yahweh." They pointed toward the huge glowing cloud hovering near the camp.

Patiently, Yahweh appealed to his squalling toddlers on their level. At twilight a vast flock of quail flew in, and the people feasted. In the morning, dew lay on everything. When the dew burned off, thin flakes like frost covered the desert floor. "*Man hu*?" people asked each other. "What is it?"

"It is the bread Yahweh has given you to eat," Moses explained. He told them to gather two quarts per person, enough for one day, and to save none for tomorrow.

The people did as they were told. The stuff was white and tasted like wafers made with honey. Not too bad. They called it manna, recalling the question, "What is it?"

SLAVES INTO SERVANTS

This whole desert journey was the beginning of a school. Yahweh had trained Abraham, Isaac, Jacob and Jacob's sons as individuals; now he had to put more than a million people through the same course. Some of them weren't even Jacob's descendants and had heard of Yahweh only a few months earlier. Nearly all of them had grown up as slaves and children of slaves.

This stage in Yahweh's plan was about transformation. First, Yahweh had multiplied Israel from a clan of seventy to a mob of thousands. But they were an unruly rabble, and Yahweh intended to make them a tight-knit, disciplined army and a united nation who saw themselves as family. At the same time, he was moving them geographically from Egypt to Canaan. And third, he was going to transform them socially and spiritually from slaves of human masters into servants of God.

To change from slaves into servants, the people had to learn to fear—and at the same time trust—Yahweh more than any other god or human. One might expect that the plagues, the Reed Sea miracle and the constant physical presence of the cloud would have convinced them, but dry mouths and growling stomachs proved otherwise. Hence, Yahweh deprived them of the sources of their basic necessities to force them to depend on him. Then each day he provided just what they needed, so as to reinforce an attitude of daily dependence. They were going to need this attitude sorely when they reached Canaan and ceased to get so many dramatic physical signs of Yahweh's presence and power.

At this point they still fell far short. As soon as water ran scarce, the mob was ready to riot. "Is Yahweh really among us or not?" they demanded. Moses panicked, but Yahweh continually came through. I am the God who is with you.

The next test of faith for the Israelites came when some desert tribesmen called Amalekites attacked. These people normally occupied the southern approach to Canaan, but having heard that a horde was approaching their territory, they sent a contingent to cut them off.

The Israelites had left Egypt armed for battle, but so far they hadn't had to fight. Moses instructed his young aide, Joshua, to array the troops. Moses himself stood on a hill overlooking the field and prayed to Yahweh all day while the armies clashed. In the end, Israel was victorious and saw yet another side of Yahweh: He was their Deliverer, their Healer, their Provider and now their War Standard. And Yahweh declared that there would be a permanent feud between Israel and Amalek. Why? Because just as he saw the serpent behind the throne of Egypt, so he knew his ancient enemy was in this attempt to crush Israel before it could be fully born.

COVENANT

So far, freedom seemed to spell nothing but deprivation to the Israelites.

For although Yahweh cared about his people's empty stomachs, he was more concerned about their empty hearts. So day passed into weary day as the nation trudged after the golden cloud through the desert.

Exactly three months from the day they left Egypt, the Israelites came to a mountain jutting 2,200 feet above the desert floor. Moses ordered them to camp, then climbed a short way alone to receive Yahweh's instructions. Yahweh told him to tell the people,

> You yourselves have seen what I did to Egypt, and how I carried you on eagles' wings and brought you to myself. Now if you obey me fully and keep my covenant, then out of all nations you will be my treasured possession. Although the whole earth is mine, you will be for me a kingdom of priests and a holy nation. (Exodus 19:4-6)

Moses took this message back to the elders of Israel—the heads of each clan in each tribe—and they recognized what Yahweh was offering. He was using the form of a treaty between a sovereign and a vassal (dependent) people that was used throughout the Middle East. Yahweh claimed to be the rightful King over all the nations of the world, even though they were in rebellion against him. So if Israel would commit to recognizing Yahweh as King, he would give them an honored place as the first nation in his eventual world kingdom. They would be his priests in that they would mediate between him and the rest of the earth's peoples.

Two key words in this treaty proposal are *obey* and *holy*. Holy means "set apart from the commonplace." Ancient Middle Eastern peoples recognized two categories of things. On one side of a chasm were common things, including humans and animals. On the other were holy beings and everything that belonged to them. As priests, the Israelites would be wholly set apart from pursuing their own ends, wholly dedicated to Yahweh's agenda.

Most ancient people thought of the holy in terms of power and inscrutability. All the divine beings were holy, from the least tree spirit to the father of the gods. Holiness did not imply morality or love at all. But Yahweh's holiness was drastically different. Since holiness was one of his chief qualities and would have to be a primary trait of his people, one of his tasks in training Israel would be to change the nation's idea of holiness. First, he had to get across that only he was holy, not the gods and spirits of the pagans. Second, what belonged to him was untouchably, radically holy. Its separation had to be taken seriously. Third, because morality was an essential trait of Yahweh, it was an essential trait of his holiness. Anyone who violated moral rules was therefore unholy and could not approach the holy God. Such a violator was "unrighteous"— out of right covenant relationship with the King because of treason. Everyone set apart for Yahweh had to take their side of the relationship seriously or face his wrath.

The elders of Israel did not yet grasp the implications of what they were getting into, so they readily agreed to make a treaty with Yahweh. They began to get an inkling when Moses ordered them to wash and abstain from sex for three days as outward signs of inward purification and separation from earthly activities. They got nervous when Moses told them to bar the people from touching the mountain lest they die. Then on the third day the mountain began to quake, smoke and fire poured forth, thunder crashed, lightning flashed and a loud trumpet blared out of nowhere. Suddenly it did not seem so appealing to be the priests who could be familiar with this holy God; the people were content to let Moses receive Yahweh's instructions and bring them back.

The Ten Commandments

So Moses climbed into the smoke and returned a short time later with a pronouncement that followed the treaty form of the day. First the great King identified himself and described the gracious deeds he had done for his subjects: "I am Yahweh your God, who brought you out of Egypt, out of the land of slavery" (Exodus 20:2). Israel had done nothing to earn this relationship. On the contrary, by liberating Israel Yahweh had earned the people's gratitude and loyalty.

Israel was supposed to express that gratitude by keeping the ten basic treaty stipulations that followed. The first four dealt with how the people would relate to Yahweh:

- You shall have no other gods before me.

- You shall not make for yourself an idol.

- You shall not misuse the name of Yahweh.

- Remember the Sabbath day by keeping it holy.

A subject could have only one king, and a wife but one husband. Yahweh wanted this relationship to have the intimacy of a marriage. He was dealing with Middle Eastern peasants, former slaves, some of whom had grown up worshiping the forces of nature depicted as beings in wood and stone. His goal was to draw them each into personal companionship with him, but they weren't ready for that yet. He was bringing them as fast and as far as they could come.

The first step was to wean them from worshiping natural forces and demons. The next was to convince them not to make idols, neither of him nor anything else. Human thinking tends to be concrete; we're not comfortable unless we have a thing we can see and touch to adore. And we are so impressed with the energies of the earth. Above all, we long for control over our world. So Yahweh said, I—the creator of the earth and all its powers—am the only one worthy of worship. Do not bow to anything else, material or spiritual. Don't confuse the maker with the made. Don't use my name in magic or casual swearing, as though you could use me to get what you want. Don't say, "God told me" when I didn't. And one day out of your week must be devoted to resting and enjoying me so that making a living won't shrivel your spirits and make you deaf to divinity.

Yahweh's last six commands described how his subjects should relate to each other:

- Honor your father and your mother.

- You shall not murder.

- You shall not commit adultery.

- You shall not steal.

- You shall not give false testimony against your neighbor.

- You shall not covet anything that belongs to your neighbor.

These commandments were intended to safeguard individuals and communities so that everyone could prosper. For instance, Yahweh knew how quickly a society would fragment when children harbored resentment against their parents and denied them care in their old age. Bitterness against parents would shackle a person to forever seeking approval or revenge in relationships. And the person who ignored elderly parents would one day find his or her own children doing the same. To honor and forgive parents—even those who had failed—was a key to inner freedom.

Similarly, in forbidding murder, Yahweh wanted to instill a value for life. No culture could long survive if its people accepted the blithe killing of unwanted children, the aged and infirm, unloved wives and personal enemies. Yahweh banned adultery in order to protect lifelong commitments between husband and wife. He knew how adultery destroyed everyone involved, leaving spouse and children feeling abandoned and numbing the adulterer's ability to commit the deep levels of his or her heart to anyone.

Yahweh forbade theft to protect property rights, but he also prohibited coveting other people's property. Like unforgiveness and unfaithfulness, coveting was a cancer in the heart, robbing a person of joy and contentment, poisoning relationships. Yahweh cared not just about his people's outward behavior but also about their inner health and character.

In addition, Yahweh banned lying, especially in court. Legal corruption, he knew, would rot the nation. Truth had to be a fundamental value.

THE KING'S LAW

After these ten basic commandments, Yahweh gave an assortment of examples of how they would apply in the daily life of peasant farmers. He elaborated on property rights and on how to show the value of a human life in the way one treated one's servants. He discussed penalties for violent crime and extolled generosity to the poor. He said a bit about how to worship him and forbade consorting with other spirits for power. More legislation would come later; this was just enough to show his subjects what he was getting at.

In short, Yahweh was setting himself up as the King and lawmaker of the nation. This was unheard of in the ancient world. No other nation claimed to have received a law code from a god or to have a deity as its authority for justice. Babylonian and Assyrian law codes recorded what some judges had done in the past, but judges were free to decide by their own opinion. Kings made and unmade laws, and in many states they decided justice according to their whims, not permanent laws. Egypt's pharaoh was considered a god on earth, so his every decree supposedly embodied truth and justice, whether or not people were treated justly or in proportion to their deeds. Thus there was no Egyptian law code at all.

But in Israel neither Moses, nor the elders, nor judges, nor even later kings would have the right to make laws. They could administer and execute laws, collect taxes, keep the peace and make judicial rulings, but Yahweh was the legislative branch of the government.

We might assume this would have led to chaos, but in fact Israel had the most fair and humane laws of its day. Many of the legal principles Yahweh laid down underlie the codes of modern nations. For instance, when Yahweh gave sample cases, he repeatedly gave motives or reasons for the just decisions to show the logic or moral value behind the decree. Justice was to be reasonable and compassionate, not arbitrary. Again, Israel's law commanded the death penalty for crimes against God and against the holiness of life, but it was strikingly humane compared to other codes. Only one law (Deuteronomy 25:11-12) prescribes the loss of a body part, the hand, as a penalty, in contrast to many instances in Babylonian, Hittite and other codes. Flogging was limited to forty lashes in Israel.

Other codes treated commoners' lives as less valuable than noblemen's. They regarded harm done to a woman, slave or ox all as harm to a man's property. For instance, if a nobleman caused the death of a noblewoman, the Babylonian code of Hammurabi said the killer's daughter had to die. If a nobleman caused a slave woman's death, he paid a sum of silver to her owner. By contrast, Israel's law protected women and slaves explicitly from being used as property and made justice the same for all social classes. Physical discipline of slaves was limited, though not forbidden, and killing a slave was punished the same way as killing a free man.

"An eye for an eye" is a well-known principle from Israel's law code. Many people suppose it was a harsh, vengeful standard, but in fact Yahweh was limiting the sternness of tribal justice. Ancient tribal custom demanded that if a man killed someone in your tribe, you killed at least him if not his whole family. If he injured you, your family tried to kill him. But Yahweh said no, a punishment must not exceed the crime. It must also not be too lenient, as in many countries where noblemen received preference. "Eye for eye, tooth for tooth" was the penalty for injuries caused by a fight between free Israelites. If a man blinded his slave's eye, he did not lose his own eye, but he did have to free the slave (Exodus 21:23-27). Property damage and accidental killing were covered by fines, not retaliation. With premeditated murder, though, "eye for eye" applied literally, because Yahweh took human life extremely seriously.

Social justice was one of Yahweh's passions. Yahweh warned judges not to show favoritism to either rich or poor, nor to let a crowd's opinion sway a decision. He forbade bribes. He warned his people not to oppress foreigners who would come to live in Israel: "You yourselves know how it feels to be foreigners, because you were foreigners in Egypt" (Exodus 23:9). He even banned the lending of money at interest to fellow Israelites. People didn't borrow money to set up businesses or buy houses in those days; they borrowed only when they were broke. Yahweh wanted his subjects to treat each other like family, lending without interest out of love. He repeatedly warned that if poor or defenseless people cried to him for help against the rich and powerful, he would avenge them.

Indeed, when Moses said, "What other nation is so great as to have such righteous decrees and laws as this body of laws I am setting before you today?" (Deuteronomy 4:8), he was telling the truth.

Questions for Reflection and Discussion

1. What does the treaty (covenant) Yahweh makes with Israel at Mount Sinai have to do with his earlier promise to make Abraham's descendants a great nation and a blessing to all the nations?

6

A COURT
FOR THE KING

Exodus 24:1–40:38

When Moses returned from the smoking mountain and re-counted the covenant stipulations, the people responded enthusiastically. Yahweh's pyrotechnics had impressed them, and they were back in their Reed Sea mood. So Moses wrote down the whole treaty and called the document "the Book of the Covenant."

The next day he held a covenant ratification ceremony. He sent young men from each of the tribes to sacrifice bulls to express their commitment. Moses sprinkled half of the blood on the altar he had built to symbolize that Yahweh forgave any past wrongdoing and accepted the offering. Then when he had reread the Book of the Covenant and the people had sworn allegiance, he sprinkled the rest of the blood on them. "This is the blood of the covenant," Moses pronounced solemnly. It was a tangible expression that this commitment was sacred and serious. To break faith after being sprinkled with the sacrificial blood would mean incurring bloodguilt (equivalent to murder) and Yahweh's judgment.

After that, Moses took Aaron, Aaron's two oldest sons and seventy clan elders partway up the mountain. It was customary for the parties of a covenant to seal it with a meal, so these seventy-four men ate and drank the covenant meal in Yahweh's presence. Then Moses took Joshua and climbed farther up the mountain, leaving Aaron and an elder named

Hur in charge until they returned. The cloud of glory settled over the mountain, looking like a consuming fire from the Israelite camp. Moses and Joshua disappeared into the cloud for forty days.

A ROYAL TENT

Yahweh spent most of these forty days giving Moses minute instructions for constructing, furnishing and staffing a royal tent. To get his people used to the idea that he was their King, He Who Is Actively Present, Yahweh would have a dwelling in the center of their camp like that of a great sheikh. The tent was called a "tabernacle" (dwelling place) and a "sanctuary" (holy place).

It was an elaborate affair, as befitted royalty. It stood about forty-five feet long by fifteen feet wide by fifteen feet high. It consisted of a sectionalized wooden framework covered by four layers of curtains (embroidered linen on the inside, then woven goat hair, then ramskin leather, then sea-cow hide). On the inside it was divided into two compartments: the Holy Place (about thirty feet by fifteen feet) and the Most Holy Place (about fifteen feet by fifteen feet). The Most Holy Place was thus a perfect cube.

Linen, ramskin and sea-cow hide were all precious fabrics. Likewise, the embroidery and even the loops to hang the curtains were of blue, purple and scarlet thread. These were royal colors because the dyes were extremely expensive (they came from shellfish and the eggs and carcasses of a special kind of worm). The tent frame was covered with gold, which was considered a perfect, royal metal because it was uncontaminated by other metals. The furnishings inside the tabernacle were also of gold.

The bases that supported the structure were of silver, made from the money that ransomed each firstborn male Israelite. Yahweh had declared that each firstborn in Israel belonged to him because he had spared them in the last plague on Egypt. Rather than sacrificing the firstborn, the Israelites had to ransom them with silver money. Thus Yahweh's tent stood on the people's ransom price.

Beginning with the base of the tabernacle's entrance, the furnishings outside the holy tent were of bronze. This is a harder metal, more suited for heavy use. It is also an alloy, so it is by definition not pure. It symbolized judgment for sin.

The tabernacle was erected on the west side of a surrounding courtyard measuring about one hundred and fifty feet by seventy-five feet. All around this courtyard, except for an entryway some fifteen feet wide on the eastern side, was a curtain almost eight feet high.

The furnishings of Yahweh's tent all symbolized important truths he wanted to impress on his people. In the Most Holy Place was a hardwood chest covered in gold called the ark (chest) of the covenant. Its pure gold lid was flanked with two golden cherubim (angels) like the winged sphinxes that often adorned the arms of Middle Eastern thrones. This "atonement cover" was the throne of Yahweh. The ark was fitted with rings so that it could be carried on poles like a litter when the camp moved.

The Holy Place contained a table on which bread would be laid as an offering of Israel's produce, a seven-branched lampstand to represent Yahweh's glory reflected in the people's holy lives, and an incense altar where the burning fragrance would symbolize the people's prayers going up to God. All this was of gold.

In the courtyard stood an altar of bronze-covered wood seven and a half feet square and four and a half feet high—large enough to burn whole bulls and rams. There was also a bronze basin in which one had to wash before entering the tent or offering a sacrifice.

The people were supposed to supply the fabric, wood and metal to construct all of this out of their own love for Yahweh. They would also continually provide the bread, oil, incense and animals as their gifts.

To staff this royal residence, Aaron and his sons would be set apart as priests—Yahweh's personal servants. They would offer the sacrifices, fill the lamp, bake the bread and so on. No one but a priest would be allowed in the tabernacle, and a priest had to be of the prescribed family, consecrated with certain intricate rites and dressed in precisely defined garments. All of this had just one point: to impress on Israel Yahweh's utter holiness.

Yahweh spelled out all of this to the last detail, including the names of the men who would oversee the construction. In some mysterious way, the tabernacle reflected the spiritual realities of heaven. Then he sent Moses back down the mountain with these instructions plus two tablets of stone. On each tablet, Yahweh had inscribed a copy of the ten basic covenant commands. It was customary to make two copies of a covenant document, one for each party. Each party usually put his copy in the presence of his god. Therefore, both copies of Israel's covenant with Yahweh were going to be kept in the ark of the covenant.

THE PRICE OF IMPATIENCE

Meanwhile, the Israelites were getting bored and concerned waiting for Moses. They finally decided that he had disappeared forever and that they would have to choose another leader and invoke another god to get them from Sinai to Canaan. So they persuaded Aaron to melt down the gold jewelry they had taken from the Egyptians and cast it into an idol in the form of a calf. (To stockbreeders, young bulls represented strength and virility, so they were standard fare for idols.) Then the people held a typical pagan festival: animal sacrifices, food and alcohol, dancing, debauchery.

Moses was at that very moment on his way down the mountain. Yahweh warned him what was going on. He said the people were like stiff-necked oxen who wouldn't respond to a pull on their yoke. He would wipe them out and let Moses father a nation.

Moses blanched. He had been serving as mediator between the King and his subjects in liberating them and giving them their laws. Now he found himself having to beg the Sovereign to forgive their treason. He reminded Yahweh of his great plan and his promises to Abraham, Isaac and Jacob, and he implored the King to relent.

This was just the response Yahweh wanted from Moses. The covenant mediator was supposed to stand between Yahweh and his people to seek mercy when the people broke the agreement. Yahweh's justice demanded that he punish rebels, but he always preferred to be merciful. They were the children of their warped father Adam, and he loved them. There was something—as yet secret—about a mediator's intercession (standing

> *The covenant mediator was supposed to stand between Yahweh and his people to seek mercy when the people broke the agreement.*

between) that satisfied the required justice and allowed mercy.

Moses sighed his relief and set off back to camp. But when he saw the orgy, he lost his temper, smashed the tablets and threw the calf into the fire. He could get nothing out of Aaron but excuses, so he waved him away and shouted, "Whoever is for Yahweh, come to me." His kinsmen, the Levites, rallied to him. He ordered them to start killing revelers until the party stopped.

The next day Moses interceded again, offering to give up his own life if Yahweh would forgive Israel. But not even Moses' life was a sufficient substitute. Yahweh had to send a plague through the camp because the price of rebellion had to be proportional to the nearness of the Holy One. But in his mercy he spared as many people as possible. Then he ordered them to set out for Canaan without him.

The people were stunned. Abandoned by Yahweh? They wept while Moses strode into the tent where he customarily met with God before the tabernacle was constructed. There he and the King had a frank exchange.

"If you're not going to go with us," Moses stated bluntly, "then don't send us. How will we be any different from any of the dozens of roving tribes? We can't accomplish your plan without you, and it's doubtful we'll survive."

Yahweh liked the way Moses never minced words. He and Abraham had been friends like that. Abraham had respected him, but he was never afraid to say what he felt and ask for what he cared about (see Genesis 18:16-33). For friendship's sake, Yahweh granted Moses' plea.

Moses followed with a personal request: he wanted to really see Yahweh. So the next day found Moses on the mountain again with a replacement pair of stone tablets. The glory descended on the peak, and Yahweh let Moses see his "back" (there's disagreement about exactly what that meant), for no one could see Yahweh's "face" and survive. As he passed by, Yahweh proclaimed his identity:

> Yahweh, Yahweh, the compassionate and gracious God, slow to anger, abounding in love and faithfulness, maintaining love to thousands, and forgiving wickedness, rebellion and sin. Yet he does not leave the guilty unpunished; he punishes the children and their children for the sin of the parents to the third and fourth generation. (Exodus 34:6-7)

Moses fell on his face and worshiped. Yahweh restated the covenant terms to reaffirm that he had forgiven Israel, but he warned emphatically that the people must not make treaties with the Canaanites but must obliterate their debauched religion. If Israel compromised, she would be sucked into the seductive cults and commit spiritual adultery against her Husband. And Yahweh, "whose name is Jealous, is a jealous God" (Exodus 34:14).

When Moses descended this time, his face shone with the reflection of God's glory. It was so bright that people could not look at him unless he wore a veil.

Chastened by the plague, the Israelites were only too glad to contribute their wealth and their time to construct Yahweh's dwelling. When it was finished, the glory enveloped and filled the tent so that not even Moses could enter it. From then on, when the cloud lifted off the tabernacle and began to move across the desert, Israel knew it was time to pack up and move out. And when the glory halted, they made camp, set up the tent and watched in awe as the cloud settled in. Everything—their diet, their moving and stopping, their whole lifestyle—was dictated to them as infants by the awesome Parent who hovered nearby, eager to see them grow up.

Questions for Reflection and Discussion

1. What were the purposes of the tent for Yahweh?

2. What aspects of the tent and its furnishings stand out to you as especially meaningful or symbolic?

3. How did Moses act as a "covenant mediator"? Why was this necessary?

7

A GENERATION LOST

Leviticus, Numbers, Deuteronomy

Yahweh was now enthroned right in the midst of his subjects. But he still couldn't wander among them as he had in Eden; he had to confine his undiluted presence behind four layers of curtains and a screened courtyard. His holiness would scorch such polluted people if he lowered the barriers. Yahweh wanted them to be holy with him—set apart from the world order that years of the serpent's influence had perverted—so that he and they could enjoy each other face to face.

But their haste to lapse into religious lechery, greed and lust for power showed they still had only the vaguest idea of the true God's character, values and expectations. Even with his people at their current distance, Yahweh would continually have to send plagues to satisfy the requirements of his holiness. Besides the laws that governed what we might call "secular" life, Yahweh gave Israel a detailed system of rituals to illustrate graphically what holiness meant. The message was that as citizens of Yahweh's kingdom, they had no secular life. All of life was sacred, set apart for his service.

The main act of worship was animal sacrifice at the tabernacle. Daily, endless blood sacrifices had to be brought to the King to maintain his approval. Why? To modern ears this sounds like senseless waste and cruelty. But Yahweh demanded it to make a point: Evil costs dearly. Whenever someone offered an animal, he laid his hands on it to identify himself with it. While he watched it being butchered and burnt, he knew that Yahweh was accepting its death in his place. He was the son of Adam and, like his father, he repeatedly rebelled against his Lord no matter how hard he tried not to. Yahweh's holiness demanded that a price be paid for treason, and the price for treason was death. But knowing his people were incapable of living up to perfection, he graciously accepted an animal as substitute for the human. In fact, he abhorred the human sacrifice practiced by other Middle Eastern peoples.

The sacrificial system was a tableau, a piece of shocking theater to teach shocking truths. Every morning and evening the priests burned a whole, perfect animal to symbolize Israel offering herself wholly to Yahweh and to atone for (cover) unintentional sin (rebellion, lawbreaking) in general. As the animal was wholly consumed in fire, so the offerers were wholly surrendered to Yahweh. When people committed some specific unintentional sin, they offered a perfect animal as their sign of confession. It paid the price and allowed Yahweh to forgive and cleanse the defilement. When restitution could be made for the sin, such as in cases of theft or cheating, they had to repay the debt plus twenty percent and also sacrifice the animal. Finally, to express thanksgiving a person gave a fellowship offering (or peace offering). Only the fat of this animal was burnt. The priests and offerers feasted on the rest to celebrate peace and friendship with Yahweh.

The typical procedure on a high holy day was to sacrifice sin offerings to deal with the people's inner corruption, then present whole burnt offerings to demonstrate total devotion to Yahweh, then finally bring fellowship offerings to express the bond between Yahweh and his children-friends. The whole thing was accompanied by offerings of grain, wine and oil to represent gratitude for Yahweh's abundant provision.

Hence, holy days were feast days, set apart for celebrating Yahweh's goodness. When Israel reached Canaan and scattered, the people were supposed to gather three times a year to commemorate how he had liberated them and brought them to their land and to rejoice over their unity in Yahweh's kingdom. Celebrating these festivals with joy was so important that better-off Israelites were supposed to finance the festivals for their servants, the poor and even non-Israelites living nearby.

Yahweh wanted his people to enjoy living in his kingdom. It was customary at that time for the king of a land to receive a tenth of each family's produce as a tithe, a royal tax. Two out of three years, Israel's tithe would fund the sacrificial system and the festivals. The third year's tithe would be set aside for those unable to make decent livings: widows, orphans and poor non-Israelites.

One holy day was not a feast day. On the Day of Atonement—the Day of the Covering of Sin—the nation fasted as a sign of mourning. In addition to regular sacrifices, two goats were offered for the wickedness of the nation. One was sacrificed, its blood brought all the way into the Most Holy Place to be sprinkled on Yahweh's throne and its body burnt outside the camp. The other was driven into the desert to symbolize that the people were driving sin from their lives. This was the only day of the year on which anyone could approach Yahweh's throne, and only the high priest could do it, bringing blood.

Thus were joy and grief intermingled in a constant rhythm in Yahweh's relationship with Israel. Evil was paid for, but the price was endless because the people never fundamentally changed. Joy was sweet in Yahweh's great mercy, but death was ever final.

HOLY AND COMMON

We might be tempted to describe these rites as Israel's "religion," as opposed to her secular life. But the line of holy and common ran through every aspect of life, just as it ran through every heart. Laws were given to teach people to "distinguish between holy and common, between the unclean and the clean."

Food was divided into clean and unclean. Unclean foods like pork, shellfish and most insects were forbidden—possibly because they tended to be unhealthy, but more importantly because Yahweh was teaching his children about distinctions. (Dietary laws also helped prevent Israel from casually socializing with pagans.)

The blood from menstruation and childbirth made a woman temporarily unclean, just as bodily discharges or contact with a corpse made anyone unclean. A person had to wash and abstain from sacrifices and sex for periods of time to regain cleanness. Skin diseases symbolized corruption, so they made a person unclean. Even mildew in a house, representing rot and decay, made the house unclean. Bodily fluids, death and skin diseases all represented the natural world that Yahweh wanted to distinguish from the perfect, holy, eternal, divine.

The rules of holy and common even descended to the most apparently absurd distinctions: do not plant two kinds of seed in your vineyard; do not plow with an ox and a donkey yoked together; do not weave wool and linen together for clothes!

In dividing the earthly from the holy, was Yahweh saying that the physical world was evil while the spiritual world was good? No. To understand these laws, we have to understand what Yahweh was working against. He was talking to a civilization that worshiped nature and used things like blood and corpses for earthly magic.

The Canaanites did not believe that one being created the world and was in charge of nature and human relations. Instead, they thought that myriad *baalim* and *elohim* (lords, geniuses, spirits) governed sun, rain, harvest, animal fertility, the planets and so on. All these "holy ones" belonged to a clan. El—the gods' father and the world's creator—had delegated control of the world to his sons and daughters, so although he was formally acknowledged, he received little worship. His son Baal, lord of sky and storm, was much more involved in human affairs. Humans could solicit his favor by feeding him with sacrifices and performing magical rituals.

Three goddesses, or three faces of one goddess, were also highly esteemed in Canaan. The mother, Asherah, ruled the home. Astarte, the lover, ruled fertility. And the virgin, Anath, ruled war and hunting. (Concepts of the triple goddess overlapped in the Middle East, so exact beliefs about each goddess varied from city to city.) These three are also known by pagans around the world as the virgin-mother-crone, birth-life-death, the new-full-old moon and other magical trinities. (They even appear in tarot cards, modern goddess worship and witchcraft.)

Other deities abounded: grain, sun, moon, dawn, sunset, sea and death. All were called "holy," but the word meant chiefly "other, beyond human." The gods did not act according to moral laws, nor were they interested in human goodness or justice. They supposedly could be persuaded to act for good or ill through flattery, begging, sacrifice or magic.

However, because they cared nothing for humans and had no morality, they were unpredictable and fearful. Personal intimacy and covenant love between human and god was out of the question.

Canaan's climate was erratic, so religion's chief goal was to influence the divine forces of nature to give sunshine, rain and fertility in desirable times and amounts. The primary method was "sympathetic magic." That is, the Canaanites acted out rituals that they wanted the deities to imitate. For instance, men performed sex acts with women holy to Baal so that Baal would water the earth. Rites with menstrual blood tapped Astarte's fertility for the land. The blood of sacrificed animals was eaten or sprinkled on the earth because blood carried the power of life. People even put their babies into ovens shaped like the mouth of the god Molech and watched as the screaming infants burned to death. Substances that symbolized the great forces of life and death—blood, semen, corpses, etc.—were mainstays of religious magic.

Hence, Yahweh made these substances "unclean" ritually so that Israel would recoil from such magic. Fertility, sex and food were all good, but Yahweh alone ruled nature and he could not be manipulated by magic. Israel needed to learn to distinguish between Creator and created, between humble petition to a loving Parent and attempts to control life. So Yahweh banned all activities associated with tapping into the god forces or natural energies of the earth or the cosmos.

> *Israel needed to learn to distinguish between Creator and created, between humble petition to a loving Parent and attempts to control life.*

Besides sympathetic magic, Yahweh also forbade mediums. Israelites must not consult spirits, whether those of dead people or discarnate beings. They could not seek his or any other god's will, nor peer into the future by interpreting leaves, fire, birds, rain, clouds or anything else. Magical incantations were forbidden. Why? First, because the spirits were not the helpful informants they pretended to be. They were really servants of the snake, luring those lusting for wealth, sex, power, knowledge or sensation into deception,

bondage and death. The price for their information was too high, and
Yahweh knew it. And second, any knowledge, prosperity or power that
Israel needed Yahweh was happy to provide. To seek those things elsewhere was to say to their Father, "We don't need you, we don't want you,
we don't trust you, we don't love you." It was to repeat Adam and Eve's
insult, attempting to take by force what Yahweh would give by grace.

Israel would not need mediums because she would have Yahweh's
written Word and his living spokespersons, his prophets. These men and
women were called by Yahweh and gifted to see the truth in events and
to understand the mind of God because of their intimate relationship
with him. If Israel needed to know the future, Yahweh would tell the
prophets and they would tell the people. If Israel needed to know God's
will these spokespersons would tell them that, too. (Moses wrote down
everything Yahweh told him, the priests interpreted those writings, and
the prophets spoke God's current will to each generation.) Israel could
tell a true prophet from a false one because a true one would speak
nothing that contradicted what Yahweh had already told Moses or what
actually happened in the world.

With a Holy God in their midst, holiness touched every aspect of
these people's lives. But with the advantages of having a God next door
went the drawbacks of having even the textile composition of one's
clothes turned into an object lesson. The book of Leviticus (the holiness manual of the tribe of Levi) underscores the message with these
refrains: "Be holy because I, Yahweh your God, am holy. . . . I am Yahweh
your God."

Questions for Reflection and Discussion

1. What were the important lessons that the sacrificial system
   acted out for the people?
2. What is holiness (see also chapter 5)? How did the holiness
   laws address the challenges of living near Canaanites? How is
   holiness still relevant for us today?

3. Technology, like magic, tries to tap into the earth's natural energies to give humans power. In fact, technology succeeds at this better than magic. Does technology raise any of the problems that make God so opposed to magic?

8

MARCH TO THE PROMISED LAND

Numbers, Deuteronomy

Yahweh gave most of this legislation while Israel remained camped at the base of Mount Sinai. For eleven months Sinai was a tent city, as populous as many ancient capitals, while craftsmen constructed Yahweh's tabernacle, the priests learned their duties, and Moses wrote down the King's instructions.

At the end of that time, Yahweh ordered Moses to take a military census of all men over twenty years old. The six hundred thousand troops were organized in divisions according to their clans and tribes. The tribe of Levi was set aside to assist the priests in caring for the tabernacle and its furnishings. (God's dealings with Levi is a good example of his mercy. The tribes of both Simeon and Levi had been sentenced to be dispersed among the other tribes because of their forefathers' crime of massacring Shechem. But God turned Levi's punishment to blessing because it was the only tribe that resisted the idolatry at Sinai. Yahweh's justice was drastic and irrevocable, but he could transmute it to mercy in the most amazing ways.) The Levites spent their days mending, cleaning, polishing and clearing out the unimaginable mess of slaughtering and burning several large animals each day. The tribe of Joseph was divided in two according to his sons, Ephraim and Manasseh, to bring the total tribal military divisions back to twelve.

Yahweh dictated the order in which the tribes trekked through the desert and how they camped. On a march, the Levites led carrying the ark, God's throne. In camp, the tribes were arranged in a square surrounding the tabernacle in the center. In this manner Israel marched to Canaan like the conquering army of God that she was. The rabble needed such discipline; they were on display before all the nations.

After almost a year at Sinai, the Israelites set out to finish the journey to Canaan. They began in high spirits, singing as they tramped, but as before they soon grew bored. It was the same old complaining: manna is dull, water is scarce, walking is tedious, wouldn't it be nice to be eating lamb and garlic in Egypt? So Yahweh sent quail again, but he also sent fire and plague to snap the mob into line. It seemed that nothing but strong discipline made a dent in these people's hard hearts.

COWARDICE

Despite all the grumbling, Moses managed to lead his ragtag outfit several more hundred miles to somewhere just south of Canaan. There he appointed a man from each tribe to a reconnaissance team. It would scout the land and bring back a thorough report: population, fortifications, soil quality, land features, agricultural produce. The people needed some encouragement to begin their conquest, and also some military intelligence.

When the spies returned forty days later, they brought a glowing report of the land and a depressing assessment of the foe. Two of the scouts—Joshua and Caleb—were hot to move into this rich land, but the other ten were scared. While Joshua and Caleb saw what Yahweh could do, the others focused on what they could not do.

Cowardice prevailed. The people swore at Moses for leading them into this jam. They debated stoning him, choosing a new leader and trying to go back to Egypt. Better to be live slaves than dead soldiers. Moses begged them to reconsider, but the complaints grew louder until suddenly the cloud of glory blazed out from the tabernacle. Yahweh thundered:

> How long will these people treat me with contempt? How long will they
> refuse to believe in me, in spite of all the signs I have performed among

them? I will strike them down with a plague and destroy them, but I will make you into a nation greater and stronger than they. (Numbers 14:11-12)

Moses had to intercede again. He based his plea on two facts: Yahweh's character ("slow to anger, abounding in love and forgiving sin and rebellion") and his plan to demonstrate that character to the nations by liberating and caring for Israel ("If you put all these people to death, leaving none alive, the nations who have heard this report about you will say, 'Yahweh was not able to bring these people into the land he promised them on oath, so he slaughtered them in the wilderness'").

Yahweh was pleased. He always responded when people showed they were betting their lives that his word and character could be counted on. So instead of wiping out the whole people, he decreed that the generation of faithless cowards would die in the wilderness, and that forty years hence, when a new generation had grown up, he would lead them into the Promised Land. Only Joshua and Caleb would survive to see Canaan, because they trusted Yahweh.

The Israelites mourned bitterly when Moses conveyed this to them. The glowing cloud terrified them, and they decided they would rather die quickly invading Canaan than spend the rest of their lives wandering through this desert. So they determined to attack the Canaanites after all.

Moses begged them not to try it without Yahweh's help. But they ignored him, and the Canaanites trounced them soundly. Sadly the survivors returned to the camp, and all the people set off wearily for the deep desert.

WANDERING

It must have been miserable trudging aimlessly through the desert for forty years. Children were born and raised on manna. The flocks were used for sacrifice, so the people may have tasted the meat of fellowship offerings and perhaps some milk, but there were no spices, no vegetables, no bread. Manna kept one healthy, but it was insipid. It was a major feat to keep idle men from brawling.

When revolt brewed, Moses never bothered to defend his authority. He always knew it was really Yahweh who was being rejected, so he left it to Yahweh to defend his own honor. Two hundred fifty upstart Levites were consumed by fire in one rebellion; 14,700 people died in another.

In all, Moses was a wise and humble leader. Yahweh loved him dearly. But with great honor and gifting went great responsibility. Moses, above everyone else, had to treat Yahweh's commands with respect. One day another of the endless quarrels over water shortage was simmering. As usual, the people shouted abuse while Moses and Aaron fell on their faces before Yahweh, who told Moses to speak to a certain rock and water would gush out. But Moses lost his temper and shouted to the gathered community, "Listen, you rebels, must we bring you water out of this rock?" Then he struck the rock twice with his staff. Water gushed out, but Yahweh was mad. Moses had publicly dishonored him by disobeying his order and acting as though his action, not Yahweh's word, were providing the water. The cost was severe: both Moses and Aaron (who had supported the offense) would die before they reached Canaan.

THREE ATTACKS

As the time of wandering drew to an end, Moses began to lead the people toward Canaan. (See map, page 348.) The Edomites denied passage through their land, so Moses circled around and approached from the east, through Moab. The Moabites let Israel pass through peacefully, but then the Amorites and, after them, the people of Bashan blocked the way. Yahweh enabled Israel to defeat both of these groups and take their land. It was fertile, well-watered real estate, especially good for livestock, so two and a half of the tribes (the tribe of Manasseh split) asked Moses if they could claim this as their promised land. Moses agreed on the condition that while the women and children settled, the fighting men would help the rest of Israel take their territory.

After securing these northern areas, Moses led the people south again to the plains of Moab, just east of the Jordan River. Right across the river was the Canaanite fortress of Jericho, strategically situated as the doorway to Canaan and the first target of the Israelite assault.

But Balak, king of Moab, didn't believe Israel intended to use his land only as a staging area for an attack westward. He had heard of the easy victories over Bashan and the Amorites and feared Moab was next. Convinced that he could not defeat Israel by force of arms, he resorted to sorcery. He summoned a certain Mesopotamian prophet for hire named Balaam to put a curse on Israel. Balaam did his best. But every time he tried to accommodate his client, Yahweh threatened to kill him, so Balaam kept pronouncing blessing over Israel.

Balaam was essentially a sorcerer. As such, he ultimately served Satan. The biblical account does not name him, but it was the snake who stood behind both attacks on Israel: the military and the occult. Both had failed, yet the serpent had one more strategy. At his prompting, Balaam suggested to Balak that Israel might be neutralized if some local women could seduce the Israelite men into pagan orgies. This ploy met with splendid success: Yahweh had to kill twenty-four thousand of his men with a plague before the Israelites turned away from the allure of paganism.

It was an omen of things to come. What force and sorcery could not do, seduction and the Israelites' own senseless moral choices could, and did. Yahweh could protect them from external attack, but his whole plan depended on humans making free choices either for or against him. In this intent, so foreign to Satan's notions of domination and subjugation, the viper thought he saw Yahweh's defeat. But Yahweh's plan had a facet so incredible, so unspeakable, that Satan never for an instant foresaw it or schemed against it.

MOSES' FAREWELL

As it happened, despite all the rebellions and debacles, six hundred thousand men of fighting age survived to enter Canaan when Yahweh finally declared that the moment had come. On the plains of Moab overlooking the promised land, Moses gathered the people to hear his final words. During the desert sojourn he had recorded for them their history (Genesis, Exodus, Numbers) and the royal law by which they were to live (Exodus, Leviticus, Numbers). Now he delivered three long speeches that together formed an impassioned exposition of Yahweh's covenant. He even used the traditional treaty format. After all, only Moses, Joshua, Caleb and a few people who had been children forty years earlier survived of all those who had seen the plagues of Egypt and the miracle at the Reed Sea. Most of this generation had been born in the desert.

The book of Deuteronomy records Moses' three sermons. He recounted Israel's failures and Yahweh's faithfulness. He reiterated the basic stipulations of the covenant and preached on the meanings of many specific laws of economics, social justice and worship. He set before the people a choice: life and blessing if they obeyed their King, death and cursing if they rebelled.

> Observe [these laws] carefully, for this will show your wisdom and understanding to the nations, who will hear about all these decrees and say, "Surely this great nation is a wise and understanding people." What other nation is so great as to have their gods near them the way Yahweh our God is near us whenever we pray to him? And what other nation is so great as to have such righteous decrees and laws as this body of laws I am setting before you today? (Deuteronomy 4:6-8)

> Hear, O Israel: Yahweh our God, Yahweh is one. Love Yahweh your God with all your heart and with all your soul and with all your strength. (Deuteronomy 6:4-5)

> He humbled you, causing you to hunger and then feeding you with manna, which neither you nor your ancestors had known, to teach you that man does not live on bread alone but on every word that comes from the mouth of Yahweh. (Deuteronomy 8:3)

> This day I call the heavens and the earth as witnesses against you that I have set before you life and death, blessings and curses. Now choose life, so that you and your children may live and that you may love Yahweh your God, listen to his voice, and hold fast to him. For Yahweh is your life, and he will give you many years in the land he swore to give to your fathers, Abraham, Isaac and Jacob. (Deuteronomy 30:19-20)

"Who is like you, O Israel, a people saved by Yahweh?" Moses concluded. Then he climbed nearby Mount Nebo and looked across the Jordan at the rich land Yahweh was giving them. He wished that after all this he could have crossed that river, but to see the land was enough. Now he was going home.

Yahweh buried him, and the nation mourned him for thirty days. But Moses had laid his hands on Joshua before his death, and the Spirit of

God that had given Moses his wisdom had fallen upon Moses' aide. Moses had been Israel's shepherd, now Joshua would be her general. And Joshua turned his face toward Jericho.

∞∞

Questions for Reflection and Discussion

1. Why is cowardice a sin in Numbers 13–14? What's the connection between faith and courage? Between obedience and courage?

2. Why do you think paganism is so persistently appealing (Numbers 25)?

3. What does it say about Yahweh that he requires his people to choose between the way of life and the way of death, knowing that they will often choose badly?

Part Two

The Rise and Fall of Israel

9

A TASTE OF
CONQUEST AND DEFEAT

Joshua, Judges

he fortress of Jericho stood on a large and fertile plain just west of the Jordan and guarded the foot of the road that climbed steeply up the Judean hills. In order to gain control of Canaan, an army first had to take Jericho to reach the road, then to conquer several more fortresses that guarded the high ground at the top of the road. From there an army could launch strikes to the south and north of Canaan while leaving a safe camp on the plains of Jericho.

Joshua knew all of this from his reconnaissance mission forty years earlier. But he didn't know how things stood in Jericho now, so he dispatched a pair of spies to reconnoiter. They slipped into the city during business hours, gathered some information, then (when it became clear that the city officials were on to them) convinced a prostitute named Rahab to hide them. A brothel was a good place for unfamiliar men to enter without attracting the neighbors' attention, and a prostitute was unlikely to be a fan of the city rulers.

The spies had guessed right: Rahab was happy to betray her city into Israel's hands. Her attitude doesn't seem callous when we understand what she was rejecting and what she was choosing. Canaanite society was divided into sharp classes. At the top were "kings," actually lords of individual walled fortresses like Jericho. The kings owed allegiance to the Egyptian pharaoh, but Egypt was having internal troubles, so in practice Egypt left the kings free to run their territories ruthlessly.

Under each king was a class of nobles and another class of priests. In exchange for their support, the king gave them lands and status. Below these was about ninety-eight percent of the population. Slaves and tenant farmers worked the lands owned by the king, nobles and priests. They lived in villages near the city. Free farmers and shepherds lived in villages farther from the city, but they paid taxes to the king and were subject to conscription without pay for wars or building projects. Crop failures might drive a family to sell its land or some of its children to the king or nobles, or a poor family might supplement its income by making its daughters prostitutes for the wealthy. Rahab probably sold her body because it was the only way for her family to survive in that system.

No wonder the Israelites considered her a good bet. Jericho was buzzing with the news that the God of these invaders had freed them from Egypt, led them through the desert and defeated the Amorite kings. The upper classes were cringing in fear, but what Rahab heard about the God of Israel inspired her with hope. She saw her chance to join a society whose God cared about oppressed slaves enough to liberate them and do mighty deeds for them. So she risked her life to save the spies in exchange for a promise that Israel would spare her family when they took the city.

ANOTHER DRY CROSSING

In Joshua's whole army, only he and Caleb had walked across the Reed Sea bed and seen the waters piled up on either side. To prove to this new generation that he was the real God and able to keep his promises, Yahweh repeated that miracle at the Jordan River.

When the Israelites with their herds, flocks and little ones halted at the edge of the gorge, they saw the green, fertile upper level at the other side. But the leaders could see that below stretched a belt of lifeless gray clay, and below that was a thick jungle. At the bottom, a thousand yards down, the river tumbled by. It was early April, and the winter rains and melting mountain snows had swollen the Jordan to a torrent.

Alone, the priests picked up the poles carrying the ark of the covenant and trekked down through the jungle to the water's edge. As their feet touched the water, the river stopped flowing from somewhere upstream. Soon the riverbed was dry, and the priests carried the ark to the middle. Joshua signaled for the people to follow. It must have taken the rest of the day to get all of the children, donkeys and flocks across.

This exercise proved two things. First, Yahweh was demonstrating that he had more power than Canaan's chief god, Baal, who was supposed to have more power than the god of sea and river. Second, Yahweh was showing that he, not Baal, had the rightful claim on the land. According to Middle Eastern custom, one could tell if an accused person was guilty by throwing him into a river. If he didn't drown, the gods had declared him innocent. Anyone in Canaan or Israel would have understood Yahweh's jest: his throne was not drowned even in the time it took for a whole army to pass through the riverbed. Yahweh was thumbing his divine nose at Baal, just as he had at Egypt's gods.

JERICHO

Joshua still didn't know how he was going to take the fortress, so he hiked over to have a look for himself. As he approached, he met a man holding a drawn sword. Grimly, Joshua challenged him: "Are you for us or for our enemies?"

"Neither," the man retorted, "but as commander of the army of Yahweh I have now come."

Joshua's eyes widened. He had imagined that he was the

> *This was Yahweh's battle against the dark spiritual forces who had usurped his earth.*

commander of Yahweh's army, that this war was human against human. Israel was the good guys; everybody else was the bad guys. Sure, Yahweh was in charge, but . . .

For the first time in more than forty years of involvement in this endeavor, Joshua's eyes were opened to the real situation. This was Yahweh's battle against the dark spiritual forces who had usurped his earth. He had humiliated them in Egypt; now he was taking on the ones in Canaan. The Israelites were the good guys only because Yahweh had chosen them as his human agents and only to the extent that they followed his orders. Joshua was the human commander, but this being (whoever or whatever he was) was evidently his commanding officer. Joshua's nose hit the dirt.

The commander outlined Yahweh's orders. Once a day for six days Joshua was to march his men around Jericho with trumpets blaring. On the seventh they would march around it seven times, then the people would shout and the walls would collapse. Every living thing in the city must be killed (except Rahab's family), and all booty would be holy to Yahweh. The strange tactics would display that this was Yahweh's battle from first to last, so he alone would receive the spoils. As the first of Canaan's cities to fall and as a center of worship for the moon god, Jericho would be a symbol of Yahweh's judgment on the whole evil culture and the spirits behind it.

The attack went just as Yahweh commanded, except for one detail. One soldier couldn't resist taking just a little of the plunder for himself. To let Israel know what he thought of cheating, Yahweh withdrew his support in the next battle against the city of Ai. After a humiliating defeat, Israel's courage melted to mush, and Joshua spent all day on his face complaining to Yahweh.

Finally Yahweh responded, "Stand up! What are you doing down on your face?" He explained the trouble and ordered the culprit and his whole household (who were presumably accomplices) stoned to death. Because Israel was a community, the corruption of one man defiled the whole group. If Israel wanted a God who accompanied her at every step and gave detailed instructions for every battle, then she must pay the high price of such intimacy with a holy God. He intended to be stern at this early stage to convince the mob to take his holiness seriously.

ALMOST VICTORY

For the next seven years, Israel did take this lesson seriously, and Joshua led Israel in a two-pronged strategy to break the northern and southern Canaanite power bases. King after degenerate king fell with his nobles to Israelite swords. Not a few local peoples decided to throw their lot in with the newcomers. The city of Gibeon, for instance, was ruled by elders who hoped the Israelites might be more pleasant masters than the Canaanite overlords. They tricked Joshua into making a treaty with them and later became loyal servants of Yahweh.

The Israelite system should have attracted most of the underclasses of Canaan. Instead of a system that drove poor people to becoming slaves of their creditors, Yahweh's law said that each extended family must have its own plot of land and that clans (groups of families) were responsible to take care of their own so that land would never be sold outside the clan. It could be rented for a period, but every fifty years it reverted to the original family. Yahweh cared about the private needs of everyday people in a way Canaan's gods never did. He even cared about the land: every seven years the land had to be left uncultivated. (Israel didn't know that land needs to be left fallow periodically to reaccumulate soil nutrients, but Yahweh knew.)

Yet the Israelites let their golden opportunity slip away. After seven campaigns, the first stage of conquest was solidified. Joshua was around ninety years old, and it was time for the tribes to divide up the land and claim their inheritances without their aging general. But the people were getting tired. Caleb's family requested its portion and set off enthusiastically to wrest it from the enemy. The rest of Judah showed up for their allotment, but those clans were much less successful in taking their property because they trusted Yahweh less, so they decided to cut their losses and settle down among the Canaanites. Live and let live.

The tribes of Joseph took the same attitude and even grumbled about the measly portion they were getting. They didn't like having to clear forests in the rocky hills, and they were afraid of the Canaanites on the fertile plains who had iron-clad chariots while Israel didn't know how to work iron. The Israelites refused to listen when Joshua told them not to fear chariots, so they settled in the hills to eke out a living and left the Canaanites to enjoy the plains. Finally, Joshua practically had to drag the other tribes to allot and move into their lands. Conquest was just too much work, or too scary, and it was easier to tolerate Canaanite neighbors. One could even learn a few things from them.

This was just what Yahweh had warned against. Living as neighbors would lead soon enough to intermarriage, then intermingling of religions, and eventually to a debasing of Israel's morals. The drinking and whoring of Canaanite worship was attractive, and Israelite farmers would figure they could hedge their bets by placating Canaan's fertility gods and worshiping Yahweh. Pretty soon their kids wouldn't be sure Yahweh and Baal weren't different names for the same god.

It was this danger that had moved Yahweh to order the execution of all Canaanites and the destruction of all religious objects. When the Israelites faltered in this mission, Yahweh started leaving them to defeat. This was partly punishment and partly a test: if Israel wouldn't exterminate Canaan, could she resist its seduction?

This was Joshua's question just before his death. He held a spectacular covenant renewal ceremony at Shechem, a natural amphitheater flanked by two small mountains. As Moses had commanded (Deuteronomy 11:29), and as they had done when they first entered the land, half the people likely stood once again on Mount Gerizim shouting the blessings for keeping the covenant, while the other half stood on Mount Ebal shouting the curses for breaking the covenant. Joshua gave a stirring speech, exhorting the nation to choose whom it would serve: the pagan gods or Yahweh. The people swore to remain faithful to Yahweh and agreed that if they rebelled they deserved the curses. They cried, "Far be it from us to forsake Yahweh to serve other gods!" (Joshua 24:16).

But Joshua died, as did the leaders who had known him, and their successors were not cut from the same cloth. Less than fifty years after

Joshua's death, Israel had degenerated so far that she looked very much like a poor imitation of Canaan huddling in the few pieces of land the Canaanites hadn't taken back.

JUDGES

So began a sordid cycle. The people's love for Yahweh grew cold, and they practiced fertility religion in order to take by manipulation the prosperity that Yahweh would have given freely. Like a husband whose wife had been unfaithful, Yahweh withdrew his favor and let raiders plunder or enslave his people. When they saw they were losing every battle and were in danger of starving to death, they cried out to Yahweh for help. Then Yahweh forgave them and raised up a military leader to liberate Israel. And when the people were comfortable again, they forgot Yahweh and went back to the debauched customs of their neighbors, and the cycle repeated.

Moses had warned the people not to say when they grew rich, "My power and the strength of my hands have produced this wealth for me" (Deuteronomy 8:17). Three generations of Israelites had sworn they would never do this and had invited Yahweh to curse them if they did. Yahweh held the children to the bargain.

The author of the book of Judges sums up the situation neatly: "In those days Israel had no king [not even Yahweh most of the time]; everyone did as they saw fit" (Judges 21:25). What everyone saw fit to do got pretty disgusting.

For instance, one Levite took a concubine, but she ran away from his shack in the backwoods of Ephraim and returned to her father's house in Bethlehem, a nice little village in Judah. So the Levite traveled to Bethlehem to fetch her back. On their way home, they stopped for the night in Gibeah, a town in Benjamin. They sat in the city square for hours before an old man noticed them and offered them his hospitality. (Hospitality was a sacred duty throughout the Middle East. It was a matter of honor to offer it to travelers.) Sometime later the scum of the town banged on the host's door, demanding that he give the Levite over to them for gang homosexual rape. The only defense the Levite and his host could think of was to send the concubine out to the men, who raped and abused her until she died on the doorstep. The Levite carried her corpse home, then cut it into pieces and sent them to the elders of the other tribes.

The tribes were scandalized, so they attacked Benjamin. Three days of slaughter and pillage followed. In the end, there weren't enough women left in Benjamin to carry on the tribe, and the other tribes refused to give wives to Benjamin, but they agreed to let the Benjaminites kidnap women from an Israelite town who hadn't shown up for the battle when called (Judges 20:1–21:24).

This was the kind of degeneracy Yahweh was trying to drive out of his people by letting raiders oppress them. But even when he raised up a deliverer, he had poor material to work with. Ehud, for instance, was an assassin. Jephthah was an outlaw bandit of confused ethics; he offered his daughter as a blood sacrifice to Yahweh. Samson was more interested in sex than national liberation. And Gideon was a coward who tried every way he could think of to get out of having to lead Israel. But as with Jacob and Moses, Yahweh enjoyed working with losers because it would be obvious to anyone that he, not the human leader, deserved credit for the victory. Yahweh even told Gideon to send home all but three hundred of the thirty-two thousand troops who had gathered to drive out countless thousands of bandits.

In fact, in an age where women were commonly treated like the Levite's concubine and Jephthah's daughter, Israel's only really noble leader in several centuries was a woman. Deborah was a prophetess in Ephraim, and people came from far and wide to put before her their legal disputes. When a Canaanite king was oppressing the northern tribes, she asked a man named Barak to lead troops against the invaders. But Barak was afraid to go without Deborah. Because of his cowardice, Yahweh showed what he thought of Israel's men by allowing a housewife (Jael) to kill the Canaanite general.

WHAT ABOUT A KING?

It was an impossible situation. The Canaanites were multiplying again, and new peoples were moving from across the Mediterranean and settling on the western shore of Palestine (Phoenicians in the north and

Philistines in the south). While they raided from the west, nomads encroached from across the Jordan. Marauders made travel between tribes, and even between villages, perilous. Canaanites still held ground between tribal settlements. Even the geography was against Israel: hills and valleys dissected the region, especially cutting the northern tribes off from Judah and Simeon in the south. In theory Israel was a confederacy united under a common faith, gathering together three times a year around the tabernacle to celebrate their love for Yahweh. But in reality it was every clan for itself, with some villages so remote that they scarcely remembered their brethren. In particular, Judah (which contained Simeon) was rarely involved in the battles and interests of the rest of Israel.

What could be done? Some Israelites wanted a king to unite the nation against her enemies. Gideon had refused to become king, saying that Yahweh ought to be Israel's King (Judges 8:23). His son Abimelech tried to make himself king by murdering his brothers and staging a coup, but Yahweh dealt with him. Moses had warned that a human king would bring Israel nothing but trouble if he were not totally committed to Yahweh's justice (Deuteronomy 17:14–20). Kings were expensive; they tended tax the people to finance grandiose wars, building projects and lifestyles. But although local elders, prophets and occasional guerrilla freedom fighters were cheaper, they were not keeping Israel from chaos. Something had to change.

<><><><><><><><><><><><><><><><><><><><><><><><><><><><><><><><><><><><><><><><><>

Questions for Reflection and Discussion

1. Like Tamar (chapter 3), Rahab is one of the women whom Matthew names as ancestresses of the promised Son of Eve (Matthew 1). What makes her worthy of that special notice? What does it say about Yahweh that he chose women like these?

2. What did Joshua learn from his encounter with the com-

10

A TALE OF TWO KINGS

Ruth, 1 Samuel, Psalms 18 and 22

Something had to be done, and Yahweh was doing it. Quietly. A famine in Judah drove a family to Moab from Bethlehem. (See map, page 349.) The two sons of the family married Moabite women. Later, the father and both sons died. The bereaved wife and mother, Naomi, returned to Bethlehem, and one of her daughters-in-law was too loyal to let her go alone.

Once they were back in Judah, bitter Naomi and faithful Ruth survived by grit and grace, Ruth gathering the stalks of grain the harvesters left behind in rich men's fields. Yahweh maneuvered things so that Ruth worked in the field of Boaz, an unmarried kinsman of Naomi's who was far more faithful to his God than most Israelites of the day. Boaz noticed that Ruth had more guts and more morals than the wealthier women he knew, so he was entirely willing to fulfill a kinsman's duty to take over Naomi's husband's property and marry Ruth to provide children for her late husband's line. He didn't care that Ruth was a foreigner whom most Israelites would consider scum; she loved Yahweh and lived like it.

The book of Ruth calls Boaz and Ruth a man and woman of excellence—jewels of loyalty and generosity in the slime pit of vice and selfishness that was Israel in the late eleventh century B.C. They were nobodies, just trying to live God's way. But because they made themselves available to him, Yahweh let them play a key, if quiet, place in his design.

Boaz was a descendant of Judah through Perez. His and Ruth's first son was named Obed. Obed had a son named Jesse. And Yahweh had plans for one of Jesse's sons.

HANNAH AND SAMUEL

About the time Ruth and Boaz were happily raising Obed, another wife was suffering the curse of barrenness less than thirty miles north. This woman's husband had a second wife, a cruel woman who teased Hannah to the point that she prayed desperately for a baby. When Yahweh finally gave her a son, she was so grateful that she dedicated him to serve at the tabernacle as soon as he was about three years old. She gave him into the care of Eli, the priest in charge.

Eli was not a bad old guy, but his sons seduced the cleaning women and extorted money from the people who brought sacrifices, and Eli did nothing but scold them. Yahweh was so incensed that he told Eli he was going to wipe out his family.

At this time Israel's main threat was the Philistines. The fight was terribly uneven because the Philistines knew how to forge weapons from iron, while the Israelites knew how to make only bronze or stone weapons. Eli's sons tried to use the ark in battle like a talisman, but Yahweh turned his back. The ark was captured, Eli's sons died and that evening Eli died of shock when he heard the news. Yahweh sent plagues until the Philistines sent the ark back to Israel, but the Israelites put it in a little town and ignored it for twenty years.

Meanwhile, Hannah's son Samuel grew up to be a priest and a prophet. Because they trusted his prophecies and legal decisions, the people began to rely on him as their unofficial leader. He managed to do what no judge before him had done: unite the unruly tribes under one religious and legal authority. Samuel led the nation back to being faithful to Yahweh, and the tide of war began to turn in Israel's favor. The prophet-priest Samuel was even willing to serve as military chieftain when the need pressed. All in all, things went well for Israel as long as Samuel was traveling from town to town settling legal cases and exhorting the people to rely on Yahweh rather than Baal and Astarte. Samuel was preparing Israel for the next stage of her life in Yahweh's plan.

SAUL

When Samuel grew old, the people grew nervous. Like Eli, he had spent so much time fathering Israel that he had failed to raise his own sons properly. When he appointed them as judges in his place, they took bribes and turned the legal system into a racket.

Israel's elders had had enough. The nation had been a mess for several centuries, and they wanted somebody they could trust to establish order. The Israelite population was outgrowing its crude villages huddled in the hills, Canaan's least farmable land. The people wanted to spread into the lush plains, and for that they needed a battle chief who could unite the tribes. Under the current system a good leader might arise, but when he died Israel was back to square one—there was no way to find a successor other than to see who turned up. The elders didn't trust Yahweh to lead them, so they demanded a human king.

Samuel was furious and warned that they would regret the decision. But Yahweh simply said, You want a king? Okay, you see how you like it. The people should have learned from Eli's and Samuel's sons that hereditary monarchy was not all it was cracked up to be.

The fact was, Yahweh had been planning to give Israel a king. But he didn't care for the people's motive: to be like the other nations. They were like eight-year-olds who just had to have what the other kids had.

Yahweh also wanted to put on record the difference between a good king and a bad one. He wanted to give Israel a taste of wise government so they would never settle for less, and he wanted to make them sick of rulers who cared more for themselves than for Yahweh or his people.

Now if it were up to you, would you choose a leader whose overdependence on people's approval led him to break a few instructions about ritual and holy war? Or a leader who committed adultery and murder, and who was such a lousy father that he let his eldest son get away with raping his daughter and his second son get away with killing the first?

Yahweh chose man number two, of course. Approval seeking cost Saul his kingdom, but Yahweh forgave David's crimes. Why? Because Yahweh looked deeper than the outward action, down to the motives and attitudes of the heart.

Saul was a tall, handsome warrior, a fine military commander, successful for years. But it became obvious that he did not possess the basic quality of leadership in Yahweh's kingdom: trust in the King of kings. Fear of losing his men's loyalty made Saul disobey Yahweh repeatedly. People's opinions and his own interests just meant more to him than Yahweh's instructions, so like Adam, Saul could not imagine letting Yahweh be in charge. Samuel eventually notified him that he was going to be replaced. Even then Saul didn't actually grieve that he had disobeyed Yahweh but only begged Samuel to keep up appearances so the elders of Israel wouldn't know the two leaders were at odds.

DAVID

Yahweh genuinely felt sorry that he had to put Israel through the misery of being led by Saul, even though the nation deserved him. In the meantime he sent Samuel to Bethlehem to anoint one of the sons of Jesse as king. This one, Yahweh assured Samuel, would remember that he was only vice regent ruling under Yahweh's authority. (Anointing with oil signified conferring Yahweh's power and authority. Priests and kings were traditionally anointed.)

Samuel liked the looks of Jesse's seven older sons, but Yahweh commented, "People look at the outward appearance, but Yahweh looks at the heart" (1 Samuel 16:7). The chosen one turned out to be Jesse's youngest, David, a teenager whose whole life had been spent herding sheep and composing songs.

But Yahweh knew what he was doing. Adolescent David had guts that came not from self-confidence but from a matter-of-fact trust in Yahweh. One day Jesse sent him to take provisions to his brothers who were off soldiering with Saul. David found them all cowering in fear of a Philistine champion named Goliath, who had challenged Israel to settle the battle by single combat. Neither Saul nor his warriors dared face this hulk with the fifteen-pound iron point on his spear shaft. But David thought it was disgraceful for Yahweh's army to cringe in their tents. It never occurred to him to doubt his God, so he was sure Goliath was dead meat for insulting Yahweh. And true to his name, Yahweh was I Am There for David. The teenager felled Goliath with a well-aimed shot from his sling.

Everybody was more than impressed with David the shepherd warrior.

But Saul, whose courage was crumbling, was also beginning to suffer fits of depression, irrational jealousy and violence. He had rejected Yahweh, so Yahweh was allowing an evil spirit to torment him. Saul's servants were getting frantic, but they remembered that young David was also known as a fine harpist. David was summoned to Saul's court to play music when the king had one of his attacks. Saul liked the boy and made him an armor bearer.

FUGITIVE SINGER

David proved brilliant in battle, and soon the people were singing victory songs about Saul and David in the same breath. That was the last straw for Saul. His paranoia attached firmly to David. Nothing anyone could do would shake it. He tried to get rid of David by sending him on suicide missions, but David always made it through. One of Saul's schemes backfired, and David ended up married to Saul's daughter. He now had a legitimate claim to the throne, and Saul was even more scared. At last he tried to run David through with his spear, but David fled.

So began a decade in which David fled from Saul, who became obsessed with chasing him down. The Philistine war languished. Saul murdered a cityful of priests for allegedly harboring David, so intent was he on foiling Yahweh's plan to replace him. But David twice declined the chance to kill Saul. He was determined to let Yahweh deal with Saul and fulfill his promises in his own way. He refused to try to take by force what Yahweh promised by grace.

During the years when David was the fugitive captain of an outlaw band in the wastelands, when he even worked for the Philistines for a while in order to stay alive, what kept him going? His secret was pouring out his fears, hopes, praises and accusations to Yahweh in songs. He lived an intensely honest relationship with his God. He braved the truth about his own circumstances and feelings:

> My God, my God, why have you forsaken me?
>> Why are you so far from saving me,
>> so far from my cries of anguish? (Psalm 22:1)

And about Yahweh's unshakable character:

Yet you are enthroned as the Holy One;
> you are the one Israel praises.
In you our ancestors put their trust;
> they trusted and you delivered them. (Psalm 22:3-4)

It was the "yet" that sustained David through years of terror and seemingly futile waiting. David's trust was not in the rock caves or fortresses he hid in, but in Yahweh, his real refuge. He could write about Yahweh as an angry thundering God:

The earth trembled and quaked,
> and the foundations of the mountains shook;
> they trembled because he was angry.
Smoke rose from his nostrils;
> consuming fire came from his mouth,
> burning coals blazed out of it. (Psalm 18:7-8)

David knew that if this wrath were directed against him, he should slink in shame. But instead, it was directed against the spiritual and human forces arrayed against him:

The cords of death entangled me;
> the torrents of destruction overwhelmed me. . . .
In my distress I called to Yahweh;
> I cried to my God for help.
From his temple he heard my voice;
> my cry came before him, into his ears.
[Then] the earth trembled and quaked. . . .
He reached down from on high and took hold of me;
> he drew me out of deep waters.
He rescued me from my powerful enemy,
> from my foes, who were too strong for me. (Psalm 18:4, 6-7, 16-17)

Yahweh was his Father. Yahweh would handle the bullies who picked on his kid, although he would let David go through just enough trouble to raise him into a man.

SAUL'S END

Yahweh did deal with Saul. This king had killed or driven off his priests because they had aided David, his prophets had deserted him to join David in exile, and Yahweh wouldn't talk to him directly, so Saul was at his wits' end when the Philistines amassed to attack Israel. David had Yahweh's constant guidance about where to go and what battles to fight, but Saul had only silence. Crazed with panic, he consulted a witch to call up the ghost of Samuel (who had been dead for some years by now) for counsel, but the spirit he met only promised that Saul and his sons would be carrion fodder the next day.

And so it was. The Philistines overwhelmed Israel, and in despair Saul took his own life. Yahweh had maneuvered David a hundred miles south of the battlefield to protect him. When news came of Saul's death, he could not rejoice in an enemy's defeat but grieved for a man he had loved, who could have been great.

Questions for Reflection and Discussion

1. What were Saul's flaws as a leader? Why do you think Yahweh didn't just forgive those flaws, as he later forgave David?

2. What were David's qualifications for leadership?

3. Where is Yahweh's promise of a Deliverer at this point in the story?

<><><><><><><><><><><><><><><><><><><><><><><><><><><><><><><><><><><><><><>

11

DAVID'S GLORY
AND SHAME

2 Samuel, 1 Chronicles, Psalms 32 and 51

*D*avid knew his Father delighted in him because he was "righteous" and "blameless" (Psalm 18:20-24). But how could David say that about himself when his faults were so glaring that they nearly brought his hard-earned kingdom down around his ears? Simple. "Righteous" and "blameless" in Hebrew did not mean that David obeyed every one of a long list of rules flawlessly. They meant that David was living up to the terms of a covenant relationship.

Those terms, expressed at length by Moses, boiled down to loving and serving Yahweh with a passion that consumed one's whole being, confessing failure and rebellion when they occurred and desiring ardently to turn from and make amends for those wrongs. Even when he committed the most appalling crimes, David remained "righteous" in Yahweh's eyes because, unlike Saul, he never tried to rationalize or evade his guilt. He always felt more horror at offending his Beloved than at being found out.

JERUSALEM

After Saul's death David's own tribesmen were quick to welcome him back from Philistia to reign over Judah. But it took seven and a half years of civil war, allegations, treachery and assassination until the ten northern tribes were ready to turn from Saul's family and accept David as king. However, while David ruled Judah as tribal chief by popular acclaim, he governed Israel (the northern tribes) only by treaty: he and the tribal elders made a covenant to fulfill certain obligations to one another.

The Philistines had left Israel alone as long as it was divided and weak, but once David (whom they knew all too well) was proclaimed king of a united nation, they attacked swiftly, hoping to neutralize him before he got his footing. However, in two decades of leading armies David had learned the same secret that had carried Joshua to victory: Yahweh was his commanding officer. David consulted him before every battle. On occasion Yahweh even sketched the combat strategy.

Once he had subdued the Philistines, David faced his real challenge: governing his unruly people. Because Judah and Israel were rivals, it was difficult to choose a capital that would not make one or the other half of the nation feel slighted. So David cast his eye on a stronghold high in the mountains in the Canaanite territory between Judah and Benjamin. Because Jebus (also called Zion) belonged to neither Israel nor Judah, it would be a neutral site for a united kingdom. The only difficulties were: (1) it was held by about thirty-five hundred Canaanites, (2) its walls were surrounded on three sides by sheer dropoff, and (3) it had its own water supply that made it invulnerable to siege.

No problem. Since the location of the entrance to the water shaft was secret, Yahweh must have disclosed it to the Israelite army, which poured through it. So David established the fortress of Zion as his citadel and built up the land around it for a royal city. He called it Jerusalem—it was probably the Salem where a Canaanite priest-king, Melchizedek, had once reigned and won Abraham's homage. In the same vicinity was Mount Moriah, where Abraham had brought his promised son to be sacrificed.

Before long the neighboring nations began to take the new kingdom seriously. The Phoenician city of Tyre was the main seaport of Palestine. Tyre depended on Israel for agricultural products and for the inland trade routes to the rich East, while Israel desired the cedar of Phoenicia and luxury products from the West. So Israel and Tyre became allies, and the king of Tyre helped David build a regal palace, the Middle Eastern symbol of kingly status.

YAHWEH'S HOUSE AND DAVID'S HOUSE

But David felt that if Yahweh was the real King of Israel and he himself was only vice regent, then Yahweh needed a palace as grand as his. His first idea was to bring Yahweh's throne to Jerusalem. David really did mean well. He sulked for three months when one of his men died because he didn't know the ark shouldn't be touched (the writings of Moses had fallen into obscurity during the centuries of chaos). But he got over it and led the final procession that welcomed the ark into the city with shouts and trumpets. Wearing nothing but the skimpy undergarment of a priest, David cavorted with wild abandon to celebrate his King's arrival in his capital. David's wife was disgusted—her father Saul would never have displayed himself with such indignity. Exactly. David didn't care what people thought of him as long as Yahweh was delighted.

He hoped to please Yahweh with a fine cedar house instead of a tattered tent. But Yahweh sent a message through the prophet Nathan that, far from David building him a house, he was going to build David a house, as he had already begun to do. David would have a son who would build a palace for Yahweh, but Yahweh would build that son's lineage into a dynasty that would never fail to give Israel a king. Nathan, quoting Yahweh, prophesied, "I will be his father, and he will be my son. . . . Your house and your kingdom will endure forever before me; your throne will be established forever" (2 Samuel 7:14, 16).

> *David would have a son who would build a palace for Yahweh, but Yahweh would build that son's lineage into a dynasty that would never fail to give Israel a king.*

Alone with his King, David marveled, "Who am I, Lord Yahweh, and what is my family, that you have brought me this far? And as if this were not enough in your sight, Lord Yahweh, you have also spoken about the future of the house of your servant—and this decree, Lord Yahweh, is for a mere human! . . . There is no one like you" (2 Samuel 7:18-19, 22).

That was an understatement. An unending dynasty? Here was a promise to rival Abraham's. But Yahweh had kept his promises to make Abraham's descendants numerous and to give them this land with rest from their enemies. David could hardly doubt Yahweh's word, since he was sitting there as king having defeated everybody from Syria to Edom and from the Mediterranean to well east of the Jordan. (See map, page 349.)

LUST AND MURDER

David was flying high. He had been reigning in Jerusalem for some years, he was well over forty, and he was beginning to enjoy palace cushions more than mats in a tent on the eve of battle. So "in the spring, at the time when kings go off to war" (2 Samuel 11:1), he didn't. He let his nephew quell an uprising out east, and he stayed home to enjoy the cool evenings in his rooftop pavilion at the summit of Jerusalem.

One evening he noticed a woman—the wife of one of his captains—bathing in a courtyard below. The predictable happened to a bored leader in midlife: attraction, seduction, pregnancy. With uncharacteristic clay feet, David tried to cover up his crime by inviting the captain home for a little "R and R" with his wife. When the man refused to sleep with her out of loyalty to his men in the field (what a slap to David!), the king secretly ordered the commander in chief to send the captain to certain death on a frontline combat mission.

After a mourning period, David married the widow, Bathsheba. She had her son, and the gossip would have died down if Yahweh had only cooperated. But he had strong opinions about kings who used their power to get away with murder. So he sent Nathan to finger David. Because he loved him, Yahweh would not take away his throne. But so that no one would say that Yahweh's grace meant license to abuse other people, David's son would die, his family would be plagued by violence, and he would suffer the same shame he had inflicted: someone close to him would one day raid his harem. A stiff penalty, but in Yahweh's order, greater honor means greater responsibility and greater cost for rebellion.

David could have had Nathan executed. Or like Saul, he could have made excuses and asked the prophet to hush things up. But instead, he simply admitted with shame that he had held Yahweh up to contempt.

Throughout his son's illness he fasted, slept on the ground and begged Yahweh for mercy. When the child finally died, he got up. His servants were baffled. But all along David was betting on Yahweh's character: while the boy lived there was still time for the mercy David had received so often, and when the boy was dead, it was time to go on trusting his God as he always had.

Why was David righteous and blameless even though he was a seducer, liar and murderer? Consider three verses of the song that tradition says he wrote while watching his son die:

> Have mercy on me, O God,
>   according to your unfailing love;
> according to your great compassion
>   blot out my transgressions. (Psalm 51:1)
>
> Against you, you only, have I sinned
>   and done what is evil in your sight;
> so you are right in your verdict
>   and justified when you judge. (Psalm 51:4)
>
> My sacrifice, O God, is a broken spirit;
>   a broken and contrite heart
>   you, God, will not despise. (Psalm 51:17)

This was not a morbid wallowing in guilt but a frank facing of truth and a trusting pursuit of restored relationship. Forgiveness. The other nations had no concept of an intimacy with a god that evoked such feelings, nor that a god could forgive a person by accepting the pain of a wrong into his own heart. Forgiveness. Yahweh so obliterated the crime that he was willing to treat David as though nothing had happened. David was blameless. But not proud, not self-confident. He knew he owed a debt to his God payable only in gratitude.

> Blessed is the one
>   whose transgressions are forgiven,
>   whose sins are covered. (Psalm 32:1)

David understood the sweet freedom of forgiveness that meant he could approach his God with confidence.

Consequences

The relationship was restored, but the effects of wrong choices could not be evaded. David's two oldest sons lost respect for him after the Bathsheba affair. Amnon, his eldest and heir, raped his half-sister Tamar. David would not discipline his son for doing what he himself had done. Like Samuel and Eli, the man who had led Israel to a golden age was a failure as a father, and he would not face it. In disgust, Tamar's brother Absalom murdered Amnon.

And again David did nothing but refuse to see Absalom for five years so that he would not be reminded of his failures and poor example. Absalom matched David's rejection with contempt: he resolved to wrest the throne out from under his father's backside. The attempt nearly succeeded and left David broken with grief and disgrace. Absalom died miserably, but not until all Israel watched as the son violated his father's concubines on the palace roof.

David's Last Years

It did not bode well for a hereditary monarchy that healthy fathering was such an unknown art. But at about fifty years old, David resolved to try again. He passed over his surviving sons in favor of a new baby of Bathsheba's named Solomon. In his fifties and sixties David could no longer travel to war, so he spent his time preparing for the palace-temple that Solomon was to build for Yahweh. He amassed absurd quantities of gold, silver, bronze, iron, cedar, stone and workmen of all kinds. He had elaborate plans drawn up, detailing everything from the size of each portico to the weight of gold in the lampstand—all of which, like Moses, he received in consultation with Yahweh.

Since the tabernacle would no longer be used, he organized the Levites as to who would supervise various temple matters and who would serve as judges and officials in the towns of Israel. In particular, he appointed certain families of Levites as temple musicians: they would write and play all sorts of worship music on stringed instruments, trumpets and cymbals.

Our current book of Psalms traces its roots to these musicians, who collected songs written by or dedicated to David. They and successive generations for some six hundred years wrote more songs that ranged from riotous celebration in praise of Yahweh to heart-rending prayers for help. David's frank and passionate writing set the tone for the way Israel would worship her God.

At seventy years old, David managed to hand over his kingdom to his barely grown Solomon. Thanks to Nathan the prophet, a coup attempt by David's fourth son was crushed. David exhorted Solomon to do three things: tie up some nasty political loose ends, build the temple and, above all, obey Yahweh. The first two Solomon accomplished smoothly. The third, well . . .

<<<<<<<<<<<<<<<<<<<<<<<<<<<<<<<<<<<<<<<<<<<<<<<<<<<<<<<<<<<<<<<<<<<<<<<<<<<<<<<<<<<<<<<<<<<<<<<<

Questions for Reflection and Discussion

1. What were David's successes? What were his failures?

2. Why did Yahweh forgive his failures?

3. What were the consequences of David's failures? Why didn't Yahweh prevent the consequences after he forgave David?

12

TWO KINDS OF WISDOM

1 Kings 1–14, 2 Chronicles 1–12,
Job, Proverbs, Ecclesiastes, Song of Songs

One thing about David's court: It was always full of prophets. The prophet Gad had joined David's outlaw band. Nathan turned up when David settled Jerusalem. David even assigned some of the temple musicians to train in "the ministry of prophesying, accompanied by harps, lyres and cymbals." (It's unclear exactly what this involved.)

When we think of prophets, we may imagine fortunetellers, thundering preachers or wild-eyed desert ascetics. Pagan prophets were all of these, as well as magicians, ecstatic mediums and plain frauds. A prophet of Yahweh, however, was different.

Yahweh was Israel's King, and judges, elders, generals and human kings were his vice regents. Their job was to lead the people according to Yahweh's covenant law given to Moses. They couldn't do whatever they wanted; they had to follow the guidelines laid down in the covenant.

In this system the prophets were Yahweh's official emissaries to the kingdom. The kings and elders were not always gifted in hearing directly from Yahweh. Instead, the King gave specific instructions through prophets. For instance, David—who was pretty good at listening to Yahweh by himself—often asked the prophets' advice when making decisions about whether and how to fight battles, what to do about the temple and so on.

Besides instructions, the prophets also conveyed Yahweh's praise or rebuke. Praise came when the leaders or people were living up to the covenant; rebuke came when they were not. Nathan brought the good news that David must not build the temple but would have an eternal dynasty. He also had to bring the bad news that David was in hot water for abusing his royal power with adultery and murder. If Israel was a building under construction, David was the foreman and Nathan was the code inspector.

David liked to hear everything Yahweh had to say—even the bad news was better heeded than ignored. So prophets were welcomed at court, and Nathan was a trusted counselor. He and other prophets got David out of more than one political mess because of their wisdom and information from Yahweh.

There were probably other prophets in David's time who lived quietly, as they had during the time of the judges, listening to Yahweh and praying for the nation. In addition, the prophets established themselves as the record keepers of the kingdom's ups and downs. The Bible mentions "the records of Samuel the seer, the records of Nathan the prophet and records of Gad the seer" (1 Chronicles 29:29) on David's reign, as well as those of Ahijah, Iddo, Shemaiah and Isaiah (2 Chronicles 9:29; 12:15; 26:22) on the reigns of later kings. In fact, the Jews call the biblical books of Joshua through 2 Kings the Former Prophets because all of those history books were written by prophets or with their input as Yahweh's official assessment of how well Israel did or didn't live up to the covenant in each generation.

Certain prophets—Moses, Samuel, Elijah—were later singled out by the Jews as especially great. They were called the *shaluchim*, the "sent ones," because they were Yahweh's special envoys to guide the nation through a transition. Moses presided as Yahweh changed Israel from slaves to servants, and Samuel oversaw the shift from confederacy to monarchy.

But all of the prophetic activity during David's reign echoes against the silence under Solomon. Nathan and Gad died and were not replaced. Evidently Solomon did not care to hear Yahweh's ambassadors assess his rule.

KING OF WISDOM

Perhaps in the beginning he did not need to. Twenty-year-old Solomon prayed for the wisdom to govern the nation justly, and Yahweh granted the request. Solomon started off as a brilliant judge and administrator. In the international luxury trade, he launched some joint ventures with neighboring states that began to bring huge profits. The temple rose magnificently in seven years, and after it followed thirteen years of construction on an opulent palace. Solomon's court became known throughout the East as a center of wisdom.

In those days "wisdom" was the art or skill of sensible living, an understanding of the right goals and the best means of reaching them. Attaining wisdom was the purpose of education throughout the East. Fathers or teachers imparted wisdom to pupils or sons by means of proverbs, pithy sayings that crystallized truth memorably through vivid figures of speech. Archaeologists have unearthed collections of wisdom from Egypt, Babylon and elsewhere that date from around the time of Solomon.

But Solomon was the master of his day. He wrote three thousand proverbs himself and collected many more from Israel and the surrounding nations. Learned men came from all over to hear Solomon's ideas about wise government, family life, even plants and animals.

Unlike his pagan neighbors, Solomon knew the essence of true wisdom:

> The fear of Yahweh is the beginning of wisdom,
> and knowledge of the Holy One is understanding. (Proverbs 9:10)

This fear was not craven cowering before an angry God but a realistic awareness that Yahweh was in charge. To fear anything—enemies, people's disapproval, failure, sickness, death—more than Yahweh was to leave the path of wisdom. The right means and ends were those that came from Yahweh and conformed to his moral requirements. Humanity was not the measure. Human reason was not ultimate. Truth was not relative.

These perceptions led Solomon to other observations such as these:

> When pride comes, then comes disgrace,
> but with humility comes wisdom. (Proverbs 11:2)

> Wealth is worthless in the day of wrath,
>> but righteousness delivers from death. (Proverbs 11:4)

From this foundation, Solomon accumulated insights into government, parenting, marriage, friendship, work, emotions and every other arena of daily life. He also wrote 1,005 songs.

The Bible contains a collection of wedding songs, called the Song of Songs, which is attributed to Solomon. The collection tells the story of a courtship, marriage and consummation. It places Yahweh's stamp of approval on passionate, erotic love within a committed marriage.

> Place me like a seal over your heart,
>> like a seal on your arm;
> for love is as strong as death,
>> its jealousy unyielding as the grave.
> It burns like blazing fire,
>> like a mighty flame.
> Many waters cannot quench love;
>> rivers cannot sweep it away.
> If one were to give
>> all the wealth of one's house for love,
>> it would be utterly scorned. (Song of Songs 8:6-7)

This song expands on the counsel to a young man in Proverbs:

> May your fountain be blessed,
>> and may you rejoice in the wife of your youth.
> A loving doe, a graceful deer—
>> may her breasts satisfy you always,
>> may you ever be intoxicated with her love. (Proverbs 5:18-19)

PRIDE AND DISGRACE

The trouble was, the more rich, powerful and respected Solomon grew for his wisdom, the more he began to rely on it instead of its source: his fear of Yahweh. Forgetting the beginning of wisdom, he soon forgot what he knew about pride, wealth and love.

It was a clever move on his part to divide Israel into twelve administrative districts for taxation and labor enlistment. In bypassing the tribal boundaries he weakened the quarrelsome tribal leaders and strengthened his central government. He was shrewd to marry seven hundred royal wives to cement alliances with all of his neighbors and to make a pharaoh's daughter his queen and build her a splendid palace of her own. It was astute of him to fortify strategic towns on major trade routes and to amass fourteen hundred chariots and twelve thousand horses to protect his country's economic and security interests.

But all of this smart politicking proved to be his undoing. Even the wealth of international trade could not finance Solomon's lavish building projects and defense spending. He had to rely on work gangs conscripted from the common people, on high taxes from the same folk and on royal bureaucrats to administer the increasingly complex system. Jerusalem was opulent, but Israel was remembering that Samuel had predicted all of this (1 Samuel 8:11-18).

Even more serious, as Solomon blossomed in the international sophisticate set, he was drawn to the exotic gods of his foreign wives. The man who wrote an ardent poem about monogamous love was ensnared by clever alliances and promiscuity. "Many roads lead to the divine" became the mentality in cosmopolitan Jerusalem, and why shouldn't the queens of Israel have altars for their gods? Soon children were being sacrificed to Molech on a hill east of the capital, and all manner of rites were being performed within.

The king's example gave license to the people to dabble in Baal and Ashtoreth worship, spiritism and whatever else they fancied. Israel was becoming like any other Middle Eastern land. Solomon had forgotten what he had prayed when dedicating the temple, the whole reason Yahweh had wanted a glorious building in the first place:

> As for the foreigner who does not belong to your people Israel but has come from a distant land because of your name—for they will hear of your great name and your mighty hand and your outstretched arm—when they come and pray toward this temple, then hear from heaven, your dwelling place. Do whatever the foreigner asks of you, *so that all the peoples of the earth may know your name and fear you*, as do your own people Israel, and may know that this house I have built bears your Name. (1 Kings 8:41-43, emphasis added)

Solomon's temple and kingdom were supposed to be setting an example that would attract the nations to Yahweh, not conforming to those nations' corrupt values.

Yahweh was not about to let Solomon wreck his plan. Because of his promise to David, he did not wrench the whole kingdom out from under Solomon and his heirs. But he did tell Solomon that the realm would be sundered after his death. He also sent a prophet to a man named Jeroboam, the head of Solomon's work gangs in Ephraim, to say that Yahweh was going to put Jeroboam in charge of the northern tribes of Israel. Jeroboam jumped the gun, launched an abortive coup to fulfill the prophecy, and had to spend the last years of Solomon's reign hiding out in Egypt.

REHOBOAM AND JEROBOAM

After thirty-three golden years under David and forty under Solomon, the flower of the nation shriveled and fell in 931 B.C. Solomon's son Rehoboam succeeded him in Jerusalem, and the elders of the people traveled there to renegotiate their covenant with Judah's tribal chief. The leader of this delegation was none other than Jeroboam. Rehoboam had been raised to be a haughty oriental monarch, not Yahweh's vice regent and the elected leader of the twelve tribes. (Failed fathering again!) The elders could see that there would be nothing but more taxes, forced labor and bureaucracy from this fool, so they thumbed their noses at him and walked out.

The people of Israel were quick to proclaim Jeroboam king to protect them from Rehoboam (who was prevented from invading them only by another prophet's warning that Yahweh wouldn't let him win). So now there were two nations with two kings: Judah (which included Simeon and Benjamin) and Israel (which included everybody else). (See map, page 349.)

The prophet had warned Jeroboam that his throne was only as secure as his loyalty to Yahweh. He was I Am With You only for those, like Joshua and David, who knew who was really in charge. But Jeroboam was like Saul. Instead of looking at the God who had made him, the son of an obscure widow, to be king in Israel, he looked at the impossible situation facing him. The people still venerated David and Yahweh, and they had gotten used to going to Jerusalem for the magnificent festivals Solomon had staged. Jeroboam was convinced that if they kept traveling to Jerusalem three times a year, they would soon return their allegiance to Rehoboam. So he devised a solution that seemed astute to human reason but proved foolish in the long run, because it bypassed the wisdom from Yahweh.

Jeroboam's scheme was to set up two national cult centers in Bethel and Dan, in the north and south of his kingdom. (See map, page 349.) In each he placed a golden calf—Syrian and Canaanite gods were often depicted standing on calves as symbols of fertility. Thus Israel's calves with no visible god riding them would represent Yahweh's throne, counterparts to the ark in Jerusalem. Jeroboam hand-picked some loyal followers to be priests and scheduled festivals to substitute for the ones in Jerusalem. He dealt ruthlessly with rebel Yahwists but gave free rein to any sort of pagan worship. Jeroboam knew that religion was either the opiate or the amphetamine of the masses, and he wanted Israel addicted to his supply.

The whole contrivance was a mockery of what Yahweh had ordained. It reminded him of Babel, and he knew who was behind it. He gave Jeroboam one chance to reconsider: he sent a prophet from Judah to denounce the new cult. To show he meant business, he split the altar at Bethel from top to bottom. Yahweh then shriveled the king's hand when he tried to assault this emissary, until Jeroboam apologized.

Still Jeroboam persisted in his rebellion, so Yahweh took his eldest son's life and decreed that not one of his other descendants would even receive a decent burial. Israel's spurned Parent had no choice but to play hardball with children who were willing to squander the hope of the human race for the sake of their own power and pleasure.

It was the same with Rehoboam. He kept up the state religion only because it supported his throne. He was glad to let Levites and other Yahweh-lovers flee from the north into his land, but he did nothing to discourage the spread of paganism that had begun in Solomon's time. Orgies and homosexual prostitution were added to child sacrifice. Rehoboam shaped up somewhat in his personal loyalty to Yahweh after

Egypt overran Judah and looted Jerusalem. But in all, Rehoboam's C-minus grade was not much better than Jeroboam's F. The prophets had gone underground while wisdom reigned in Solomon's court, but they were back in force in the divided kingdom as both halves teetered toward disaster.

WARNINGS ON WISDOM

True wisdom is as much a gift from Yahweh as revelation, but the case of Solomon proves that abused wisdom is disastrous. As wisdom flourished in Judah and Israel for centuries after Solomon, later writers exposed and refuted the most dangerous abuses.

Ecclesiastes. One wise man looked around him at an increasingly worldly culture. Its people believed in God, of course, but they saw him as a far-off Creator, someone who didn't matter in day-to-day life. The real world was about getting and spending—a first-class education, work, accomplishments, wealth, status, pleasure.

To shake his society to its senses, the wise man wrote a reflection on its approach to life. He called it "The words of the Teacher, son of David, king in Jerusalem." He may have been Solomon, or he may have been saying, here's what we can learn from a reflection on Solomon's life:

> "Meaningless! Meaningless!"
>> says the Teacher.
> "Utterly meaningless!
>> Everything is meaningless." (Ecclesiastes 1:2)

The Hebrew word translated "meaningless" means mist or vapor, something fleeting, here now and then gone in the sun's heat (see how it's translated in Proverbs 21:6 and 31:30). Education is good, yes, but it doesn't offer ultimate meaning to life. Work too is good, and so is achievement, but to strive after these things as if they can give meaning to your life is to strive after mist. Life is as brief as morning dew. Wealth, status and pleasure don't last. Death comes to the smart as well as the stupid, the high achiever and big spender as well as person who lives simply. If all you look at is this life "under the sun," then "surely the fate of human beings is like that of the animals; the same fate awaits them both: As one dies, so dies the other" (Ecclesiastes 3:19).

How then shall a wise person live? The Teacher draws two main conclusions. First, although this world offers no ultimate meaning, it was created good and can be enjoyed with humility. Get married, he says. Work. Enjoy a good meal with family and friends. Just don't attach the hunger of your soul to any of these good things.

Second, don't approach life as if God is irrelevant. God is present here and now, and he is not mere mist. He is far more solid than the things that look so solid but are not. In the last two sentences of his book, the Teacher gives his response to the strivings of the worldly:

> Fear God and keep his commandments,
>> for this is the duty of all mankind.
> For God will bring every deed into judgment,
>> including every hidden thing,
>>> whether it is good or evil. (Ecclesiastes 12:13-14)

Ultimate meaning can be found only in God, and he will judge our deeds done under the sun. Work and wisdom and honesty are not futile because Yahweh is unfolding a plan in what we do, and death is not the end. The life of obedience outlined by Moses is worth living now and promises a rich future. Pie in the sky when you die? Absolutely. But, contrary to what the world would say, that future pie is worth living for.

Job. Another Israelite was fed up with people who took the teachings of wisdom as iron-clad promises from a legalistic God. Solomon had written, "The righteous person is rescued from trouble, and it falls on the wicked instead" (Proverbs 11:8), along with many more proverbs in the same vein. Such sayings were meant to be pithy statements of how the world works in general and in the long run, not universal laws. But some people who wanted to nail God down and get the rules straight so they would feel secure took the proverbs as absolutes. The righteous prosper and the wicked suffer—that's God's justice. So if you're suffering, you must be wicked. Right?

Wrong. There is a snake in the grass. Disgusted with small-minded people who made a mockery of Yahweh, this unknown Israelite told the story of Job, a completely righteous man—so good you could hardly believe it. And as the proverbs promised, he was rich, healthy and loved. But Satan made the accusation that the legalists hadn't thought of: Job isn't righteous because he loves Yahweh; he's good out of pure self-interest. Virtue pays, the serpent charged. Yahweh buys loyalty with goodies. If Yahweh were to take away the benefits, Job would spit in his face.

This was a severe allegation. The whole human experiment was designed to demonstrate to the cosmos that Yahweh was a Lover who longed to be freely loved by an uncoerced bride, that he deserved to be trusted even in the dark. So Yahweh took Satan up on his dare.

> *The whole human experiment was designed to demonstrate to the cosmos that Yahweh was a Lover who longed to be freely loved by an uncoerced bride, that he deserved to be trusted even in the dark.*

However, when Job lost his wealth, his family and his health, he had no idea that he was a living test case that those who love Yahweh do so just because they love him, not because he buys it. Nor did his friends. They quoted him all the proverbs about how if he was suffering, he must have done something wrong. When Job protested that he hadn't done anything to deserve this treatment, his friends furiously denounced him for calling God unjust. To them, if God was in control, life had to be fair always. Everything that happened to you had to be a direct result of whether you'd been good or not.

In the end Job silenced his accusers by calling upon Yahweh to appear and judge his case. He didn't even really care whether his health recovered, so long as he could have an honest, face-to-face relationship with the real God.

Job's friends expected lightning from heaven to swallow Job up for such a challenge. And when Yahweh appeared in a mighty storm, his response did flatten Job, but not as his friends expected. In an avalanche of questions, Yahweh demonstrated that he indeed had both the wisdom to know how to run the world justly and the power to accomplish what he decided.

It was not for a divine lack of understanding or ability that life was unfair, he told Job. Life was unfair because the enemy had corrupted it. There was no way to get rid of evil in the world by force without annihilating everybody, and that Yahweh was unwilling to do. He had another plan, and in the meantime, the good guys would suffer right along with the bad. Sometimes they would suffer more, because the enemy wanted to make the good guys bitter against Yahweh, or at least miserable in their faithfulness. But when the wise were confused in their distress, they wouldn't make petty rules about God to rationalize what was happening. They would, like Job in the end, bow in awe and trust at the One whose wisdom, power and goodness far surpassed their wildest imaginations. Job summed up what he had learned as follows:

> Then Job replied to Yahweh:
> "I know that you can do all things;
>> no purpose of yours can be thwarted. . . .
> My ears had heard of you
>> but now my eyes have seen you. (Job 42:1-2, 5)

Job no longer needed answers to his questions. To glimpse Yahweh once was more than enough for a lifetime of faith in the dark.

Several centuries after Solomon, his proverbs and those of other wise men were collected into the book of Proverbs. That book remains an invaluable guide to practical living. Wisdom stands alongside revelation as a priceless gift from God. But Ecclesiastes and Job remind us that wisdom must be understood in light of who Yahweh is. He's the God whose thoughts and ways are so far beyond our minds that they cannot be reduced to legalisms to make us feel safe. But he's also the God who is right there with us, infusing our every day with meaning. Life is not fair, but it matters deeply because of who its Author is.

Questions for Reflection and Discussion

1. What is wisdom? In what ways was Solomon wise? In what ways was he unwise?

2. What does the book of Ecclesiastes add to our understanding of wisdom? What does the book of Job add?

3. Why did Israel split into two kingdoms, Judah and Israel? Where should we look for Yahweh's promise of the Son of Eve (Son of David) from this point forward?

13

◇◇

POWER
ENCOUNTERS

1 Kings 15–2 Kings 12; 2 Chronicles 13–24

*I*srael and Judah split because petty despots fancied themselves grand
monarchs and refused to submit to a King who had the whole people's
interests at heart. The result was pathetic. For two centuries Israel and
Judah played a triangle game with Syria. Two of the nations allied against
the third until it was defeated. Then the two turned on each other. When
one feared conquest, it sent money to the third to make a treaty, and the
cycle repeated. This went on until Egypt and Assyria grew strong enough
to play, too, and between them they gobbled up the three others. (See
map, page 348.)

In the meantime the game bled the resources—human and financial—
of all three players. Judah fared best because its rugged topography made
it less accessible, because it had a stable ruling dynasty and because
Yahweh was faithful to his promise to David. Israel was battered by coups
and assassinations—in two hundred years it went through twenty kings
from nine families, while Judah went through twelve (including one
usurping queen) from one family during the same period. At that point
Assyria destroyed Israel but Judah survived.

The prophetic author of 1 and 2 Kings assessed each ruler according
to the covenant standard. Using David as the standard for an A, he eval-
uated the Judan kings' faithfulness to Yahweh (from Rehoboam to the

Babylonian captivity) and came up with ten Fs, two Ds, one C, three Bs, three A-minuses and only one fairly solid A: Josiah. The bright spots in Judah were unparalleled in Israel; all her kings failed. Yahweh did not grade on a curve.

Only one royal family in Israel really succeeded in becoming a dynasty, and it proved to be the most dangerous of all to Yahweh's plan. Through that family the snake nearly succeeded, not only in corrupting Israel to the point of no return but also in exterminating the house of David in Judah. The tactics were military force and politics, but also witchcraft and deception on an unprecedented scale. Yahweh fought back as he had not done since the days of Moses and Joshua. Open demonic activity invited open divine response, and (as the serpent well knew by now) Yahweh's plan depended on the lineage of David.

OMRI

For fifty years after the split, things degenerated. Judah endured two worthless kings, then began struggling back under the long reign of Asa. Israel went through five kings, spent six years in civil war, then finally settled down to eleven stable years under the victor, Omri.

Omri was as shrewd as Jeroboam and realized that to compete with Judah he needed a capital of equal splendor. So he bought a hill near Shechem, named it Samaria after its former owner and built a citadel on it to rival the fortress of Zion. Omri began, and his son completed, work on grand palaces, administrative quarters and homes like those Solomon had built in Jerusalem. In Samaria the houses of the rich priests, nobles and bureaucrats who served the thriving kingdom were divided from the poor neighborhood by a wall. (Jerusalem definitely had uptown and downtown. The best real estate was upwind from cooking and sewage odors. But nobody had thought of a wall.)

Omri put Israel on the map. His dynasty lasted only forty-four years, but a century and a half later the Assyrians were still calling Israel "the house of Omri." Omri did his best to copy Solomon's Egyptian-style administration.

He also imitated Solomon in making foreign alliances. He married his son Ahab to the Phoenician princess Jezebel. When Ahab became king he topped Jeroboam by building a temple for Jezebel's god Baal in Samaria itself and dropping all pretense of worshiping Yahweh. Baal became the official state god—a mockery of Yahweh's kingship in Jerusalem.

AHAB, JEZEBEL AND ELIJAH

In response, Yahweh brought in the big guns. Ahab's predecessors had tolerated Yahweh's prophets and hadn't executed them even when they graphically prophesied the kings' deaths. They took Yahweh seriously enough not to mess with his envoys. At this time the prophets were grouped in companies—communities in which one who felt called to serve Yahweh could reside and learn with other likeminded people. They lived in austerity on the fringes of the increasingly depraved Israelite society to protest the nation's materialism, and generally they didn't bother the king unless Yahweh had a message for him (which wasn't often). Probably they spent most of their time imploring Yahweh not to let their country go to the dogs.

However, Jezebel was a practicing witch, an all-out viper's daughter and enemy of Yahweh. But Yahweh had been grooming a prophet of the stature of Moses and Samuel. Elijah, whose name meant "Yahweh is God," was a tough desert dweller in camelhair shorts who arrived in Samaria one day with an official notice: Israel belonged to Yahweh. If her kings and priests did not recognize him as their Sovereign, they were guilty of treason. If they thought Baal the storm god was better than the gods of Egypt and Canaan whom Yahweh had dealt with in the past, they were mistaken. And to prove that Baal, Jezebel and every pagan priest from Hamath to Jericho shouting together couldn't squeeze one drop out of the sky, there would be neither dew nor rain in Israel until Elijah said so.

That was it. Elijah walked out. He went out east alone and Yahweh provided him with food until the brooks all dried up. Then he went to Sidon (Jezebel's home territory) and Yahweh directed him to a starving widow. He stayed with her while Yahweh miraculously replenished her supply of oil and grain. When her son fell ill and died, Yahweh enabled Elijah to raise him from the dead. Yahweh's point: Unlike Baal, I can take care of my own. And if my people want to spit in my face, I can find faithful people to bless in the seedbed of paganism itself. Remember, my covenant with Israel is for the sake of the nations.

> *I can find faithful people to bless in the seedbed of paganism itself. Remember, my covenant with Israel is for the sake of the nations.*

SINGLE COMBAT

Nearly three years passed and Ahab didn't get the message. Jezebel began massacring Yahweh's prophets until Ahab's chief of staff resorted to hiding a hundred of them in two caves and bringing them supplies secretly. Yahweh could have let the nation starve, but he had compassion even on traitors. So he sent Elijah back to face Jezebel's prophets.

The challenge was simple. Jezebel's 850 prophets would set up one bull for a burnt offering, and Elijah would set up another. The god who sent fire to consume his sacrifice was the real God; the other was a fake. The people gathered at the site on Mount Carmel and agreed to take this single combat as proof.

Baal's prophets exhausted themselves in ecstatic dances, shouting and slashing themselves to arouse their god to act. Elijah poked fun (Shout louder! Maybe he's asleep, busy, traveling!) to underscore the absurdity of carrying on like this for a nonexistent god. Finally, as evening was coming, Elijah arranged his sacrifice and told the bystanders to pour water on it until even a trench around it was filled. Nothing up my sleeve.

Then Elijah prayed briefly, and lightning struck his sacrifice and consumed the bull, the wood and even the water in the trench. The people fell prostrate and cried, "Yahweh is God!" At Elijah's order they slaughtered the priests of Baal.

Elijah sent them off to eat while he prayed for rain. When at last a cloud appeared on the horizon, he told Ahab to get down the mountain before the storm stopped him. And full of the Spirit of God, Elijah ran before Ahab's chariot some twenty miles to Jezreel.

Ahab could not have had a more solid incentive to abandon his wife's god and lead the nation back to Yahweh. But although he was stubborn, he lacked real backbone. He could put on a good macho show to cover up his essentially weak masculinity, but Jezebel controlled him. Ahab informed her of the events on Carmel. She sent a death threat to Elijah. Ahab did nothing.

Elijah was crushed. As he saw it, Yahweh had played his trump card and it had made no ultimate difference. Like many people he apparently assumed that if Yahweh demonstrated his majesty publicly, everyone would turn to love and faithfulness. But with the witch still in charge there would be no national repentance. He had failed. The snake had won.

But Yahweh had known since Eden that power would not win love. He had made a real offer and had stripped Israel of the excuse that he was absent and silent, but the results did not surprise him. And while he loved this crusty prophet, he couldn't have him sulking in a cave in the Sinai desert. (Ironically, Elijah had fled to Horeb, where so many years ago Yahweh had twisted a discouraged Moses' arm into leading Israel out of Egypt.) This time Yahweh showed his envoy a little object lesson.

> *Yahweh had known since Eden that power would not win love.*

Fireworks isn't my trump card. I can come in storm and wind when I want to. But you know that mostly those aren't my style.

Mostly I come in a whisper to people like you who are willing to listen. And there are seven thousand more in Israel who are listening. So don't give up. I haven't. We're not going to beat this snake with pyrotechnics. You'll see: It's only going to take a whisper.

ELISHA

But it was going to be a loud whisper for a while with opponents like Jezebel still at large. Yahweh gave Ahab every chance, miraculously intervening in battles against Syria and sending prophet after prophet to encourage him or get in his face. He did humble himself before Yahweh enough to die in battle instead of murder. But he kept letting his wife cajole him into acting like a Phoenician tyrant, and he had no respect for Yahweh's messengers.

Ahab's eldest son carried on his tradition; he died without leaving an heir, having consulted a Philistine god for healing and trying to murder Elijah. His brother Joram succeeded him. Early in Joram's reign Elijah was taken into heaven in a flaming chariot, and his office as Israel's head prophet passed to his protégé, Elisha.

Elisha had the nerve to ask for a double dose of Elijah's spirit (a.k.a. Yahweh's Spirit). And Yahweh—who likes that kind of spunk if it accompanies humility and love—granted the request. Elijah had prayed and sweated for a national cleansing, and Elisha now led one into being. Elisha did twice as many spectacular miracles as his mentor.

The miracles were eye-catching exhibits of Yahweh's character. Some, such as a famine, trumpeted judgment against Israel's depravity. Many more displayed his compassion for the innocent (helpless widows and hungry prophets) who suffered for that depravity along with the guilty. Some miracles protected Israel and Judah from destruction by Syria. And one was yet another reminder that Yahweh's plan concerned more than twelve tribes.

Syria's commander-in-chief received healing from leprosy because he humbled himself enough to obey a seemingly childish instruction from Elisha. This adversary of Israel went away with such respect for the God of Israel that he took back some dirt in order to worship him on his native soil. It was a disgrace: the glory of Yahweh was under the noses of Israel's leaders every day and they failed to perceive it while a foreigner was overcome by it on his first encounter. Who were the real chosen people?

Yahweh gave Joram twelve years of Elisha's miracles to catch on to what Israel was supposed to be about—being a light to people like this Syrian officer. Joram did take down the phallic symbol in honor of Baal that had adorned the capital in Ahab's day. But it was a weak gesture, and finally Yahweh told Elisha to put an end to Omri's dynasty.

JEHU

The selected instrument was Jehu, an Israelite army commander and opportunist. After being anointed by one of Elisha's prophetic students, Jehu led his men out to meet Joram and his nephew Ahaziah, the king of Judah, as they were recovering from battle against Syria. He killed them both in Jezreel and had Joram's body thrown onto a plot of land that Joram's father, Ahab, had stolen from someone he'd murdered. He then made short work of Joram's mother, Jezebel. Next came a bloodbath of the remaining seventy male heirs of Ahab, all of their supporters and every Baal-worshiper Jehu could find.

Yahweh rewarded this thoroughness with a promise to give Jehu a four-generation dynasty. But Jehu was no more faithful to Yahweh than Jeroboam had been, so Yahweh allowed Syria to slowly whittle Israel away. There would be blood and more blood until the nation recognized the one on whom its life depended.

ATHALIAH AND THE ATTEMPTED TAKEOVER OF JUDAH

All the same, Yahweh worship was legal again in Israel and the poison of Jezebel was neutralized. But not before it had infected Judah. This was the serpent's real goal.

Let's catch up on events to the south. Early in the reign of Ahab, when Jezebel was just getting rolling, Jehoshaphat inherited the throne of Judah. Like his father Asa, Jehoshaphat was basically a good king, appointing honest judges and doing his best to quell the Baal worship that Rehoboam had encouraged. Under Asa and Jehoshaphat there were basically good relations among the priests who taught the law of Yahweh, the king who administered the law and the prophets who assessed how well the nation and its leaders were keeping the law.

But Asa and Jehoshaphat had one weakness: when threatened with war, they tended to make foreign alliances rather than trusting Yahweh. Prophet after prophet rebuked both father and son for doing this. Yahweh enabled these kings to win miraculous victories when they took the risk of allying with him only. But they didn't get the message.

This no-alliance rule wasn't a petty whim of Yahweh's. It was given to prevent the near disaster that occurred when Jehoshaphat allied with Ahab. Jehoshaphat married his son Jehoram to Ahab's daughter Athaliah. Now unity among the twelve tribes was a great idea, but this was neither the time nor the method with Israel such a cesspool of witchcraft.

The result was that Athaliah (who was a daughter of Jezebel in every way) corrupted Jehoram. Her Jezebel style was evident when early in his reign Jehoram murdered all of his brothers so as to have no rivals for the throne. Things got so bad that Elijah himself wrote a warning to Jehoram, but the king ignored the letter and contracted an illness sent by Yahweh to punish his wickedness. Jehoram was such an appalling king that his people refused even to give him a royal funeral or bury him in the royal crypt.

All of Jehoram's sons but one—Ahaziah—had died in a Philistine attack. His mother, Athaliah, controlled his every move, so he would have been as poisonous a king as his father except that when Jehu seized the kingship of Israel, he killed Ahaziah along with Joram.

When Athaliah saw that the Yahwists had killed both her nephew Joram and her son Ahaziah, she was ripe to fulfill her viper lord's scheme. She set about slaughtering every surviving person descended from David, including her own grandsons. When they were apparently all dead, she proclaimed herself queen of Judah.

If Athaliah had succeeded, the Davidic lamp would have been extinguished and the kings of Israel would have claimed Judah when she died, because she was a daughter of an Israelite king. There would have been no son of David to fulfill the prophecies, and Israel would have been a united pagan nation.

But Athaliah's sister-in-law had hidden an infant son of Ahaziah. For six years a priest named Jehoiada nurtured the child while Athaliah ruled. At last Jehoiada staged a quick coup and crowned Joash.

Joash ruled well until Jehoiada's death. And even though later he turned rotten and murdered Jehoiada's prophet-son for denouncing him, and even though his own officials eventually assassinated him in return, the house of David survived in his sons.

Questions for Reflection and Discussion

1. What role did Yahweh's prophets serve (see also chapter 12)? How did Elijah fulfill that role in the northern kingdom (Israel)?

2. Elijah and Elisha were among the very few prophets who performed miracles. What purposes did their miracles serve? Why do you suppose Yahweh didn't do that in every generation?

3. How did the evil queen Athaliah pose a threat to the promise about the Son of David? How was the threat defeated?

14

ENFORCING
THE COVENANT

2 Kings 13–17, Amos, Hosea, Jonah

hroughout Israel's history Yahweh geared his tactics to fit the situation. His use of prophets is a case in point. When David had needed counselors who would guide and support him in his commitment to serve Yahweh, his Lord sent Gad and Nathan. When Solomon wanted no prophets, he got none. When the nation split, the southern prophets continued to follow the pattern of Nathan to the degree that the kings imitated David. Prophets, priests and kings worked together in the good times. In the bad times the prophets were often silent, as under Solomon.

Things were different in the northern kingdom. The trouble there was not just a diluting of Yahweh worship but a total sellout to Baal or Jeroboam's state-run pseudo-Yahwism. The lines between good and evil were sharp. The enemy's tactics included open witchcraft. Open supernatural assault demanded overt confrontation—in other words, the power displays of Elijah and Elisha.

In the background there were always "the sons of the prophets," members of the prophetic communities who supported the plan through hidden intercession and who recorded key events for posterity. Indeed, even Elijah and Elisha spent most of their ministries in this hiddenness.

But interestingly, Yahweh did not instruct the prophetic communities to collect the sermons of their leaders. We have few or no recorded public messages of the prophets from 1400 to 800 B.C.

This pattern shifted around 800 B.C. The biblical books from Joshua through 2 Kings (minus Ruth, which is a short story) are the Former Prophets—the history of Israel and Judah from a prophetic viewpoint. But the books from Isaiah to the end of the Old Testament (minus Daniel, a special case) are the Latter Prophets—collections of public prophecies delivered between about 760 and 460 B.C.

Why the change? Why do we have the collected messages of Isaiah, Jeremiah and Amos but not those of great prophets like Samuel and Elijah? And why did the miracles fade out—such as nature miracles like preventing or bringing rain, and divine guidance for battle? (Isaiah did give one miraculous sign that was immediately fulfilled—Isaiah 38:7. But he was no Elisha.)

PUBLIC NOTICES

To understand what Yahweh was doing, we need to remember that the prophets were his ambassadors for covenant enforcement. They pointed out violations of the terms to which Israel had agreed under both Moses and Joshua. The prophets also notified the people about the consequences of their choices. Those consequences—blessings for obedience and curses for disobedience—had all been spelled out through Moses and accepted by the people. So there was nothing cruel about Yahweh letting them take effect.

Up until 760 B.C., Yahweh was patient with generation after generation of treacherous, callous children. The prophets proclaimed only limited consequences for evildoing. There was no need to record their messages in detail. The gist sufficed to let later generations learn from what had happened.

But from 760 until 460 B.C., Yahweh wanted a permanent record of his memoranda. This was not a time for power encounters through prophets (although angels were occasionally deployed) but for a legal record of repeated warnings of covenant violation.

The reason was that Yahweh had decided to unleash the full consequences for rebellion. He was going to obliterate the nation. As a just ruler, he wanted a permanent record that he had done everything possible to turn his people from their disastrous course. He wanted to leave later generations in no doubt of the lengths to which he had gone to restore his people. The prophets' messages during these three centuries fell into two patterns:

> To: Israel/Judah
> From: Yahweh
> Subject: Covenant violations
>
> You have violated our agreement at Sinai in the following ways: _____. As you recall, the consequences we agreed upon for such betrayal were _____. This note is to inform you that the consequences will be imposed if you do not change your attitude.

Yahweh sent this message repeatedly for fifty years before destroying Israel, then for another hundred before demolishing Judah. In the meantime, and even more after the destructions, he also addressed this to the destitute survivors:

> To: Israel/Judah
> From: Yahweh
> Subject: Pardon for covenant violations
>
> Because I am a compassionate Father and I love you, I am going to forgive your crimes and restore you to a glory you can hardly imagine, as follows:
>
> _____.

Just two basic messages repeated over and over. Sounds simple—and boring. Yahweh knew his people wouldn't respond to dry memos, to some code enforcer citing paragraph 9.5.1 of a law book. And he had too much personality for that anyway. So instead, he sent his emissaries with ironic, scathing, lyric, funny, grieving poems to recite. Middle Easterners were accustomed to hearing poetry—they found it more gripping and memorable than lectures. Like good songs, the prophecies would stick in the people's minds.

So each book of the Latter Prophets is a collection of poetic messages spoken by a prophet. In some cases the oracles may have been collected or even recorded by the prophet's followers. Rarely do we know the exact circumstances in which the prophet delivered a given poem. Nor are we usually sure even where one prophecy ends and the next begins. Most modern translations guess at the divisions between oracles, but in the original Hebrew they are all run together. We have no way of knowing whether two adjacent messages were delivered days or years apart, or to the same or different audiences. It is clear from the few recorded dates that the collectors weren't concerned with putting the prophecies in chronological order.

Add these uncertainties to the fact that we aren't used to reading poetry anymore and you can see why the prophets are hard to interpret. They use colorful, figurative language, jump from subject to subject and don't even say whether they are talking about the present, the near future or the far future. They can be talking about a situation in their own time, then shift without warning as they glimpse something in a distant century, for a prophet sees from Yahweh's perspective of eternity. It's like taking an aerial view of a highway rather than driving along it. Maybe we'd rather have memos.

But since we don't, we'll try to see what Yahweh was trying to get across to his people through each of the latter prophets. We'll begin with those in the northern kingdom because they lasted only until 721 B.C.

A Bull Market in Israel

The prophets were quiet in Israel from the time Jehu became king in 841 B.C. until about 797 B.C. During that time the kings tolerated Jeroboam's fake religion, but Baal worship wasn't totally taking over as it had under Ahab. Yahweh let Syria gnaw at Israel until Syria virtually took over. Not even this slow hemorrhage got the people's attention.

So Yahweh tried another tack. Assyria, far to the northeast of Syria, had been a looming threat since Ahab's day. (See map, page 348.) Jehu had had to pay Assyria tribute to keep his throne. But afterward Assyria fell on hard times internally. It barely managed to defeat Syria in 805 B.C. but was exhausted in the effort. Assyria's weakness and Syria's defeat were crucial, for they left a power vacuum for Israel to fill. Around 795 B.C. a prophet named Jonah foretold that Israel would soon retake all the territory that had been lost since the time of Solomon—quite a bit of real estate.

Jeroboam II inherited the crown of Israel in 793 B.C. and set about fulfilling Jonah's words. With both Syria and Assyria weak, and with Israel controlling the major north-south trade routes, the nation exploded into financial and military prosperity. But only the powerful profited. They became fabulously rich as merchants then employed sharp lawyers to acquire the land of small farmers. They built huge houses, furnished them extravagantly and held endless dinner and drinking parties. Those who lacked either the money, intellect or connections to play legal hardball found themselves landless and destitute day laborers.

Worst of all, the wealthy attributed their success to Yahweh's favor. They reveled in being the chosen people, and business at the shrines of Bethel and Dan boomed. Worship services were packed. The prime topic of sermons was "when Yahweh has his day"—when he would come and permanently defeat Israel's enemies.

Business was also good at pagan shrines. As the nation grew increasingly worldly and materialistic, it was easy for people to celebrate the festivals of both Yahweh and other gods. Yahweh worship had never been too pure in Israel anyway. People liked to hear the old stories about Abraham and Jacob—the ones that made them feel important—but they also enjoyed the earthier pleasures of fertility rites.

AMOS

It made Yahweh grind his teeth to be marketed. Israel had not learned to take him seriously in the fireworks on Mount Carmel nor in oppression by Syria. He gave the nation about thirty-five years of prosperity under Jeroboam II to muster some gratitude, and when it was clear that nothing but smugness was forthcoming, he sent Amos.

Amos was in the livestock business a few miles south of Jerusalem. He was informed on the law of Moses as well as on international affairs. He had never been part of a prophetic community, but when Yahweh told him to take time off to carry a message to the northern kingdom, he did so.

Biting irony was the tone of the speeches Yahweh gave Amos. Amos stood outside the shrine at Bethel or in the thoroughfare of Samaria and announced, "This is what Yahweh says: . . . " He caught the crowd's ear by declaring how Yahweh would judge the pagan nations for atrocities against Israel, then won applause by denouncing Judah, and finally zeroed in on his real target:

For three sins of Israel,
    even for four, I will not relent.
They sell the innocent for silver,
    and the needy for a pair of sandals.
They trample on the heads of the poor
    as on the dust of the ground
    and deny justice to the oppressed. . . .
Now then, I will crush you
    as a cart crushes when loaded with grain. (Amos 2:6-7, 13)

Was Israel Yahweh's chosen people? Undoubtedly. But election has a price:

You only have I chosen
    of all the families of the earth;
therefore I will punish you
    for all your sins. (Amos 3:2)

Amos got into big trouble with the authorities by describing rich women lounging with chilled wine—as if they were Israel's top breed of cattle—and for predicting that Assyria would soon chew Israel to bits. But when threatened, Amos coolly informed his accuser of the fate he and his family would soon face for their vileness.

The prophet did not enjoy these hard words. Yahweh deliberately selected messengers who would grieve and pray for the wicked rather than revel in their destruction. But he who at Bethel had transformed deceitful Jacob into humble Israel could not tolerate Jacob's descendants celebrating at Bethel by transforming "justice into bitterness" (Amos 5:7). Pride and self-congratulating religion disgusted him.

Most of Amos's oracles graphically detailed the obliteration Israel could expect. But in a final prophecy, Yahweh granted him a glimpse of hope:
    In that day,

"I will restore David's fallen shelter—
    I will repair its broken walls
    and restore its ruins—
    and will rebuild it as it used to be." (Amos 9:11)

With Yahweh, even the end is not final because a promise is never broken.

HOSEA

Israel's elite ignored Amos the doomsayer, so eventually Yahweh sent the prophet home to take care of his livelihood and collect his messages for posterity. Meanwhile, Yahweh was preparing a different stripe of man to present his plea in a startlingly different way.

Toward the end of Jeroboam's reign, Yahweh asked an ordinary guy named Hosea to marry a woman he knew would be unfaithful. She bore him three children, and Yahweh gave each of them symbolic names. The firstborn was called Jezreel after the place where Jehu had massacred Ahaziah, Joram and all of Joram's male relatives. This was a warning that Jehu's dynasty would soon be as dead as Joram's. The other two children were named "Not Loved" and "Not My People." (Imagine growing up with the name Not Loved!) Then Hosea's wife ran off, became a prostitute and ended up a slave. And Yahweh told Hosea to buy her back and love her as Yahweh loved the Israelites, even though they were prostituting themselves with fertility gods.

The whole wild scenario was an object lesson for Hosea's neighbors and a chance for Hosea to truly share Yahweh's anguish at being jilted by the people for whom he had poured himself out. Like an enraptured husband, Yahweh had showered his nation in affluence. But she had seen it all as payment from her paramours, the gods of prosperity and power. Now, through the prophecies of a man who had been there, Yahweh could weep at how as a lover he had wooed Israel, how as a spurned husband he had let her chase her suitors and end up trapped in prostitution, and how incredibly he would allure her again when the consequences

> *Through the prophecies of a man who had been there, Yahweh could weep at how as a lover he had wooed Israel, how as a spurned husband he had let her chase her suitors and end up trapped in prostitution, and how incredibly he would allure her again when the consequences of her betrayal hit home.*

of her betrayal hit home. Not Loved would become Loved, and Not My People would again become My People.

Hosea pulled no punches in cataloging Israel's whoredom:

> I will not punish your daughters
>> when they turn to prostitution,
> nor your daughters-in-law
>> when they commit adultery,
> because the men themselves consort with harlots
>> and sacrifice with shrine prostitutes—
>> a people without understanding will come to ruin! (Hosea 4:14)

He talked of marred ecology, drunkenness, debauchery and unjust lawsuits. But he also affirmed Yahweh's mad passion even for such degenerates:

> How can I give you up, Ephraim?
>> How can I hand you over, Israel? . . .
> My heart is changed within me;
>> all my compassion is aroused. (Hosea 11:8)

If his bride would only abandon her strategies for living without him, Yahweh promised to forgive everything.

Hosea was from Israel, but his book is dated according to the reigns of Judah's kings. The dates show us that he suffered his marital troubles toward the end of Jeroboam II's reign but that he addressed his adulterous country all the way to the end.

Jeroboam II ended a glorious forty-one-year rule in 753 B.C. His son Zechariah succeeded him with all due pomp—it was still a bull market in Israel. Six months later Zechariah lay dead in a bloody public assassination. His killer held the throne for one month before another army officer, Menahem, murdered him in another coup. Menahem managed to hold the crown for ten years by paying off the king of Assyria with money from a tax that crippled Israel's upper class. A shrewd young king had led Assyria out of hibernation and into a series of well-executed military campaigns that led to Menahem's doorstep. Israel really had no choice but to buy Assyria off. (Other than casting itself on Yahweh's mercy—a plan that occurred to nobody but Hosea. He predicted that bribing Assyria would fail in the long run.)

There were those in Israel, however, who thought there ought to be a third alternative: tough it out against Assyria while ignoring Yahweh. An officer named Pekah set up a counter-government in the part of Israel that lay east of the Jordan River. He led a civil war first against Menahem and then against his son Pekahiah, who kept up his father's pro-Assyrian policy for two years. At last Pekah managed to assassinate Pekahiah. Pekah promptly rebelled against Assyria, and (one didn't need to be a prophet to foresee it at this point) Assyria promptly overran Israel and conquered everything except the capital city and its environs. Captives were deported to other corners of the empire. To avert total disaster, an officer named Hoshea murdered Pekah, declared himself king and surrendered to Assyria.

Hoshea lasted for nine years. But when Assyria discovered that he was secretly conspiring with Egypt to throw off the Assyrian yoke, the siege engines rolled again for the last time. After a hideous three-year siege, Assyria took Samaria and deported 27,290 people—virtually all who failed to flee to Judah. Six kings, but only thirty-one years, had passed since Jeroboam II's death.

The prophet Hosea must have escaped, for his book was apparently compiled in Judah. He lived to see his mission fail utterly as Yahweh dealt with his adulterous bride.

JONAH

Possibly there was one man who would have been more devastated by these events than Hosea. Back around 795 B.C., young Jonah had predicted Jeroboam II's victories and the abundance that would follow. Toward 750 B.C., things were crumbling and Assyria was on the rise. And Yahweh gave this patriotic prophet an incredible assignment: "Go to the great city of Nineveh and preach against it, because its wickedness has come up before me" (Jonah 1:2). Now Nineveh was a major city of Assyria—soon to be its capital. If Jonah had believed that Yahweh was properly nationalistic and vindictive, he would have set off whistling. But Jonah knew that Yahweh could not be trusted. Nineveh was bound to repent, Yahweh would forgive, and that would be disgusting.

In Jonah's defense it should be noted that the Assyrians were not nice people. When they conquered an area, they demolished buildings, burned trees, slaughtered animals, skinned captives alive, impaled corpses on stakes, stacked heads in heaps, tortured and mutilated captured leaders, deported whole populations to other parts of their empire to discourage nationalist uprisings and generally practiced rule by terror.

So in order to avoid giving the message that might cause Nineveh's repentance and deliverance, Jonah caught the first boat to the other end of the Mediterranean world. However, Yahweh sent a storm. Jonah let the sailors throw him overboard to save themselves, and Jonah spent three days in the belly of a large fish thinking things over. In the end he cried out to Yahweh, who had the fish vomit him onto land.

While inside the fish, Jonah wrote a poem of thanksgiving and resignation ending, "What I have vowed I will make good. I will say, 'Salvation comes from Yahweh'" (Jonah 2:9). Then he went to Nineveh, and sure enough, the Ninevites responded to his warning by instantly repenting.

Jonah was furious. He accused Yahweh, "Isn't this what I said, Yahweh, when I was still at home? That is what I tried to forestall by fleeing to Tarshish. I knew that you are a gracious and compassionate God, slow to anger and abounding in love, a God who relents from sending calamity" (Jonah 4:2).

So Yahweh gave him a little lesson in which he provided a vine to shade Jonah and then shriveled it with heat. When Jonah protested his harshness, Yahweh replied, "You have been concerned about this plant, though you did not tend it or make it grow. . . . And should I not have concern for the great city of Nineveh, in which there are more than a hundred and twenty thousand people who cannot tell their right hand from their left— and also many animals?" (Jonah 4:10-11).

How it galled Jonah and grieved

> *Yahweh wanted no one to forget the purpose of his covenant: "All peoples on earth will be blessed through you."*

Yahweh that Assyria responded to a single message from a prophet while Israel ignored the records of Moses, the miracles of Elijah and the warnings of Amos and Hosea. It was unspeakable that repentant Nineveh became Yahweh's agent to destroy stubborn Israel. But while Yahweh had chosen Israel as his bride, he was not her national pet. He loved all nations—even wicked Assyria—and he wanted no one to forget the purpose of his covenant: "All peoples on earth will be blessed through you."

Questions for Reflection and Discussion

1. Why did Yahweh appoint a group of prophets to write down their messages?

2. Why did he let the Assyrians destroy the northern kingdom of Israel?

3. Why did Jonah hate the Ninevites? What was Yahweh's attitude toward them? How would you describe his general attitude toward those outside his covenant people?

15

MEANWHILE DOWN SOUTH

2 Kings 15–16; 2 Chronicles 26–28;
Isaiah 1–11; Joel, Micah

*J*udah was not much better than Israel during the eighth century B.C. One year after Jeroboam II took over in the north, Uzziah became king in the south. He benefited from the weakness of Assyria and Syria—and from his new control of trade routes through his territory—in just the same ways as Jeroboam did. During his fifty-two-year reign Uzziah fortified Jerusalem, built towers and cisterns for his livestock holdings, expanded his army, strengthened his defenses to the southeast and southwest and developed trade by land and sea. Agriculture also boomed. But as in the north, legal maneuvering increasingly concentrated wealth and power in the hands of the upper class while the poor grew poorer and poorer.

Uzziah started out devoted to Yahweh, but like Solomon he let success go to his head. One day he decided to emulate the old Jebusite priest-kings like Melchizedek. When he entered the Holy Place of the temple to burn incense, Yahweh struck him with leprosy. Yahweh had separated the roles of prophet, priest and king on purpose, and he was not about to let Uzziah upset the balance of power.

Having reached beyond what was rightfully his, Uzziah lost even what he had. Lepers were quarantined as contagious, so Uzziah spent the last decade of his life as king in name only. His son Jotham dictated policy and ran the daily business of state.

Jotham took over in 750 B.C., about the time Amos started making trouble up north. Jotham was not a bad king: he respected Yahweh worship, continued renovating Jerusalem and fought some successful battles. While Israel convulsed in one coup after another, Jotham kept his house stable. But he was not concerned enough to discourage either the fertility cults with their magic and debauchery or the ruthless legal tactics of his upper-class supporters. Greatness scored higher with Jotham than ethics. So as strong as the nation was, it was like a kingdom built on a net and suspended over a crevasse. With business booming, nobody wanted to notice that the net's moral fiber was being slowly chewed away by the moths of pleasure and self-interest.

JOEL

Nobody, of course, but the prophets. The book of Joel has no date—it may have been written at any time in Judah's history because it addresses the situation Judah's prophets were up against for centuries. The gist of Joel's message was that Yahweh would send a plague of locusts to prod complacent Judah into repentance. It was the same basic message Jonah took to Nineveh: turn or pay.

Locusts don't seem too threatening to modern city dwellers, but farmers of Joel's day had reason to dread a scourge that could strip a tree in minutes, a field of grain in hours. Yahweh's people were fond of talking about "the day of Yahweh" when he would destroy their enemies, but like Amos Joel warned that the day would strike at home first. This locust plague was a small-d "day of Yahweh," and it would be bad enough that the nation had better do some serious soul-searching.

But the locusts were only a foretaste. In one of those prophetic time shifts, Joel saw through the immediate situation to the big-d Day of Yahweh at the end of the age, when he would pour out his Spirit on anyone who was open, offer salvation from disaster to the nations and judge both them and his people according to the integrity of their hearts.

Yahweh showed Joel awesome special effects, including, "blood and fire and billows of smoke. The sun will be turned to darkness and the moon to blood" (Joel 2:30-31). But "everyone who calls on the name of Yahweh will be saved" (Joel 2:32).

ISAIAH'S COMMISSION

Did Judah pay attention, as Nineveh had? Maybe—they were not destroyed when the Assyrians flattened Samaria. But the change didn't stick. In 740 B.C., the year Uzziah finally died, Yahweh appeared in a vision to a young member of the royal court named Isaiah. He was

> *Joel saw through the immediate situation to the big-d Day of Yahweh at the end of the age, when he would pour out his Spirit on anyone who was open.*

not much older than eighteen, but well-born, well-educated and well-connected. He was on his way to the top until Yahweh burst in. Here is Isaiah's account:

> I saw the Lord, high and exalted, seated on a throne; and the train of his robe filled the temple. Above him were seraphim, each with six wings: With two wings they covered their faces, with two they covered their feet, and with two they were flying. And they were calling to one another:
>
> "Holy, holy, holy is Yahweh Almighty;
> the whole earth is full of his glory."
>
> At the sound of their voices the doorposts and thresholds shook and the temple was filled with smoke.
>
> "Woe to me!" I cried. "I am ruined!" (Isaiah 6:1-5)

Isaiah knew himself to be a man with a dirty mouth—full of malice and deceit like his countrymen. But one of the seraphim seared his mouth with an altar coal, and in that instant of agony Isaiah was prepared for a mission. "Whom shall I send?" asked a voice. Isaiah answered, "Send me!"

His mission was to tell his people what they didn't want to hear until— just like Pharaoh—they thoroughly calloused their hearts against the God to whom they didn't want to listen. Isaiah's task was to expose their willful blindness and deafness by doing everything he could to sway them, and failing. His job was to fail.

Fun. And what he would have to hang on to for the next six decades was that memory of the thrice-holy Lord, the thundering voices of the angels and the scalding coal against his lips. That, and an ongoing jumble of hints about events from tomorrow to eternity. Isaiah came away from this experience with a favorite title for his God, not a very popular one among his lighthearted kinsmen: the Holy One of Israel.

THE BUBBLE BURSTS

While Jotham was toiling to prolong the prosperity, a rejuvenated Assyrian army under King Tiglath-Pileser was beginning to swallow up kingdoms north of Israel. (See map, page 348.) It didn't take a prophet to see what was coming. But no matter how Isaiah tried to get through to him—lyrical parables with heavy punch lines (Isaiah 5:1-7), mournful laments (Isaiah 1:4-9; 5:8-30) or sharp rebukes (Isaiah 3:13-26)—Jotham and his administration were not interested. Isaiah carefully recorded his reproofs of haughty women, ruthless moguls and "champions at mixing drinks," even though nobody cared.

But their bubble was bursting. In 735 B.C. Jotham made his son Ahaz co-regent, possibly because Jotham was ill. Israel and Syria had allied against the Assyrian peril, and they threatened that unless Judah joined them, they would invade and put their own man on Judah's throne. Jotham refused to play ball, but he was also too smart to ally with Assyria. For three years Judah's well-financed army kept Israel-Syria at bay while Jerusalem's complacence oozed away.

AHAZ

Then Jotham died in 732 B.C., leaving Ahaz in control. Weak, amoral and vain, he was not the leader the nation needed in this crisis. Yahweh bored him; he preferred the pleasures of Baal. And he was terrified that Syrian siege engines might roll up to his window any day. Cornered and thinking himself clever, he decided to put an end to this anxiety by hiring Tiglath-Pileser to get his neighbors off his back. He would become an Assyrian vassal, of course, but so what? It was inevitable anyway. Better to spend some cash than be overrun.

By now, Isaiah was well-known as a prophet in the capital. No doubt Ahaz would have gotten rid of him if he had not been an aristocrat and backed by Yahweh. But Isaiah was swimming upstream in this administration.

Yahweh told Isaiah to tell Ahaz his scheme was madness. Don't worry about Israel and Syria, he said—they were small potatoes. The real menace was Assyria. "Be careful, keep calm, and don't be afraid. . . . If you do not stand firm in your faith, you will not stand at all" (Isaiah 7:4, 9). You're on thin ice, and your only hope is a real God.

Ahaz was not impressed. So, Isaiah said, you don't believe Yahweh can handle it? Okay, ask for a miraculous sign—anything. Ahaz wouldn't do it. If it came true, he'd be obliged to believe in this inconvenient God and his unmanageable prophet. So Isaiah gave him a sign anyway: a certain virgin would have a son and would name him Immanuel, "God Is With Us." This meaning was already implicit in the name Yahweh ("I AM actively present"), but now the reality was being revealed even more explicitly. Before this child reached his teens Assyria would wipe out Syria and Israel, and when the boy became a teenager he would have nothing but curds and honey to eat because war would have ravaged Judah and made agriculture impossible.

The virgin may have been a new wife whom Isaiah or another courtier was about to marry. If so, and if Immanuel was born about a year later, Isaiah's prophecy came true right on schedule: thirteen years later Syria and Israel no longer existed and Judah's agriculture was in shambles. (Did even Isaiah know that his sign would have another fulfillment seven centuries later that would dwarf this one?)

Ahaz went ahead with his plan. He sent Tiglath-Pileser a

> *Did even Isaiah know that his sign would have another fulfillment seven centuries later that would dwarf this one?*

fortune in treasures, and Assyria obliged him by sacking and deporting Syria and most of Israel. Then Ahaz traveled to Damascus to meet his Assyrian lord. He was genuinely impressed by what he saw, and even sent his priest sketches of the Assyrian royal altar to copy and install in Jerusalem.

This was the beginning of full-dress paganism in Judah. Ahaz ordered Yahweh's temple closed. Hereafter, official state sacrifices would be offered on the new altar. The old bronze altar of Yahweh he would keep, however, for divination (as though Yahweh would have anything to do with him). Other altars began to proliferate around town, and soon Ahaz was sponsoring child sacrifice, sexual rites and spirit channeling.

Isaiah was shaken. He could see what Israel was reaping for her crimes; refugees were pouring into Judah every day with new tales of atrocities. And Judah was plunging headlong into the same insanity. The palace buzzed with intrigue (a coup? a treaty with Egypt?). The people were drowning their panic in alcohol, sex and politics. But Yahweh told Isaiah:

> Do not call conspiracy
>   everything this people calls a conspiracy;
> do not fear what they fear,
>   and do not dread it.
> Yahweh Almighty is the one you are to regard as holy,
>   he is the one you are to fear,
>   he is the one you are to dread.
> He will be a holy place;
>   for both Israel and Judah he will be
> a stone that causes people to stumble
>   and a rock that makes them fall. (Isaiah 8:12-14)

Yahweh gave Isaiah an awful glimpse of the dark times ahead. But he also let him see a light that would pierce the shadows from Galilee in the northern kingdom.

> For to us a child is born,
>   to us a son is given,
>   and the government will be on his shoulders.
> And he will be called
>   Wonderful Counselor, Mighty God,
>   Everlasting Father, Prince of Peace.
> Of the greatness of his government and peace
>   there will be no end. (Isaiah 9:6-7)

Snapshots barraged Isaiah: Israel's destruction, Assyria's ultimate defeat, the emergence of a faithful remnant from the nation's ashes, and that larger-than-life future King:

> A shoot will come up from the stump of Jesse;
>> from his roots a Branch will bear fruit.
> The Spirit of Yahweh will rest on him—
>> the Spirit of wisdom and of understanding,
>> the Spirit of counsel and of might,
>> the Spirit of the knowledge and fear of Yahweh—
> and he will delight in the fear of Yahweh. (Isaiah 11:1-3)

Offspring of Eve, Lion of Judah, son of David—Isaiah doubtless knew the prophecies. But Mighty God? Everlasting Father? Isaiah faithfully recorded the promises and spent his time rearing his family and a circle of followers who would stay faithful to Yahweh even in the dark.

MICAH

One of Isaiah's allies in these grim days was a small-town prophet named Micah. His little book tells the same tale as Isaiah's early messages (there are even some word-for-word overlaps), except from the viewpoint not of a courtier steeped in political intrigue but of a villager who daily watched wealthy landholders extort the family farms out from under their owners. As Hosea had shared Yahweh's grief at Israel's adultery, Micah wept with Yahweh that the same poison was infecting Judah. Prophets for hire harassed Micah for predicting disaster, but he could say only what he saw. He may have been a country bumpkin, but Yahweh showed him not only the fall of Samaria before it occurred, but also Babylon taking Judah into exile, Yahweh freeing a remnant and the reign of the Davidic king in the last days. Micah added another piece to the puzzle about this King: he would be born in David's hometown of Bethlehem.

<hr />

Questions for Reflection and Discussion

1. What is "the day of Yahweh" (day of the Lord)?

2. How would you summarize Isaiah's messages to the political

leaders and situations of his day? In what ways are they relevant in any dangerous time?

3. What do we learn from Isaiah and Micah about the promised
Son of David?

16

JUDAH SEALS
HER FATE

*2 Kings 18:1–21:18; 2 Chronicles 29:1–33:20;
Isaiah 13–66*

Somehow, Isaiah was appointed chaplain for crown prince Hezekiah. He weathered the Ahaz administration for eight years, then another twelve in which father and son reigned together. His one goal as a statesman was to groom Hezekiah to be a real Davidic king.

Faithful waiting paid off. When Ahaz died in 715 B.C., Isaiah found himself in midlife as a trusted royal counselor at last. Hezekiah was utterly devoted to Yahweh. His first act as king was to reopen the temple, which his father had closed. It took the Levites weeks to clean out the years of accumulated grime, dispose of the occult objects Ahaz had collected and get things running again. Then Hezekiah held a lavish rededication ceremony modeled on Solomon's, and after that a two-week Passover festival. He even invited Israelites who had managed to survive the Assyrian deportations six years earlier. It was a glorious expression of the chosen people reunited in obedience to Yahweh.

Hezekiah looked and acted like Solomon reborn—the young Solomon in his temple-building days. Everyone hoped that this renewed devotion would lead to another golden age. They resented it when Isaiah continued to point out that the renovation was only skin deep: overt occultism might be dwindling, but materialism, greed, treachery—all the old vices—were still going strong.

So Isaiah's life was still far from easy. The other counselors disdained him for exposing their hypocrisy. They were pro-Yahweh for political expedience only. And Hezekiah, although honestly devout, was also a rash and idealistic patriot. It galled him that Judah was still vassal to pagan Assyria. Each time he paid his annual tribute he was reminded of his father's mistakes.

Some of his advisors proposed that Judah ally with Egypt to throw off the Assyrian yoke. Isaiah unleashed his complete verbal arsenal against this counsel, which amounted to relying on what people could manipulate—intrigue and military hardware—rather than on Yahweh. He cried,

> Woe to those who go to great depths
>   to hide their plans from Yahweh,
> who do their work in darkness and think,
>   "Who sees us? Who will know?" (Isaiah 29:15)

> In repentance and rest is your salvation,
>   in quietness and trust is your strength,
>   but you would have none of it.
> You said, "No, we will flee on horses."
>   Therefore you will flee!
> You said, "We will ride off on swift horses."
>   Therefore your pursuers will be swift! . . .
> Yet Yahweh longs to be gracious to you;
>   therefore he will rise up to show you compassion. (Isaiah 30:15-16, 18)

Again and again Isaiah faced off against Hezekiah's ministers, countering their ridicule with steely-eyed messages.

But his efforts came to nothing. When a new Assyrian king was engaged in securing his position in 705 B.C., Egypt, Judah and several other vassals seized the chance to revolt. In the first year all was quiet when Jerusalem sent no tribute. King Sennacherib was busy stabilizing his throne in his new capital, Nineveh. The second year was fine.

In 703 B.C. Hezekiah fell seriously ill and survived only because Yahweh answered his desperate prayers. Then envoys arrived from Babylon (see map, page 348), another Assyrian vassal, ostensibly to congratulate Hezekiah on his recovery but actually to urge him to join a military campaign against their overlord. Strongly tempted to agree, Hezekiah entertained the diplomats regally. He even gave them a tour of his entire royal treasury to show that he was as much to be reckoned with as his ancestor Solomon. Isaiah was aghast when he heard about the incident. In a flash he saw it all: troops marching, overrunning Jerusalem, sacking the palace, carrying everything back to Babylon. It would not happen yet, but sometime after Hezekiah's death.

Hezekiah was used to these premonitions from his old teacher. He was still basking in his restored health and the admiring murmurs of the Babylonian entourage. "The word of Yahweh you have spoken is good," he told Isaiah. But he was thinking something else: "There will be peace and security in my lifetime."

Rude Awakening

Selfish fool! For all his patriotism and loyalty to Yahweh, Hezekiah's real goal was a successful, pain-free life. He wanted to make the history books as a great king without having to endure hard times. So far, faithfulness to Yahweh had paid off handsomely, but his faith was about to receive its first real test.

By 701 B.C., Sennacherib had gotten things together at home and was ready to deal with rebels. His army swept through Syria and Samaria to Judah and began to gobble up city after city. Soon he reached Lachish, thirty miles southwest of Jerusalem and the last stop before the capital itself. Panicking, Hezekiah sent a message of capitulation and an offer to pay as much tribute as Sennacherib asked. The king's price was eleven tons of silver and a ton of gold. Hezekiah had the gold plating stripped from the temple doors to fulfill it.

But Sennacherib had no intention of going home without beating the nationalism out of Hezekiah. He continued his siege of Lachish and dispatched officials to demand complete surrender. They urged the guards on Jerusalem's walls to turn against Hezekiah, detailing the pathetic state of Judah's army, the failure of every other nation's gods to resist Assyria and the horrors of famine that would come with a long siege. They even pointed out that Yahweh's own prophets (such as Isaiah) had predicted this Assyrian invasion.

The Jerusalemites steeled themselves against this psychological warfare, and Hezekiah sent a message to Isaiah: Ask Yahweh to hear how the Assyrians have mocked him and to rebuke them.

Sennacherib had made this a test case of his power versus Yahweh's. Yahweh accepted the challenge. While Hezekiah kept praying desperately each time Sennacherib sent another threatening message, Yahweh told Isaiah what he thought of the Assyrian king. One night Yahweh sent an angel with bubonic plague to decimate the Assyrian army, and he followed that with some news from Nineveh that obliged Sennacherib to call off his siege and hurry home. As Yahweh had promised, he never returned. Twenty years later his sons assassinated him in his temple.

YAHWEH AND THE NATIONS

The dispute between Sennacherib and Yahweh hinged on whether Yahweh had the power—which the other gods lacked—to defeat this human king. Yahweh accepted this duel in order to demonstrate (for anyone paying attention) that he was not just another national deity but the Ruler of the Nations, and not just in the abstract but in the details of each nation and life.

Yahweh made a strong point of this fact to Isaiah, a statesman embroiled in international politics. He gave Isaiah prophecies of judgment on every one of the nations around Judah at one time or another. They are collected in a long section in the first part of Isaiah's book (chapters 13 through 23 in the traditional divisions). These prophecies of judgment culminate (in chapter 24) in a vision of the whole earth laid waste—ecological holocaust because humans, the earth's stewards, have defiled it in their self-absorption.

But always Yahweh comforted Isaiah with glimpses beyond desolation: a banquet Yahweh would spread for his own among all peoples when he would wipe away every tear and swallow up death forever.

MANASSEH

Judgment and joy seesaw in Isaiah 24–35. The prophet must have grown dizzy in those late days of Hezekiah between the tense statecraft and wild insights from Yahweh. Only a pitiful remnant of Judah survived the onslaught of 701 B.C., and the king, in his late fifties by now, was not the confident patriot he once was. After five years he appointed his twelve-year-old son, Manasseh, as co-regent. He lived another decade, but we hear nothing of more reforms.

Manasseh became sole king upon his father's death in 687. He reigned fifty-five years, longer than any other king of Israel or Judah. He was Yahweh's curse on a persistently rebellious people. They had played church for twenty-eight years under Hezekiah without pausing in their unethical business practices, so Yahweh gave them the king they deserved. Manasseh reinstituted the ways of Ahaz and then some. He put pagan altars and a fertility pole in Yahweh's temple, sacrificed his own infant son, consulted mediums and practiced sorcery. Those who opposed him he executed.

Among the executed were probably some of the prophets who announced that Yahweh was going to wipe out Judah as he had Israel because Manasseh was worse than the Canaanites had been. It was the rampant bloodshed, more than anything else, that Yahweh refused to forgive.

ISAIAH'S LAST ASSIGNMENT

Isaiah was getting on toward seventy years old, fifty of which he had spent toe to toe with three kings and their charlatan counselors. Now, as Manasseh showed his colors, Yahweh pulled his chief prophet back from the front lines to record some tidings for future generations.

His first glimpse had come that day when Hezekiah crowed about the Babylonian envoys. All the destruction that was still a century away had flooded in on him. But it was not primarily his job to foretell those days. Instead, he scribbled oracle after oracle about the times after the destruction. Chapter 40 opens with "Comfort, comfort" for a Jerusalem demolished for her crimes and for the people carried off to Babylon. Isaiah saw a highway built through the desert on which Yahweh would come to lead his people back to their land.

Why did Yahweh announce this return 160 years before it happened? Yahweh was trying another tactic in his appeal to the nations, including the returning remnant. His displays of power had not convinced them to abandon worthless idols; perhaps his foreknowledge would. Repeatedly

Isaiah saw a law court in which Yahweh sat now as judge and prosecutor, now as defendant. He summoned the nations to face him with their charges that he was weak or unworthy of worship. In his own defense, Yahweh pointed to a warrior from the east named Cyrus, whom Yahweh would raise up to deliver his people even though he knew nothing of the Holy One. Who but the King of the Earth could predict what he would do 160 years before it occurred, a century before it even appeared necessary? Who else could foretell the fall of an empire before it had risen and name both the empire and its conqueror?

THE SERVANT

Besides his preannounced deeds, Yahweh called one other witness into court: Israel. He viewed them not as Israel and Judah, two political entities, but as Israel, his people. "My servant," he called them, a term he had previously used only of men like Moses, Joshua and David, for in the Middle East a king's "servant" was a trusted royal envoy. And to drive home the intimacy, he added, "whom I have chosen, you descendants of Abraham my friend." And he repeated the covenant commitment: "I am with you." I am Immanuel. I am Yahweh.

"You are my witnesses," he told his people as the nations gathered to hear them testify to the fact of his identity. "I am he. Before me no god was formed, nor will there be one after me. I, even I, am Yahweh, and apart from me there is no savior" (Isaiah 43:10-11).

The scene shifts. The witnesses are in court to account for their failure to keep the covenant and be real witnesses to the nations. Yahweh's servants have failed in their mission.

Now there is another Servant: Israel but not Israel, with a strange mix of qualities: a ruler filled with Yahweh's Spirit like the judges of old, but gentle to the weak and bringing justice not only to Israel but to the nations. Yahweh tells this Servant,

> It is too small a thing for you to be my servant
>> to restore the tribes of Jacob
>> and bring back those of Israel I have kept.
> I will also make you a light for the Gentiles,
>> that my salvation may reach to the ends of the earth. (Isaiah 49:6)

Yet the Servant is not quite the liberator one might have expected after David. He is one who "know[s] the word that sustains the weary" (Isaiah 50:4), who endures abuse and continues to serve:

I offered my back to those who beat me,
   my cheeks to those who pulled out my beard;
I did not hide my face
   from mocking and spitting.
Because the Lord Yahweh helps me,
   I will not be disgraced. (Isaiah 50:6-7)

Servanthood is less and less attractive, even for those who follow the Servant. It is a confusing picture, made worse in the final song (Isaiah 52:13–53:12). On the one hand,

See, my servant will act wisely;
   he will be raised and lifted up and highly exalted. (Isaiah 52:13)

But on the other hand, consider this:

His appearance was so disfigured beyond that of any human being
   and his form marred beyond human likeness. . . .
He was despised and rejected by mankind,
   a man of suffering, and familiar with pain.
Like one from whom people hide their faces
   he was despised, and we held him in low esteem.
Surely he took up our pain
   and bore our suffering,
yet we considered him punished by God,
   stricken by him, and afflicted.
But he was pierced for our transgressions,
   he was crushed for our iniquities;
the punishment that brought us peace was on him,
   and by his wounds we are healed. . . .
Yahweh has laid on him
   the iniquity of us all. (Isaiah 52:14; 53:3-6)

How could it be that "he was cut off from the land of the living" and "assigned a grave with the wicked, and with the rich in his death," yet "he will see his offspring and prolong his days, and the will of

Yahweh will prosper in his hand"? Somehow this Servant would be the ultimate guilt offering, the perfection of all the bulls and rams offered in the temple, bearing in his own body the crimes of humanity. Yet "after he has suffered, he will see the light of life and be satisfied."

> *Somehow this Servant would be the ultimate guilt offering, the perfection of all the bulls and rams offered in the temple, bearing in his own body the crimes of humanity.*

One wonders what Isaiah made of these prophecies. Did he think the Servant was a renewed Israel, suffering for the crimes of the nations? Did he envision some great prophet like Moses? Did he connect the Servant Songs to his visions of the Davidic king decades earlier? How could he reconcile the affliction and triumph, the death and the life after death?

THE KINGDOM

The third thing Yahweh talked to Isaiah about at length was the restoration of his kingdom. Alongside the highway, Isaiah kept seeing the desert blossom as Yahweh irrigated it with springs and pools for his thirsty ones. Yahweh said this water represented his Spirit that would restore life to a dead people and knit them to him in faithfulness.

Another image Yahweh used was the barren woman (Zion) whom he had rejected for her adultery but whom he would take back to himself and bless with many children. Isaiah saw Zion's sons and daughters streaming home from exile, followed by the mighty of the nations bearing lavish gifts. Peace and abundance would reign among a righteous people devoted to their deliverer. They would not even need the sun anymore because Yahweh would be the source of light in their midst.

Yahweh painted the restoration in glowing colors: a new sky and a new earth in which a century would be a short lifespan, farmers would cultivate their lands in safety, wolves and lambs would live at peace together and, above all, the intimacy of Eden would return.

THE INVITATION

Yahweh did not show this to Isaiah to satisfy his curiosity. He was laying up a storehouse of promises for the remnant who would return to Judah after exile in Babylon. They would have hard times, and they would be tempted to slip back into the callousness that was getting Judah into trouble now. So interwoven among the threads of glory were invitation and warning. Isaiah quotes Yahweh:

> Come, all you who are thirsty,
>> come to the waters;
> and you who have no money,
>> come, buy and eat! . . .
> Why spend money on what is not bread,
>> and your labor on what does not satisfy?
> Listen, listen to me, and eat what is good,
>> and you will delight in the richest of fare. . . .
> Surely you will summon nations you know not,
>> and nations you do not know will come running to you,
> because of Yahweh your God. (Isaiah 55:1-2, 5)

For just as the Servant's job is to be a light to the nations, so those who return to Yahweh will also receive that task, which was always Israel's purpose. "For my house will be called a house of prayer for all nations" (Isaiah 56:7).

Yahweh knew already what the returnees would fall into: bloodshed, deceit, plots, avarice, corrupt courts—the same old song. He would raise up prophets like watchmen on the walls of Jerusalem to intercede for the city as Moses had done, but many of

> *Whoever the Servant is, and whatever his followers do, one thing is certain. The Redeemer—the Kinsman who buys his people out of slavery (Yahweh himself)— will come to Zion.*

them would be lazy. Isaiah's messages swing from hope to judgment and back again. But even though his last word details the agony of those who spurn Yahweh in the last days, the closing chapters as a whole ring with joy because vindication does not ultimately depend on human faithfulness:

He saw that there was no one,

    he was appalled that there was no one to intervene;

so his own arm achieved salvation for him,

    and his own righteousness sustained him. . . .

The Redeemer will come to Zion. (Isaiah 59:16, 20)

Whoever the Servant is, and whatever his followers do, one thing is certain. The Redeemer—the Kinsman who buys his people out of slavery (Yahweh Himself)—will come to Zion.

Questions for Reflection and Discussion

1. What were Hezekiah's strengths and weaknesses as a leader? How did Isaiah try to help him?

2. Whom does Yahweh call "my servant"? What does he say through Isaiah about his servant?

3. What do we learn about the promise from the later chapters of Isaiah?

17

STROLLING
TOWARD DISASTER

2 Kings 21:19–23:27; 2 Chronicles 33:21–36:8;
Jeremiah 7–20; 26; Nahum; Habakkuk; Zephaniah

Yahweh managed to catch Manasseh's attention toward the end of his life. Manasseh got involved in a Babylonian rebellion against Assyria and was dragged off by the Assyrians to Babylon itself. His time in prison led to some change of heart regarding Yahweh, and he prayed to the God of Israel for deliverance. After he was pardoned and sent home, he tried to take Yahweh more seriously and reduced his own pagan practices, but he did virtually nothing to reform his people.

He died at the ripe age of sixty-seven, and his twenty-one-year-old son, Amon, took over. Amon, who had not had the pleasure of walking to Babylon with a hook in his nose, had not seen the light about Yahweh. He was such a vile king that after two years his officials assassinated him and tried to take over, but the coup was put down and Amon's son, Josiah, was crowned.

ZEPHANIAH

About the time eight-year-old Josiah became king, one of his older cousins began receiving some public prophecies. Zephaniah was a great-great-grandson of Hezekiah and familiar with the court and current politics. Observing the wreckage left by Manasseh and Amon, he blasted

Jerusalem with several brief oracles. His visions focused now on the atrocities committed by his nation's leaders, now on the destruction they would reap, now on the day of Yahweh at the end of the age. His poetry is stark:

> Their blood will be poured out like dust
>   and their entrails like dung.
> Neither their silver nor their gold
>   will be able to save them
>   on the day of Yahweh's wrath. (Zephaniah 1:17-18)

Zephaniah saw the fate of Judah's enemies—even Assyria—as well as that of Judah herself, since Yahweh played no favorites. He heard Yahweh's astonishment that even the city where he had put his name did not respond to his correction. Yet like most of his prophetic brothers, he closed with a song of triumph about the day when Yahweh would forgive and restore.

JOSIAH

Temporary relief was in sight, for like Joash two centuries earlier, Josiah had the benefit of virtuous tutors. At the age of sixteen he committed himself to seek Yahweh, and at twenty he launched a campaign to morally disinfect Judah and Israel. First he had his father's and grandfather's paraphernalia, such as phallic symbols and astrological gear, thrown on the garbage heap. He tore down the altars of child sacrifice and expelled the male prostitutes from Yahweh's temple. Then he traveled across his land and even to Samaria and Bethel desecrating shrines and slaughtering pagan priests. (He rebuked priests of Yahweh who were officiating outside Jerusalem, but he didn't kill them.) At last he went home (to the relief of large sections of his people) and set to work repairing the temple, which had had no upkeep for a century.

JEREMIAH

Twenty-year-old Josiah launched his religious purge in 627 B.C. The following year when it was well under way, Yahweh called a young priest (or priest-in-training) only slightly older than Josiah to be a prophet with an international portfolio. Jeremiah gave the stock response to a calling (Who, me? I'm no public speaker. I'm nobody!), and Yahweh gave his standard retort: Don't be scared. I am with you.

Jeremiah had the distinction of receiving possibly the very worst assignment of any prophet. Many had to prophesy Judah's destruction; Jeremiah got to do it for forty years, during most of which he endured death threats and imprisonment and at the end of which he got to savor every bitter moment of famine and slaughter.

His first seventeen years were tolerable, because Josiah was alive and working for the same ends. He made the job of restoring Judah's integrity seem possible, and he protected Jeremiah from active persecution. Jeremiah could stand in Jerusalem's marketplace and express Yahweh's grief over his wanton bride, his sorrow that rather than drink from Yahweh's fountain his people preferred to dig their own wells to slake their thirst for security and importance. Yahweh's envoy was free to accuse Judah's finest of murder and graft. Those were the years when Yahweh begged shamelessly, "Return, return." But few listened.

THE BOOK OF THE COVENANT

One day during the temple renovations, the priest in charge was fetching money to pay the workmen. In a back storeroom he discovered a scroll, which he passed on to Josiah's secretary.

Josiah was appalled when he heard the scroll read, for it turned out to be some or all of Moses' writings—the Book of the Covenant with its commands, blessings for obedience and curses for treachery. It was obvious to Josiah that Samaria lay in ruins and his own nation was barely hanging on against crop failures and the ever-present threat of Assyria all because they had scorned their King.

The book of Moses made it clear that crimes on the level of Manasseh's and Amon's would lead to destruction. (It's a hint of how low things had fallen that Moses' writings were utterly unknown in Josiah's day.) Josiah dispatched four of his officials to a prophetess to inquire what Yahweh was going to do about these crimes and curses.

She reported that, yes, Yahweh was indeed going to obliterate Judah for its villainy, but because Josiah had humbled himself before Yahweh, he would take the king's life before the destruction took place so that he would not have to suffer through it.

Wonderful news. Josiah called a mass meeting of the elders of Judah and the entire population of Jerusalem to renew the covenant. He had the book of Moses read and made the people pledge to obey it. Then he threw the greatest Passover celebration in history: 41,400 animals were sacrificed as burnt offerings or as fellowship offerings.

No doubt Yahweh appreciated Josiah's attempt, but he knew his fickle people were simply following their leader to avoid his wrath and would revert to their old ways as soon as they had a more compliant king. So Yahweh continued to move nations into position like chess pieces for his checkmate of Judah. For Jeremiah, the visions and sounds of an army swarming toward Jerusalem were like nightmares. He obediently reported what he saw, but he also wept:

Oh, my anguish, my anguish!
    I writhe in pain.
Oh, the agony of my heart!
    My heart pounds within me,
    I cannot keep silent. (Jeremiah 4:19)

Yahweh told him he would save Jerusalem if Jeremiah could find one honest person in the city. But as hard as he looked, he failed. Yet daily, it seemed, other prophets were coming out with grandiose pronouncements of Yahweh's favor and protection, and the priests spoke pious platitudes.

NAHUM AND THE RISE OF BABYLON

Nahum was one of the few true prophets of this period who had something popular to say. He had the job Jonah wanted: he received a technicolor preview of Nineveh's fall. The city had abandoned its earlier repentance and reached new heights of brutality in the 640s and 630s. Nahum's staccato style throbs as Nineveh, soaked in blood and sorcery in its lust for gold and power, is crushed, then blown away like locusts in the wind.

Josiah's magnificent Passover was in 622 B.C. In 612 Nineveh fell to an

alliance of Media and Babylonia. (See map, page 348.) The surviving Assyrian forces regrouped, but after three years of fighting they were
pushed west across the Euphrates. The Egyptians (who wanted to be rid
of Assyria for good) allied with Babylonia and began to march north to
squeeze the Assyrians from the other side. Josiah feared Egypt would
swallow Judah up if Assyria were defeated, so he led his army out to cut
Egypt off. But as Yahweh had promised, the thirty-nine-year-old monarch
died in battle. Egypt and Babylonia, under the brilliant general Prince
Nebuchadnezzar, cut down the remains of the Assyrian army. The neo-
Babylonian Empire was dawning.

JOSIAH'S FIRST TWO SONS

When a bleeding Josiah arrived in Jerusalem and later expired, the whole
nation mourned bitterly. Jeremiah composed laments for the lost king
that were national treasures for centuries. But times were tense. Jehoahaz,
Josiah's second-oldest son, was quickly chosen as his successor.

However, the Egyptian pharaoh paused on his way home from
smashing Assyria to arrest Jehoahaz, imprison him in his military headquarters in Syria, appoint his elder brother king, impose a stiff vassal
tribute upon Judah and carry Jehoahaz back to Egypt to die.

Jehoiakim, Josiah's eldest son, then reigned eleven cruel years. Dishonesty, oppression, ambition and injustice were the order of the day,
along with renewed idolatry and debauchery. For the first four years Jehoiakim was a vassal of Egypt.

HABAKKUK

The prophet Habakkuk was disgusted with the way Judah behaved
during the late years of Josiah and the early ones of Jehoiakim. It looked
to him as though Yahweh was going to let the rich nobility squeeze the
life out of the poor forever. Habakkuk finally got fed up with praying for
justice and complained to Yahweh: "Why do you tolerate wrongdoing?"

Yahweh coolly responded that he was about to punish Judah's wickedness by overrunning the land with an even more ruthless people: the
Babylonians.

That's worse! Habakkuk protested. You're the Rock, the Holy One.

"Your eyes are too pure to look on evil, You cannot tolerate wrongdoing."
How can you let such vicious people who worship themselves be your
instruments of justice? How can you let the wicked triumph?

This question was burning in the mind of more than one prophet who
had heard the predictions about Babylonia. So Habakkuk stationed
himself like a watchman to hear what Yahweh wanted him to tell the rest
about this complaint.

Yahweh was not the least offended that his servants were challenging
his methods. He told Habakkuk to take a memo and save it for later generations who would also wonder about his justice. He detailed both the
Babylonians' offenses and the judgment he would eventually impose on
them. Habakkuk would have to be patient, but in due time the wicked
would get theirs.

Like Job, Habakkuk stood in awe when Yahweh actually showed up
to answer his complaint. He composed a song exalting Yahweh's power
as a deliverer. He concluded, looking around at the way aristocrats were
raping the land and looking forward to even worse devastation when the
Babylonians arrived:

> I heard and my heart pounded,
>> my lips quivered at the sound;
> decay crept into my bones,
>> and my legs trembled.
> Yet I will wait patiently for the day of calamity
>> to come on the nation invading us.
> Though the fig tree does not bud
>> and there are no grapes on the vines,
> though the olive crop fails
>> and the fields produce no food,
> though there are no sheep in the pen
>> and no cattle in the stalls,
> yet I will rejoice in Yahweh,
>> I will be joyful in God my Savior. (Habakkuk 3:16-18)

JEREMIAH'S COMPLAINTS

We don't know whether Jeremiah got to hear this interchange between Habakkuk and Yahweh, but we do know that he was asking

rather the same questions early in Jehoiakim's reign.

Here's why: Yahweh told him to stand in the temple doorway and rebuke the worshipers for coming there after making shady business deals all week. He added that both temple and city would be ravaged because of this behavior. The priests and others whose livelihoods depended on the temple demanded that Jeremiah be executed. The crowd agreed vehemently at first, until some elders argued that Hezekiah hadn't executed Micah for saying essentially the same things. Jeremiah was released—a close call since Jehoiakim had another prophet hunted down and executed at about this time. And shortly thereafter, Jeremiah heard of a plot among his fellow priests—his relatives—to murder him.

Jeremiah was devastated. Yahweh had ordered him not to pray for this worthless nation, but Jeremiah just couldn't bring himself to stop. He wept and wrote heart-rending laments about the sufferings he saw coming to Judah. He couldn't understand why he was being treated like a traitor. So he told Yahweh he'd like to have a word with him about his justice: "Why does the way of the wicked prosper? Why do all the faithless live at ease?" (Jeremiah 12:1).

Yahweh's incredible response was, you think it's bad for you now? Just wait!

Later, when Jeremiah complained again, Yahweh promised that the day would come when Jeremiah's enemies would come crawling to him for counsel. But he also added that Jeremiah had better give up the pity parties. The only real comfort Yahweh had to offer was the honor of a noble mission and his old promise: I am with you.

Incredibly, as Jeremiah continued to pour out his pain, he also continued to draw enough strength from Yahweh's presence to see his galling job to the end. He both yelled and trusted when a priest had him beaten and restrained overnight in the temple.

His offense that time was gathering a crowd at the Potsherd Gate, smashing a clay pot and declaring that Yahweh would smash the nation just like that. Yahweh was continually giving him these bits of theater, like the time when he had to bury a linen belt until it rotted to symbolize how pure-white Judah, which had been the belt around Yahweh's waist, would be ruined.

Questions for Reflection and Discussion

1. How would you describe the situation in Judah in the time of King Josiah?

2. Habakkuk wanted to know how a good God could tolerate wrongdoing and even act through evil people. How did Yahweh respond to Habakkuk's question?

3. What do you think it would be like to be in Habakkuk's and Jeremiah's situation, having to "wait patiently for the day of calamity"?

18

BABYLON'S TRIUMPH

2 Kings 24:1–25:30; 2 Chronicles 36:9-23;
Jeremiah 21–25; 27-52; Lamentations; Obadiah

ehoiakim was a smug vassal of Egypt from 609 until 605 B.C. In that year Jeremiah announced that for twenty-three years he had been warning Judah, and now the warning period was over. Judah was about to begin seventy years of captivity in Babylon.

At about the same time, Jeremiah got a series of words predicting the same judgment on Judah's neighbors: Egypt, Philistia, Edam, Moab, Ammon. And he got a long, spectacular preview of Babylon's end after the seventy years were up. None of this comforted him much.

That year, 605 B.C., Prince Nebuchadnezzar defeated Egypt soundly (at the same place where the two nations had fought as allies against Assyria four years earlier). Just as he was sweeping south to absorb Samaria and Judah (see map, page 348), news arrived that his father had died and he was now king of the Babylonian Empire. To assert himself as the new overlord, Nebuchadnezzar confiscated some of the holy objects from the temple and some of the young men from royal and noble families. The latter would be trained to serve in the growing Babylonian bureaucracy that administered the empire. (Among these noble captives were Daniel and three of his friends, about whom we'll hear more later.)

It was possible that this shock might soften the people's hearts, so Yahweh made another appeal. He told Jeremiah to record all of the messages he'd been given about both Judah and the nations, then read them aloud in public. So Jeremiah dictated and his secretary, Baruch, recorded everything. Then, because Jeremiah was under house arrest, they agreed that Baruch would take the scroll to the temple to read it on an opportune day when the people would be gathered there.

Their opportunity didn't come until the following winter. One December day found Baruch at a temple gate reading Jeremiah's scroll. The son of Jehoiakim's secretary of state heard him and ran to tell his dad what was going on. Jehoiakim's cabinet ministers were aghast when they heard Baruch's oration and told him, "You and Jeremiah, go and hide. Don't let anyone know where you are." Then they told the king about the scroll. Jehoiakim had it read aloud, and every few minutes he sliced off the section he had heard and threw it in his fireplace. His officials begged him to take Jeremiah's words more seriously, but he just sat in grim silence until the scroll had been entirely read and burned. Then he sent some of his men to arrest Jeremiah and Baruch.

But the two were successfully hidden. After they heard Jehoiakim's response, Yahweh told them to rewrite the scroll and add a word for the king: because of his contempt for Yahweh, his lineage would be cut off and his body unburied.

BABYLON'S SECOND ATTACK

So Jehoiakim and his people were unmoved. They played the role of an obedient vassal to Babylonia from 604 to 602 B.C. However, in 601 Nebuchadnezzar took on Egypt again but failed to break her. That encouraged Jehoiakim to rebel, even though Jeremiah warned against it. Babylonian troops and their allies arrived swiftly to quell Judah's uprising with a series of raids.

When the raids failed to subdue Judah, Nebuchadnezzar himself arrived with his army to besiege Jerusalem. In 598 Jehoiakim died (cause unknown) just before the Babylonians completed their siege. The city fell on March 16, 597. It was looted, and ten thousand people were deported this time. King Jehoiachin, Jehoiakim's son, was among the captives. Nebuchadnezzar put Jehoiakim's uncle Zedekiah on the throne as his puppet king.

JEREMIAH VERSUS THE FALSE PROPHETS

Zedekiah was as weak as Jehoiakim was spiteful. Jerusalem overflowed with "prophets" claiming that within two years Babylon would be defeated, the temple articles and captives taken by Nebuchadnezzar would be returned and Judah would be restored. In 593 Yahweh told Jeremiah to wear an ox yoke around to drive home the point that the yoke of Babylon was there to stay. Eventually one "prophet" splintered the yoke in a public quarrel with Jeremiah, claiming that Yahweh was going to break the yoke of Nebuchadnezzar within two years. Jeremiah accused that man of being a false prophet and announced he would die that year for preaching rebellion against Yahweh. Two months later the man was dead. For the time being, Zedekiah heeded Jeremiah and stayed loyal to Babylon.

That same year (593) he sent envoys to Babylon and even visited there for reasons unknown. Jeremiah sent a letter with the envoys to the Jews in exile, telling them to settle down and pray for the prosperity of their pagan towns, for they would be in exile for a total of seventy years. He warned them to ignore the prophets with the two-more-years prediction but encouraged them that another fifty-eight years of exile was not forever:

> For I know the plans I have for you . . . plans to prosper you and not to harm you, plans to give you hope and a future. Then you will call on me and come and pray to me, and I will listen to you. You will seek me and find me when you seek me with all your heart. I will be found by you . . . and will bring you back from captivity. (Jeremiah 29:11-14)

The exiles didn't think a hope and future fifty-eight years away was good enough news. A prophet in Babylonia wrote to the chief priest in Jerusalem, demanding that he imprison Jeremiah for telling the exiles that they would be gone seventy years. (The Babylonian contingent had its share of false prophets.) Jeremiah predicted the false prophet's death.

BABYLON'S THIRD ATTACK

It didn't take long for an ambitious new pharaoh to stir up a pro-Egyptian faction in Jerusalem. Zedekiah succumbed to it (despite Jeremiah's reproof) and revolted. So for a third and last time Nebuchadnezzar set out for Jerusalem, determined to swat this pesky city for good. He arrived on January 15, 588 B.C.

Zedekiah panicked and sent several of his officials to beg Jeremiah to seek information from Yahweh or ask him to do what he did back in Hezekiah's time, a century earlier.

But Jeremiah retorted that Yahweh was now doing what he had been predicting for years. He added that anyone who resisted Nebuchadnezzar would die, but anyone who surrendered would survive. Yahweh would protect those who had been taken into exile, but those who stayed with Zedekiah he would reject. And if the king and his men really wanted help from Yahweh, let them show it by reforming the corrupt courts, ceasing to rub out their enemies, paying workmen fair wages, cutting back on their luxurious lifestyle and giving justice to the many oppressed poor in the city. Jeremiah also denounced Jerusalem's prophets for simply telling her leaders what they wanted to hear. They were the worst of all, putting their own words into the mouth of the living God.

But as the siege wore on and things looked darker and darker, Yahweh began to give Jeremiah some hopeful messages. Yahweh was going to discipline but not destroy his people. Eventually he would punish their captors. Once again they would be in covenant relationship to their Bridegroom, their Father, their God. Yahweh spoke as he did to Isaiah in his latter years:

> I have loved you with an everlasting love;
>> I have drawn you with unfailing kindness.
> I will build you up again,
>> and you, Virgin Israel, will be rebuilt. . . .
> The days are coming . . .
>> when I will make a new covenant
> with the people of Israel
>> and with the people of Judah. (Jeremiah 31:3-4, 31)

But these messages of hope were for future generations. To Zedekiah's face, Jeremiah's message was that Nebuchadnezzar would burn Jerusalem to the ground, but first Zedekiah had a chance to die and be buried honorably.

A PAUSE IN THE FIGHTING

A moment of respite came when Egypt marched out to aid Judah, and Nebuchadnezzar had to suspend his siege until he could beat off the Egyptians. Zedekiah begged Jeremiah to pray that the Babylonians wouldn't come back, but the seer said it was useless. In hopes of pleasing Yahweh and gaining some willing soldiers, Zedekiah declared that all Hebrew slaves in Jerusalem were free. At first his officials and the other slave owners agreed to this, but afterward they changed their minds. (After all, Nebuchadnezzar was withdrawing. Maybe they could have their lives and their slaves, too.) Jeremiah said this was just more proof that this people had no intention of obeying Yahweh (whose law required that Hebrew slaves be freed after seven years) and repeated his word of destruction.

Jeremiah took the opportunity provided by the lull in fighting to try to get to his hometown to settle some family matters. However, the captain of the guard arrested him at the gate, accusing him of trying to desert to the enemy. Zedekiah's officials imprisoned him as a traitor, despite his protests.

Zedekiah secretly released him for a private audience. The king wanted to know what Yahweh had to say, but he feared his officials, who hated Jeremiah. But all Yahweh had to say was, "You will be handed over to the king of Babylon." Zedekiah didn't dare release Jeremiah, but he did grant him a less miserable prison and a reasonable food ration until supplies in Jerusalem ran out.

However, Zedekiah's officials were still fuming that Jeremiah was telling the people they would survive if they surrendered but would die if they resisted. The bureaucrats told the king this was sheer treason and undermined morale. They finally convinced him to let them throw the prophet into a cistern. (They wanted to kill him without overtly having his blood on their hands.) The sixty-year-old prophet spent days up to his hips in mud in an abandoned well.

PROMISES

Nebuchadnezzar had soon dealt with the Egyptians and was back at Jerusalem's gate, as grim as ever. The defenders tore down their luxurious houses in order to hurl the stones at the builders of siege ramps. The grain ran out and people started eating anything they could find. Jeremiah sat in jail, once again receiving words from Yahweh that contradicted everything his senses told him.

For decades Jeremiah had heard messages of doom while Judah lounged at ease. Now when catastrophe was imminent, Yahweh instructed him to buy his cousin's field back home in order to keep it in the family. Jeremiah did what he was told but asked what on earth Yahweh was thinking. Ah, Lord Yahweh, he said, you can do anything. You know everything that goes on in people's hearts. You've done miracles to keep your covenant with us through thick and thin. You've been totally right to send these Babylonians to obliterate us. I know you can do anything, but if you're going to destroy and exile us, why am I buying this field?

Yahweh responded, "I am Yahweh, the God of all mankind. Is anything too hard for me?" (Jeremiah 32:27). Yes, in justice he was going to smash Judah, but because of his unearthly love he was going to forgive and restore his people, even transform their hearts so that they would be able to be faithful. Jeremiah might never get the use of that field, but his descendants would.

I am Yahweh who made the earth, he said. "Call to me and I will answer you and tell you great and unsearchable things you do not know" (Jeremiah 33:3). Great and unsearchable things: how he would heal his people, restore them to peace and security and raise up an unending heritage of the royal and priestly lines. Above all, "a righteous Branch" would "sprout from David's line." Zedekiah's name meant "Yahweh is my righteousness," but he failed to live up to that name. But the Branch and his city would be called "Yahweh Our Righteousness" in truth.

> *The goal of all of this was the original plan: Yahweh would have the seed of a people passionate for him. A faithful Jerusalem would be his bait to draw the nations.*

The goal of all of this was the original plan: Yahweh would have the seed of a people passionate for him, and "this city will bring me renown, joy, praise and honor before all nations on earth that hear of all the good things I do for it" (Jeremiah 33:9). A faithful Jerusalem would be his bait to draw the nations.

THE END

By July of 586 the famine was so bad in Jerusalem that mothers were cooking their babies. Jeremiah urged the king to save himself by surrendering, but Zedekiah was paralyzed with fear of both his officials and those Jews who had already deserted.

On August 14, 586, the attackers finally broke through the wall. Zedekiah tried a desperate escape, but Nebuchadnezzar caught him and executed his sons before his eyes, then blinded him and hauled him off to Babylon. The invaders burned the temple and every prominent building to the ground, took everything of value, smashed the walls and took captive all but the poorest, who would keep the land productive so that it could be taxed.

RAGE AND WEEPING

Poets poured out their response to the calamity of 586 B.C. At least one of those poets was a prophet. Obadiah denounced the Edomites for gloating at Jerusalem's destruction and aiding her enemies. His rebuke stands as a permanent warning to those who watch others suffering Yahweh's discipline: "You should not gloat over your brother in the day of his misfortune" (Obadiah 12), for your own discipline may not be far behind.

Five songs of grief have been collected for us in the book of Lamentations. The songwriter(s) aren't named, although tradition points to Jeremiah. In the first four songs the verses begin with the successive letters of the Hebrew alphabet. The first song sees Jerusalem weeping like a destitute queen, who is now a hideous wretch.

> Her filthiness clung to her skirts;
>> she did not consider her future.
> Her fall was astounding;
>> there was none to comfort her.
> "Look, Yahweh, on my affliction,
>> for the enemy has triumphed." (Lamentations 1:9)

The third songwriter wails his grief in tightly crafted verses, but he also finds the "yet" of David. Surveying smoking rubble, starving infants, corpses everywhere, he writes:

> I remember my affliction and my wandering,
>> the bitterness and the gall.
> I well remember them,
>> and my soul is downcast within me.
> Yet this I call to mind
>> and therefore I have hope:
> Because of Yahweh's great love we are not consumed,
>> for his compassions never fail.
> They are new every morning;
>> great is your faithfulness. (Lamentations 3:19-23)

The final song is a mix of confidence, questioning and humility, knowing that only Yahweh can bring such a people to real repentance:

> Restore us to yourself, Yahweh, that we may return;
>> renew our days as of old.
> unless you have utterly rejected us
>> and are angry with us beyond measure. (Lamentations 5:21-22)

To Egypt

The commander of the Babylonian imperial guard, who was in charge of cleanup operations, had heard of Jeremiah. Both he and Nebuchadnezzar knew the prophet had been counseling submission for years, and they suspected that here was a man of great character, if not divine appointment. So when the commander found Jeremiah in prison awaiting deportation, he freed him. He offered the old man hospitality in his own home in Babylon, but Jeremiah, loyal to the end, insisted on staying with the survivors in Jerusalem.

Nebuchadnezzar had appointed as governor a Judan named Gedaliah who, like Jeremiah, had long advocated nonresistance to the Babylonians because their conquest was a judgment from Yahweh. The commander committed Jeremiah to Gedaliah's protection. Gedaliah set up an office in Mizpah, a few miles north of Jerusalem, and urged the farmers to gather the harvest that was just coming ripe.

But a surviving relative of Zedekiah assassinated Gedaliah and more than a hundred of his supporters, took captive the rest of Gedaliah's group (including Jeremiah) and tried to flee the country. Another group of Jewish army officers intercepted the assassin and freed the prisoners. Then, terrified of Babylonian reprisal, they begged Jeremiah to ask Yahweh what they should do next.

Yahweh promised to protect them if they stayed in Judah and took care of his land. He also promised that if they fled to Egypt because they didn't trust him, the death they feared would come upon them there. Sure enough, the officers had no intention of trusting Yahweh and staying in Judah. They had already made up their minds and were only hoping for someone to justify their decision. They had the gall to accuse Baruch of inciting Jeremiah to say the wrong thing. Then they forced Baruch, Jeremiah and the rest of the remnant to go with them to Egypt.

Poor Jeremiah. It wasn't long before the new arrivals in Egypt met earlier Jewish fugitives and all were practicing a mix of Jewish, Egyptian and Babylonian religion. In particular, they were making cakes in the shape of Ishtar, the Babylonian goddess, and burning incense to her. Jeremiah marveled—hadn't they learned anything from the cataclysm they had just been through? Yes, they said, we've learned that things started falling apart back home when we stopped worshiping Ishtar, and we're not going to make that mistake again.

Postscripts

In 561 B.C., some twenty years after Jeremiah's death, a new king of Babylon declared an amnesty for the Judan captives there. He released Jehoiachin from prison and assigned daily rations from the royal household to support Jehoiachin and his five sons. The lineage of David was hanging on by a hair.

Questions for Reflection and Discussion

1. Babylon attacked Judah three times and took away captives each time. After each attack, about how many people were taken away, and who were they?

2. Why do you suppose the people didn't believe Jeremiah and turn back to Yahweh after the first attack?

3. How does the poet of Lamentations view Yahweh? What place does lamentation have in the Christian life?

4. With Judah destroyed and the royal family dead or captive, what do you think happens to the promise about the Son of David?

Part Three

EXILE AND RETURN

<><><><><><><><><><><><><><><><><><><><><><><><><><><><><><><><><><><><><><>

19

A PROPHET IN EXILE

Ezekiel

The exile was Yahweh's judgment on his people, but he used the tragedy productively. These few generations did more to transform Judaism (the faith of the people of Judah) than all the centuries since Joshua. A few key people spearheaded the transformation. The prophet Ezekiel was one of them.

EZEKIEL'S CALL

A handful of Jews were taken to Babylon in 605 B.C., but thousands went in 597. (See map, page 348.) They clung to the hope that any day Yahweh would work a miracle and bring them home. They eked out livings in their makeshift settlements along the canals of the Euphrates River, and they were largely unwilling to face any responsibility they may have had for their sufferings.

Among them was a priest-in-training named Ezekiel. On his thirtieth birthday, he was eligible to be anointed as a full-fledged priest. But in Nippur, a Babylonian city a thousand miles from Jerusalem, there was not much for a priest of Yahweh to do. No temple, no sacrifices. The only work was teaching the writings of Moses.

But Yahweh had another assignment for this priest. As you might recall, in the year 593 B.C., King Zedekiah sent envoys to Babylon and later went there himself. Jeremiah wrote to the exiles, advising them to settle in for another fifty-eight years and ignore those among them who were prophesying a speedy return. Many of the exiles were furious at Jeremiah's letter, and one "prophet" called for his death. Yahweh blasted young Ezekiel with a vision.

Ezekiel saw a blazing windstorm, in the midst of which were four living creatures glowing with fire. Each had four faces and four wings, and they stood as the four corners of a square, outstretched wings touching. Resting on their spread wings was a crystalline expanse, upon which stood a sapphire throne. On the throne Ezekiel could make out a "figure like that of a man" gleaming like white-hot metal and fire. This was a physical representation of the glory of Yahweh. The Presence that had led Israel through the desert, indwelt the tabernacle and inhabited Solomon's temple was now appearing to an exile in Babylon.

Ezekiel had the usual response to such a sight: he hit the dirt. Yahweh breathed his Spirit into the prone form so that Ezekiel could stand up, then began issuing instructions to his new prophet, whom he addressed as "son of man." "Son of" in Hebrew parlance signified someone's essence. A "son of iniquity" was a thoroughly wicked person. A "son of Abraham" was a person with a character like Abraham's. And "son of man" (or "son of Adam") referred to an utterly human, Adam-like person, in contrast to the Holy God.

Yahweh appeared to Ezekiel in this terrifying way to strengthen him for a harsh task. The Jewish exiles were rebellious. Yahweh had a woeful message for them, just like the one Jeremiah was giving the Jews back home. Ezekiel would need the same tough hide Jeremiah had to withstand abuse from people who didn't want to hear what he had to say.

Free to Choose

Yahweh compared the prophetic task to that of a watchman stationed on the heights of a city to inform its people about approaching couriers or the progress of a battle. Jeremiah was posted in Jerusalem to warn about the coming destruction. Ezekiel's job was to notify the exiles that each of them was as individually accountable for his own actions as Jerusalem was as a whole for hers.

The exiles were saying they were suffering for their parents' crimes, or for the nobility's corruption—it was always someone else's fault. Yahweh wanted them to face the fact that in his sight, they would all live or die by their own virtue or vice. It's true that Yahweh let parents' sin taint their children's lives, for no man is an island. But the children always had enough freedom to choose darkness or light. Even people who had been wicked since birth retained the freedom to choose to change. They may not have had enough power to break ingrained habits on their own, but they had enough to reject them in principle and wholeheartedly seek Yahweh's help to reject them in practice.

In their heart of hearts, the exiles suspected that Yahweh enjoyed saddling people with inherited sin and then zapping them for it. To this Yahweh retorted, "Do I take any pleasure in the death of the wicked? . . . Rather, am I not pleased when they turn from their ways and live?" (Ezekiel 18:23).

LIVING MESSAGE

Like Hosea, Isaiah and Jeremiah, Ezekiel often had to live his message. First, Yahweh made it impossible for him to speak except when giving a direct message from his Boss. This silence went on for seven years until Jerusalem's destruction. This symbolized the nation's refusal to listen.

Yahweh also told him to build a clay model of Jerusalem under siege (the real siege was as yet five years off) and to lie on his side in front of it one day for each year of the treason of Israel and Judah. For 430 days Ezekiel had to lie there eating nothing but vegetarian patties baked on cow dung (a taste of famine food). In this way he embodied what Yahweh had suffered for 430 years. For it was really he who had borne the nation's

> *Ezekiel, the son of man, was a living picture of what Yahweh was willing to bear for love of treacherous children.*

evil all those years, and he who would suffer with his people every anguish of siege, starvation and slaughter. Ezekiel, the son of man, was a living picture of what Yahweh was willing to bear for love of treacherous children. And like Hosea, the prophet was able to enter into the intimacy of Yahweh's grief and share it with him as a friend.

THE GLORY DEPARTS

The next year Ezekiel saw a dreadful thing: in a vision of Jerusalem he watched the glory rise from the temple and depart. Out the front gate of the city it went, and it stopped over a nearby hill called the Mount of Olives. Jerusalem had abandoned Yahweh; now he was abandoning her. Ezekiel cried out in horror.

COVENANT SENTENCE

Ezekiel directed some scathing tongue-lashings. Jerusalem was a woman Yahweh had found as an abandoned baby, raised tenderly and finally married and adorned as a queen. But she had used her fame and wealth to become a whore and attract gigolos, so Yahweh was handing her over to be torn apart by her lovers. Ezekiel described both idolatry and international intrigue in graphic, lewd imagery.

Ezekiel fought the same battle Jeremiah was fighting against the false prophets who predicted that everything was going to be okay. Real prophets, said Ezekiel, would be repairing the gaps in the moral and spiritual wall of the city so that it could stand against all upheavals in the day of Yahweh. But instead, when the leaders of Judah built a flimsy wall, these prophets simply whitewashed it to look like a solid piece of justice and commitment.

Every bleak picture, though, held its ray of hope. One day, when Yahweh's adulterous bride was humbled, he would take her back as his wife. He would take his sheep from the false shepherds and give them a true shepherd: a son of David. Over and over he explained the purpose of both destruction and restoration: "Then they will know that I am Yahweh."

NEWS OF THE END

In August of 586 B.C., Yahweh told Ezekiel that the next day he would lose the delight of his eyes: his wife. He was not to show any sign of mourning, for on that same day the exiles would lose the delight of their eyes and their hopes would crumble: Jerusalem would fall. In his silence, Ezekiel could share his grief only with Yahweh. For if lying on his side before a model of Jerusalem had let Ezekiel taste Yahweh's suffering, here was the ultimate empathy: both God and this "son of man" saw their beloved brides die that day. They wept together alone.

Five months later the first captives arrived with news of the final desolation of the Holy City. For seven and a half years Ezekiel had been unable to speak except when delivering a message from Yahweh. Now his tongue was loosed to greet the refugees. All this time his job had been to urge the exiles to turn from the self-centeredness to which, insanely, they still clung, despite the ordeals they had suffered. His tactic had been to predict destruction as a sign of Yahweh's rage.

But now that the worst had happened, Yahweh gave him a new assignment: to sketch out yet more of the glorious future so that hope might accomplish what warning had not. Again he gave Ezekiel a series of visions: Israel was like a valley of dry bones, but Yahweh would breathe into them until they were again a great army. He would bind Israel and Judah together again into one nation under one Davidic king.

> I will give you a new heart and put a new spirit in you; I will remove from you your heart of stone and give you a heart of flesh. And I will put my Spirit in you and move you to follow my decrees and be careful to keep my laws. Then you will live in the land I gave your ancestors; you will be my people, and I will be your God. (Ezekiel 36:26-28)

World powers would amass to destroy the new kingdom, but Yahweh would reduce their armies to carrion. Yet Yahweh was quick to reiterate the purpose:

> It is not for your sake, people of Israel, that I am going to do these things, but for the sake of my holy name, which you have profaned among the nations where you have gone. I will show the holiness of my great name, which has been profaned among the nations, the name you have profaned among them. Then the nations will know that I am Yahweh . . . when I am proved holy through you before their eyes. (36:22–23)

Yahweh's eye was ever on the nations.

Yahweh's eye was ever on the nations.

ENIGMA

The final section of Ezekiel's book is a vision of what it would mean for a holy God to dwell among his people. The prophet saw the temple rebuilt in Jerusalem according to a plan of mammoth proportions—the entire complex covered a square mile with wide buffer zones between it and the rest of the city. Yahweh's holy place was utterly separate from the commonplace city of getting and spending that surrounded it. No longer would Yahweh's house sit cheek-by-jowl next door to a palace like Solomon's. In fact, the priests and Levites would have about twenty-one square miles each around the temple precincts to form a further buffer between the holy and the common. The city itself would be only a quarter the size of the holy area.

Ezekiel saw the glory move back into Yahweh's dwelling place just as he'd seen it abandon Solomon's temple before Jerusalem was burned. He also saw a river flowing out of the temple, giving life to everything it touched. He saw how Yahweh would redistribute the Promised Land in equal portions to the twelve tribes—no more of this concentrating wealth in the hands of a few. And finally, Yahweh renamed the city. It would no longer be called Yerushalayim (Jerusalem), but Yahweh-Shammah: Yahweh Is There.

Questions for Reflection and Discussion

1. What did it mean when Yahweh called Ezekiel "son of man"?

2. How did Ezekiel's personal life mirror what both Yahweh and the people in Jerusalem were experiencing? What impact do you think Yahweh wanted this to have on the exiles?

3. What does Ezekiel add to our understanding of the promise?

20

AMBASSADOR TO A PAGAN COURT

1 and 2 Kings, Daniel

*W*hile Ezekiel was berating his countrymen in their impoverished villages, Yahweh was doing something quite different with four Jews who had been taken to Babylon back in 605 B.C. A rapidly expanding empire prompted Nebuchadnezzar to recruit administrative staff from among the conquered nations. It wasn't easy to find people with the intellect and basic education to master the classical literature of Babylon (written in an ancient and complex language), the official language in which state business was done (Aramaic), and the intricacies of Babylonian magic, divination and dream interpretation. A royal administrator had to know all of these, and he had to be physically perfect and handsome in order to fittingly represent his master.

So in each captured country, Nebuchadnezzar's officers selected a few young noblemen who showed potential for such studies. In Judah they found four. These teenagers agreed to have their names changed as a sign of submission to Nebuchadnezzar, even to receive names derived from the names of Babylonian gods. They agreed to study the literature of sorcery and nature worship even though Yahweh had forbidden such practices. They were apparently secure enough in their commitment to and understanding of Yahweh that they could immerse themselves in their neighbors' thought world without having their own convictions undermined. (These four, at least, had benefited from the labors of Zephaniah, Habakkuk and Jeremiah.) Their firm foundation enabled them to serve as Yahweh's ambassadors to a pagan court, ambassadors who understood the people they were reaching well enough to speak their language and touch them where they lived.

THE LIMITS OF CONFORMITY

The four captives were willing to do all this in order to identify with the culture to which Yahweh had sent them, but thereafter they repeatedly drew lines they would not cross. Over and over they had to discern between the conformity that won them an audience in the culture and the conformity that would have meant selling out and losing their message.

The first line they drew was refusing to eat the king's food. Young administrators-in-training were housed outside the palace but they were fed from the royal kitchens to signify that they were the king's servants. However, the king's meat and wine were routinely offered to pagan gods before being served, and in the Middle East, regularly eating someone's food was powerfully symbolic of swearing allegiance to him. The four young Jews just could not in good conscience eat food that linked them to Babylon's gods so firmly.

So Daniel, their leader, maneuvered their steward into feeding them vegetarian diets and no wine. Yahweh confirmed this stratagem by giving them better health than their colleagues who ate the king's food. He also demonstrated the truth of the old proverb "The fear of Yahweh is the beginning of wisdom" by enabling his ambassadors to excel in all aspects of their training in wisdom by the end of their two-year course.

This limit to conformity was private, but later the four Jews had to risk their lives to maintain their principles. At one point Nebuchadnezzar experimented with uniting his multiracial empire under one state religion and commanded officials from all of his provinces to bow down before a statue he erected. Daniel's three friends were reported to the king and thrown into a furnace for refusing to worship the state idol. These three told Nebuchadnezzar flatly that their God was able to rescue them from the flames, but even if he chose not to, he deserved their loyalty. When miraculously the flames did not consume the men, Nebuchadnezzar was so awed that he praised this powerful God and on the spot declared Judaism legal in his empire.

Decades later, Daniel found himself in a similar position. Jealous fellow courtiers, out to get Daniel, convinced a new king to decree that for a month no one could worship anyone but him, knowing that Daniel would ignore such an order. That time, God demonstrated his power to protect his own by preventing a den full of lions from devouring Daniel.

MESSAGES FROM THE GOD OF HEAVEN

Most of the time, however, Daniel and his friends were able to go about their duties in a corrupt pagan government, serving Yahweh and his justice in quiet ways. But in a few key instances, Yahweh employed Daniel as his spokesman to these people who knew nothing about him.

Daniel's book reflects his (and Yahweh's) sensitivity to speak in ways his hearers could grasp. When addressing non-Jews, Daniel avoided Yahweh's personal name and instead used titles that his hearers would understand: God, the God of heaven, the God of my ancestors, the great God, the Most High God. The whole middle section of his book is written in Aramaic rather than Hebrew to demonstrate God speaking to all nations in the international language. And when God wanted to get messages across to the kings Daniel served, he used dreams and omens because Babylonians were prepared to hear from the gods in this way.

God wanted to give Nebuchadnezzar a chance. The king was insecure about having risen so fast to become lord over a huge empire, so God gave him a dream in which the kingdoms of the world were represented as "an enormous, dazzling statue." Nebuchadnezzar's kingdom was the statue's head of gold (the first and greatest). But after him would follow kingdoms of ever-decreasing glory represented by other parts of the statue made of silver, bronze and iron. The feet of the statue were iron mixed with clay: strength and fragility mixed. And finally would come an eternal kingdom founded by God, not humankind, that would smash and replace all human kingdoms.

The message: Your human empire is secure for a time, O Nebuchadnezzar, but the God of heaven is lord over all nations and the whole scope of history. For a time he will allow human kingdoms to rise and

186 STORY OF STORIES

fall, but at the end of time he will sweep them all away and establish a
kingdom that will last.

God enabled Daniel to interpret this dream for Nebuchadnezzar at
the very beginning of his career. The young Jew could hardly have been
more than twenty, but he proclaimed the truth about God's supremacy to
a man who held Daniel's life in his hands. Daniel was quick to credit God
rather than his own skill for the interpretation, since it was only God's
answer to desperate prayer that gave Daniel the insight to explain the
dream and save his own life.

Sadly, the king responded only by recognizing Daniel's God as a powerful deity in a pantheon of gods. So some forty years later God sent him
another dream, which Daniel again had to interpret: unless Nebuchadnezzar acknowledged that he was subordinate to the God of heaven and
showed it by ceasing to oppress his own subjects, God would reduce
him to insanity until he yielded. This is just what happened. But although Nebuchadnezzar did eventually admit that God was in charge of
the world, he seems to have died before he truly understood what that
fact implied.

THE CHANGING OF KINGDOMS

Just as Nebuchadnezzar had dreamed, the Babylonian Empire was a flash
in the pan that God raised up briefly to discipline his people. He had
promised Babylon's fall to Habakkuk, Jeremiah and Ezekiel. He had told
Jeremiah it would happen seventy years after the captivity began. He had
even told Isaiah the name of the man who would do the job.

Sure enough, in 549 B.C., a Persian king named Cyrus defeated his
overlord and became king of the vast Median Empire north and east of
Babylon. Two years later he absorbed Asia Minor, west of Babylon, and
cast his eye on Babylon itself.

By that time the king of Babylon was Nabonidus. But Nabonidus had
made enemies among the priests of Babylon and had fled to Arabia,
leaving his son Belshazzar in charge. So Belshazzar ruled the Babylonian
Empire while Cyrus jaunted around building his own empire. By 540 B.C.
Belshazzar saw he'd made a fatal mistake in letting his army go to seed,
but it was too late. In the autumn of 539, with the Medo-Persian army

on his doorstep, Belshazzar was losing his grip. To drown his terror he threw a wild banquet, even calling for the sacred vessels of Jerusalem for his drinking cups.

Toward the end of this drunken feast, the horrified ruler saw writing appear on the wall opposite him: words about weights of money. His mother told him to summon an old magician named Daniel to interpret the message. Daniel explained that God had weighed Belshazzar's worth and found him wanting. That very night Babylon fell to Cyrus.

WIDER VISIONS

With experiences like these, there was no doubt in Daniel's mind who was in charge of the volatile world he lived in. But what about the other Jews scattered around the Middle East? Some were making good livings in commerce and manufacturing; others were barely surviving.

Jeremiah and Ezekiel were dead, and Yahweh sent no emissary to replace them. But one or more prophetically minded Jews sorted through the annals written by the prophetic communities since Solomon's time and wrote a sweeping history to answer the question in everyone's mind: Why did Yahweh let this happen? In this book, which we call 1 and 2 Kings, the author traced how the kings of Israel and Judah failed to lead their people to keep the covenant. He showed that the exile was the natural result of rejecting their Lord.

Some priests began to understand that keeping the covenant was essential, and they started codifying the books of Moses and the prophets into a system of religious practice that could hold its own against pressures to assimilate into local culture. If Yahweh kept his promise to restore them, they were determined never to break the covenant again.

But all of these activities were focused on the Jewish community, which was carefully insulating itself from the alien world around it. Daniel could not afford such a narrow perspective, and God's focus had always been wider. Also, now that Judah would never again be an independent state but would be continually subject to the pagan kingdoms of Nebuchadnezzar's dream, God had to prepare his people to survive under regimes that would make it difficult for them to live his way.

In the furnace and the lions' den, Daniel and his friends had received foretastes of what would happen when the interests of a secular state clashed with loyalty to the true God. These four forerunners escaped miraculously, but it would not always be so. Living in the corrupt world without being absorbed by it would demand the toughest kind of faith. So Yahweh gave Daniel four visions to encourage the generations that would follow him. They echoed the glimpses Isaiah and Ezekiel had had of the far-distant future, but they also represented to a new kind of prophecy, which we call apocalyptic (from the Greek word *apokalypsis*, "revelation" or "unveiling"). In weird, symbolic pictures, Yahweh sketched highlights of what he had in store.

THE SON OF MAN

Daniel's four visions were built on Nebuchadnezzar's dream of the statue. He received the first two while Belshazzar was still reigning. In the first he saw four wild animals that represented the four kingdoms. The ruler of the fourth kingdom spoke boastfully of his power, but God appeared as the judge of rulers and kingdoms, and the fourth animal was slain. Then appeared "one like a son of man" who received from the judge authority to rule and even be worshiped by all nations in an everlasting kingdom.

Who was this "son of man" with whom Yahweh would share his worship? Yahweh had used the term for Ezekiel to emphasize the prophet's mere humanness. But this son of man was the ultimate human, the true son of Adam promised at the beginning, the one who alone of all his brothers and sisters bore the image of God untainted. He was not just the son of David, a king for a tiny nation, but king of all.

Wonderfully encouraging, but there was an ominous note. The fourth kingdom would be crushed, but not until after its king had blasphemed God and oppressed his servants cruelly. Those who remained faithful even to death, however, would reign with the son of man.

BABYLON, PERSIA, GREECE

Daniel received a second vision in 551 B.C., just as Cyrus was beginning to put Persia on the map. This vision zeroed in on the second and third of the four kingdoms. The first was Babylon; its days were already numbered. Persia was number two, and Greece (which was just starting to be noticed as a power) was number three. An angel described to Daniel one of the kings of the Greek empire: a conniving despot who would war against God and his people. This vision so appalled Daniel that he spent days in bed, sick and exhausted.

Suffering and Perseverance

Daniel's third vision came just after Cyrus conquered Babylon in 539 B.C. Daniel had been reading Jeremiah and figured that the seventy years of exile were about over, so he went to Yahweh with mourning and fasting, begging him to forgive and free his people. As faithful as he had always been, Daniel saw in himself the same corruption that stained his people. He confessed passionately and threw himself on Yahweh's mercy. In response, an angel came to say Yahweh was granting his request. Jerusalem and the temple would be rebuilt, but beyond that, sixty-nine weeks of years remained until an anointed king would come. He would then be killed and there would be war, the destruction of the temple, treachery and abominations before justice would be inflicted on a false ruler.

Two years later, Daniel was fasting to understand what he had seen, and a fourth vision came: an angel so terrifying that Daniel was overwhelmed and had to be strengthened repeatedly just to stand up and talk. This warrior angel was battling the spirit princes who stood behind the earthly kingdoms arrayed against God's people. He gave Daniel more details of Persia and Greece (astonishingly accurate as to what would happen in the 200s and 100s B.C.). Proud kings would rise and be dashed to dust, and one particular king would exalt himself to divine status, ravage Israel and finally be crushed. In those terrible times the people of God would suffer horribly, but "the people who know their God will firmly resist" and "those who are wise will instruct many" (Daniel 11:32-33). Then the angel spoke of the end of the age, when after cataclysmic distress the dead would be raised to either eternal life or eternal shame.

Kings and Kingdoms

The details of all this were opaque to Daniel. From our hindsight we can see the rise and fall of Babylon, Persia, Greece and a fourth kingdom: Rome. We know of a wicked Greek king, Antiochus IV, who set himself up as divine and persecuted the Jews in Israel. But we also find elements of Daniel's visions that look past that king. It appears that Antiochus was going to be a foretaste of many rulers who would tyrannize God's people for refusing to worship false gods, and of a final ruler who would be the epitome of this type. In the face of such oppressors, the message of the visions is clear: "The people who know their God will firmly resist."

Questions for Reflection and Discussion

1. What are some things Daniel and his friends needed in order to be Yahweh's representatives in a pagan culture?

2. What are some ways in which we today need to adapt to our culture in order to communicate the message about Yahweh? What are some ways in which we need to avoid conforming?

3. What did Yahweh reveal to Daniel about the present and the future? Who was the "son of man" in his vision?

21

RETURN TO JERUSALEM

Ezra 1–6, Haggai, Zechariah

*I*n 539 B.C. King Cyrus of Persia rode victorious through the gates of Babylon having absorbed most of the Middle East into his empire. He had never even heard of the God of Israel, but Yahweh had selected him carefully nonetheless, revealing his mission and even his name centuries earlier to Isaiah:

> This is what Yahweh says to his anointed,
>> to Cyrus, whose right hand I take hold of
> to subdue nations before him
>> and to strip kings of their armor . . .
> I will go before you
>> and will level the mountains;
> I will break down gates of bronze
>> and cut through bars of iron. . . .
> For the sake of Jacob my servant,
>> of Israel my chosen,
> I summon you by name
>> and bestow on you a title of honor,
>> though you do not acknowledge me.
> I am Yahweh, and there is no other;
>> apart from me there is no God. (Isaiah 45:1-5)

Cyrus viewed politics and religion in a way utterly unlike his Babylonian predecessors. Convinced that sheer force could not make a large empire stable, he sought to win his diverse subjects' good will by tolerating their cultural distinctives. Instead of forcing everyone to worship Persian gods, he encouraged each nation to seek its own gods' favor for him. He sent people back to their homelands, returned confiscated religious objects and financed the rebuilding of temples. This policy was so successful that his successors continued it.

So only months after Yahweh told Daniel his prayers were granted, Cyrus issued an edict that Jews in his empire could return to Jerusalem and rebuild their temple. A bare fifty years had passed since the city's destruction and not quite seventy since Daniel's capture. In response to prayer, Yahweh had mercifully trimmed the time of suffering.

Only about fifty thousand of the exiles decided to make the trek back to Judah. The rest—the majority—preferred to stay where they had settled, bought houses and built businesses. After all, many had been born in Babylon and knew Judah only as a story.

But those who stayed behind were glad to help finance the resettlement. Cyrus's treasurer counted out every last gold dish and silver bowl that Nebuchadnezzer had carried off from the ruined temple. And the returnees were on the whole a prosperous bunch with slaves and considerable personal funds. It was a promising start.

For fifty years and more, the priests and Levites had been poring over the books of Moses and the prophets, analyzing what had gone wrong. This time they were determined to take Yahweh seriously and do everything by the Book.

TEMPLE FOUNDATIONS

The returnees took about three months to settle into villages around Judah. Then in the autumn of 537 B.C. they gathered in ruined Jerusalem to celebrate the Festival of Tabernacles. The temple site was a heap of rubble, but they rebuilt the altar and began offering the sacrifices precisely as laid down in Leviticus, the priestly handbook. If their primary reason for existing as a people was to be "a kingdom of priests and a holy nation" (Exodus 19:6) as a model to the other nations, then worshiping Yahweh took top priority. Hence, on top of planting their first crops in a land quite different from Babylon, the community's chief task that first wet winter was to line up craftsmen and material to begin rebuilding the temple in the spring. There was a bittersweet celebration when the foundation was laid in May of 536: the young shouted for joy, while the old who had seen Solomon's temple wept.

Everything was going great until a delegation arrived from Samaria (the region that used to be called Israel but was now named after its former capital). They were pleased as punch to welcome their new neighbors and help them build a Yahweh temple. Why, they'd been worshiping Yahweh ever since they came to Samaria! But the Jews knew that these Samaritans were equal opportunity religionists imported from all over the Middle East by the Assyrians. They would be glad to support a Yahweh cult along with their other gods and thereby slowly assimilate the well-heeled newcomers into their system.

So the Jews turned the delegation down flat. They welcomed with open arms anyone who wanted to join them to serve Yahweh exclusively, but "open-mindedness" and "many paths to the divine" had gotten the covenant nation in hot water the last time, and they had no intention of repeating that mistake.

Rebuffed, the Samaritans showed their true colors. They launched a campaign of intimidation, ridicule and threats to discourage the rebuilders. They even hired professional help to cut supply lines and cause trouble with the legal authorities. They had no intention of letting a distinctly Jewish state become a power in the region.

The campaign succeeded, but only because the Jews were not really prepared for the realities of recolonization. They had marched out full of idealism, their ears ringing with the words of Isaiah and Ezekiel about restoration. They probably expected the land to sprout abundance of its own accord, and certainly to support them in the comfortable lifestyle they had been carving out in Babylon. A few poor crop years and a little scorn from their neighbors, and they were no longer in the mood to build a temple. Priorities shifted to self. When the people had nicely paneled houses and full stomachs, then it would be time again to think about building a house for Yahweh.

THE TEMPLE RESTARTED: 520 B.C.

So things sat for sixteen years. In the meantime Cyrus died in 530 B.C., and his son Cambyses secured the throne by murdering his brother and hiding the body. Cambyses had soon swallowed Egypt into his empire, but then he died suddenly in 522. In the ensuing struggle for power, one of Cambyses' officers and distant relatives, Darius, gained the upper hand. But he had all kinds of trouble stabilizing his reign. For two years he contended with rebel factions, two of which claimed to be led by Cambyses' vanished brother. It was a credit to Darius's talent and toughness that he finally managed to impose order by the middle of 520.

In August of that year Yahweh knew the time was ripe to prod his people back into action. A series of disastrous harvests due to drought and hail had gotten their attention. The despondent community was a pale shadow of the cocky crew who had first set out from Babylon seventeen years earlier.

A prophet named Haggai announced that the crops would keep failing until the people started building Yahweh's house instead of pouring everything into their own houses. A temple was a national focal point—an essential if Judah was to remain distinct as Yahweh's nation against intense pressures to merge into the surrounding culture.

Haggai's calm reasoning stung the community's two leaders into action: Governor Zerubbabel (a grandson of King Jehoiachin, and therefore a potential Davidic king) and Joshua (or Jeshua), the high priest. They promoted the building project in earnest while Haggai cheered them on: "Be strong!" "I am with you, declares Yahweh."

To those who didn't think much of the stark brick-and-beam structure after seeing the splendor of Solomon's temple and of the temples in Babylon, Haggai painted a grand picture of how Yahweh would shake the heavens and the earth and overturn kingdoms. "The desired of all nations" would come, the prophet said, and the glory of this house would be greater than that of Solomon's. From the day the rebuilding began, the harvests would start turning around. And most importantly, Yahweh had chosen Zerubbabel as his "signet ring," his pledge of full payment on the promises about the son of David.

ZECHARIAH

Haggai delivered just four messages in four months. Once construction was well under way, his job was over. But that same autumn a young priest named Zechariah took up the task of encouraging the builders. The following February he received a series of strange visions—angelic horsemen, horns and craftsmen, a woman in a basket—symbolic messages to spur the Jews on. Yahweh was going to overturn the oppressing nations, cleanse Judah and fill Jerusalem to overflowing. Zechariah saw Joshua in his high priestly robes bloodstained with the crimes of his people. The robes were stripped off him and replaced with clean ones, and Yahweh repeated his promise to send the son of David: "1 will remove the sin of this land in a single day" (Zechariah 3:9). Did anyone wonder what would have to take place on that single day to remove the land's sin?

Zechariah saw two olive trees providing oil for a lamp: king and priest, anointed with Yahweh's Spirit, fueling the holy service of his people. He saw Joshua crowned as king: the royal and priestly offices intermingled in a way impossible under Moses' law, since kings had to come from Judah and priests from Levi.

> *Did anyone wonder what would have to take place on that single day to remove the land's sin?*

The meaning of all this was not clear, especially statements like, "'I am coming, and I will live among you,' declares Yahweh . . . 'and you will know that Yahweh Almighty has sent me to you'" (Zechariah 2:10-11). God sending God?

But on the whole, it sounded as though any day now Persia would be overthrown, Jerusalem would be again the resplendent capital of an independent nation and a son of David would reign. Some of the prophecies gave the distinct impression that Zerubbabel himself might be that king (although what to make of a king with a priestly role of cleansing sin?).

In any case, it was all upbeat enough to keep the builders going when the next round of threats to their project surfaced. Another delegation arrived, this time from the Persian provincial governor. The empire had been in disarray for two years, and any sign of a local uprising—such as building fortifications with large blocks of stone—demanded investigation. The Jews quaked when the governor made out a full report, including names of those involved, and sent it to the Persian capital.

But Yahweh had everything under control. First he moved the governor to let the Jews continue building until a verdict came from King Darius. Then he moved Darius to the same attitude as his grandfather. Cyrus's original decree authorizing state aid in the building of the Jewish temple was found in the archive of a remote Persian city. So Darius ordered the governor not only to permit the construction but even to finance it out of local taxes. Darius even decided to pay for the daily offerings so that both these citizens and their God would support his regime. Palestine was a key region, what with Egypt so volatile, and it was in Darius's best interest to please his subjects so easily.

With ample funds, the Jews finished the temple in less than three and a half years. Zechariah kept up morale in Yahweh's double-edged fashion. On the one hand, he predicted extravagant blessings: Jerusalem full, all the exiles restored, abundant crops, non-Jews streaming to Jerusalem to seek Yahweh. But there was a catch. Zechariah relayed Yahweh's instructions to the people:

> These are the things you are to do: Speak the truth to each other, and render true and sound judgment in your courts; do not plot evil against your neighbor, and do not love to swear falsely. I hate all this. (Zechariah 8:16-17)

Whether the people would share in this glorious future depended on their response.

HOPE DEFERRED

Nonetheless, it was a bright day in 516 B.C. when Joshua and Zerubbabel dedicated the new temple, just seventy years after the destruction of the first one. Those who remembered the opulence of Solomon's temple found the bare-bones replacement disappointing. There was no gold, there was one lampstand instead of ten, and the ark of the covenant had been lost and had to be replaced by a slab of stone. The dedication ceremony squeezed the impoverished community to the limit, but even so it was stark compared to Solomon's lavish affair (seven hundred animals versus twenty-two thousand). Yet although the kingless nation under

Persian domination was a pale shadow of its former glory, the people were full of hope.

But year passed into year. Jerusalem remained in ruins and Darius showed no signs of falling off his throne. To keep the people going, Yahweh gave Zechariah an even wilder series of prophecies, encouraging but bewildering in their contradictions. He told of an army (the Greeks?) sweeping through Palestine and routing Judah's enemies, then of the Jews battling victoriously against the Greeks, and he gave more glimpses of national greatness. The people would abandon their corruption. Yahweh would come himself to battle against their enemies and reign as King in their midst. The nation would be so pure that even the horses' gear would bear the insignia of the high priest's turban: "Holy to Yahweh." Yet the Davidic king would come on a donkey, a symbol of peace, rather than on a war horse when he triumphed over the oppressors. How could a man of peace defeat Israel's enemies? Zechariah also saw the king as a shepherd rejecting his rebellious flock and its greedy shepherds and tossing away his wages: thirty pieces of silver, the price of a slave.

With hindsight we know Zechariah was seeing jumbled-together events that would happen over the course of one century, five centuries, even twenty-five. Why didn't Yahweh spell things out more clearly? The Jews got the understandable impression that "soon" meant "in our lifetime," or at least not centuries and millennia away. When Zerubbabel died and nothing earth-shattering seemed to be happening, the Jews not surprisingly cooled in their spiritual fervor. They kept up the temple sacrifices, but it all became more and more a matter of religious duty than of passionate devotion.

Yahweh couched his messages as he did knowing that his people would grow fickle through disappointment. What if he had told them back in 520 B.C., "Build this temple now, even though you're going to live in poverty and oppression for five and a half centuries until the king comes, and even then he won't be the military general you wanted, you'll sell him for a slave price, and you'll have another couple thousand years to struggle through"? Surely the Jews would have thrown up their hands right then and said, "This is too much. What's in it for us?" So instead Yahweh told them just enough to encourage them, just enough to give them a chance to respond if they trusted him. He could have burst in right then, ousted Persia and dropped the Jews into the lap of luxury. But that would have been just what Satan had said about Job: Yahweh buys love. He didn't want the kind of love that had to be bought. He wanted the Abrahams who would hang on in the dark.

> *Yahweh didn't want the kind of love that had to be bought. He wanted the Abrahams who would hang on in the dark.*

This generation of Jews were not Abrahams. After Zechariah's final prophecies the Bible falls silent on that generation, and we hear nothing more of the restored community for sixty years. By that time rot and complacency had settled in, and while Yahweh was not finished with the nation, there was no more hinting that glory was just around the corner. What would have happened if that generation had kept the faith through the years of hard work and waiting under foreign oppression?

Questions for Reflection and Discussion

1. What challenges did the first group of returning exiles face, both in the situation and in themselves?

2. How do you typically deal with disappointment and delay?

3. What does Zechariah add to our knowledge of the promise?

◇◇◇

22

LOOKING TOWARD
THE FUTURE

Ezra 4:6-23; 7:1–10:44;
Nehemiah; Esther; Malachi

*M*eanwhile, the scene shifts back to the Persian capital, where Yahweh was beginning to deal with a quiet threat to his people's existence.

Darius was a superb leader. He solidified the Persian Empire from India to northern Sudan, improved the bureaucracy, instituted the use of coins, standardized weights and measures, introduced a new law code and took a strong interest in his subjects' welfare. But he also imposed burdensome taxes to support his administration and building projects, such as his lavish palace at Susa, his new capital.

Darius's son Xerxes (pronounced "Zerk-seez") succeeded him on his death in 486 B.C. The new king was bold, ambitious, handsome, stately and thoroughly self-indulgent. The empire was crumbling under Darius's taxes, but Xerxes lacked his father's diplomatic skill. He burned Athens, took sacred treasures from Egypt, destroyed temples in Babylon after a revolt and denied a Jewish request to rebuild the walls of Jerusalem. He seduced his niece, abandoned his sister-in-law to death for rebuffing his advances and wiped out his brother's whole family. When a bridge he commissioned collapsed in a tempest, he ordered the sea flogged and had the builders beheaded.

It took Xerxes a couple of years to quell revolts in Egypt and Babylon after his father's death. Then he spent a while finishing his fabulous citadel at Susa. But by 483 he was ready to tackle empire building. He invited all the prominent men of his domain to spend six months in Susa, to admire his wealth and power and to help him plan a campaign against Greece. The culmination of that visit was a seven-day debauch before the launch of the war.

On the seventh day Xerxes summoned his loveliest possession, his queen, to display herself for his guests. She refused to come, possibly because she objected to the manner in which she was to be displayed. But the Persian nobles agreed that such conduct undermined wifely submission, so Xerxes deposed his wife and declared that he would choose a new queen upon his return from Greece.

The Greek venture was catastrophic. Xerxes gave the Greeks two of their most glorious historic victories. When his army limped home in 479 B.C., Xerxes was ready for the distraction of a new batch of girls for his harem. So his attendants planned a beauty contest in which the prettiest girls from across the empire were commandeered, given beauty treatments and allowed to spend one night with the king. When Xerxes found one that suited him, she would be queen. The rest would spend the remainder of their days locked in the hot, cramped harem, living like nuns.

One of the unlucky ladies was Esther, a Jew from the tribe of Benjamin. She found favor with the eunuch in charge of the harem, who coached her on how to win the king's notice. Sure enough, she became queen in January of 478 B.C.

An orphan, Esther had been raised by her cousin Mordecai. Upon becoming queen she had him appointed as a judge, and while sitting among the other officials one day Mordecai overheard a plot to assassinate Xerxes. He told Esther and she told Xerxes, who executed the plotters and recorded Mordecai's service in his record book.

Sometime later, Mordecai irritated one of Xerxes' officials by refusing to bow to him. This official, named Haman, was a descendant of the king of Amalek whom Mordecai's ancestor Saul was supposed to have executed six centuries earlier (1 Samuel 15). Haman was also an insufferable boor, and Mordecai saw their rivalry as a symbol of the war between the sons of the snake and the sons of God.

Haman saw it that way, too. He wheedled Xerxes into issuing an irrevocable edict authorizing pogroms against a certain unnamed race. The Jews mourned when they heard of the edict issued on April 17, 474. Mordecai urged his cousin to intercede with the king. But Esther knew her husband's volatile moods. Initiating contact with him could mean instant death, and she hadn't seen him in a month. Mordecai's response was curt:

> If you remain silent at this time, relief and deliverance for the Jews will arise from another place, but you and your father's family will perish. And who knows but that you have come to your royal position for such a time as this? (Esther 4:14)

A mind with a plan lay behind the destiny of every Jew; Esther's choice was whether to accept the risks of her assignment or fail in the purpose for her existence. She accepted.

As it turned out, her shrewd tactics and some "coincidences" won the execution of Haman and a second edict that the Jews could protect themselves against anyone who tried to carry out the previous irrevocable edict. As Haman had anticipated, March 7, 473, was a bloodbath, but it was the Jewish people's enemies, not the Jews themselves, who were destroyed.

The book of Esther was probably written sometime between Xerxes' death in 464 B.C. and the end of the Persian Empire in 331, most likely by a Jew living in one of the Persian cities. The hairbreadth deliverance is celebrated annually as the Feast of Purim, when the book is read. But the most notable feature of the book is that it does not name or allude to Yahweh even once. Fasting is mentioned, but not the prayer that certainly accompanied it. The coincidences—that it was Esther whom the harem officer and the king favored, that Mordecai happened to overhear a conversation, and on and on—are simply left to dangle as "well, that's what happened." Nothing is attributed to Yahweh's intervention. It's as if the writer is saying, that's how life looks from down here. We see what happens; we can only guess where Yahweh's hand is touching.

The God who dealt with Pharaoh through technicolor plagues could deal with a tyrant like Xerxes by placing a gutsy woman in the right place at the right time.

EZRA

Xerxes' successor, Artaxerxes, again had to deal with revolts in Egypt. To maintain order and loyalty in Palestine, he authorized a priest named Ezra to lead a second party of Jews back to Judah in 458 B.C., and then to enforce the Jewish law on all Jews there. Artaxerxes also made a grant to pay for sacrifices in return for the goodwill of the Jewish God and people.

Ezra was an impassioned student, practitioner and teacher of Moses' law. He soon whipped temple worship into shape and began teaching Moses' instructions. The people were shocked to find out how many things they were doing that directly contradicted Yahweh's laws. Some of the leaders admitted to Ezra that many Jewish men had married non-Jewish women, who were now leading their husbands and children to practice the mixed local religions. It may have been (as happened a generation later) that the men were even divorcing their Jewish wives in order to marry into the families of influential local landowners. But at the very least they were endangering the existence of a nation devoted to Yahweh.

Ezra did not rebuke the men. He was consumed with the horror of how this disregard must make Yahweh feel. He tore his clothes and hair as signs of mourning and sat in silence for hours, appalled. Then he went to the temple in his torn robes, fell to his knees, and sobbed a prayer of confession. He knew Yahweh had every right to wash his hands of this mob and bring in another batch of exiles through whom he could fulfill his plan.

His grief cut the people's hearts deeper than any accusation; they came to him weeping and promising to divorce their foreign wives. A committee of the leading Jews sat for three months reviewing each family's case and found 110 men guilty of marrying wives who had not converted to worship Yahweh exclusively. The committee decided these persistent idolaters had to be divorced. It was a human tragedy of mammoth proportions, but spiritual purity (not ethnic purity) was the reason for this community's existence.

NEHEMIAH

For twelve years Ezra strove to keep the unruly Jews in line. By 446 he had made enough progress that they were ready to try rebuilding Jerusalem as a proper national capital. But three local non-Jews informed Artaxerxes that if this city were restored, the Jews would almost certainly revolt and try to set up an independent state. Since he had quelled a Palestinian rebellion in 454 B.C., Artaxerxes took the warning seriously and ordered the work halted until further notice. The Jews' enemies went a step further and demolished and burned what had already been rebuilt.

The Jews were mortified, but Yahweh had an ace up his sleeve. Back in Persia, one of Artaxerxes' trusted officials happened to be a Jew of faith and nerve called Nehemiah. When Nehemiah heard that the reconstruction had been wrecked, he spent four months fasting and praying for Yahweh to do something. By April of 445, he knew he was that "something." Through prayer and natural shrewdness he worked out his whole strategy before approaching Artaxerxes with it. Miraculously, the king agreed to send Nehemiah as the new governor of Judah with a royal escort, letters to the local Persian officials and even a requisition for timber from the royal forests.

Upon his arrival in Jerusalem, he inspected the demolished walls and again had a plan entirely mapped out before presenting it to the Jewish leaders. Their new governor's take-charge confidence impressed them, and they summoned their people from around Judah to help build the city wall.

The governors of Samaria and Ammon, however, were not pleased. They were used to running the region, and this new Jewish governor would be a pest once he had a defensible city. But Nehemiah dismissed both their ridicule and their threats: "The God of heaven will give us success."

The Jews flocked from their villages and set to work. When scorn failed to daunt the builders, their enemies tried raids. Nehemiah countered with his typical spiritual-practical approach: "We prayed to our God and posted a guard." The work halted temporarily for a total call to arms, but thereafter the builders were able to make progress as long as their weapons were at hand. It was a grueling two months in which Nehemiah got little sleep and rarely changed his clothes.

The next problem was internal. Nehemiah had diverted the people from farming to building, and many of them were already in economic trouble. They'd had to mortgage their land to feed their families during a bad crop year, and if their harvests failed this year, their creditors would take everything. Certain farmers had even sold some of their daughters to support the rest of their children, and the Jewish buyers were selling the girls to pagans. These peasants were dedicated to Nehemiah's cause, but as the saying goes, "you can't eat walls."

Nehemiah was shocked that Jews were willing to buy the land and even the children out from under their countrymen with the attitude that business is business. He had himself been lending money, but he was now convinced that even fair lending was improper when a brother's life was at stake. He made his fellow rich men swear that everything that had been foreclosed on or bought from a debtor would be returned, that interest would no longer be charged on loans, and that anything a fellow Jew could not pay back would be treated as a gift. To set an example, Nehemiah went so far as to refuse to take a salary from taxes on his people. For the next twelve years he lived off what he had earned in Persia. (That included supporting a household of 150 people plus guests.) To him, sacrificial concern for his people was a leader's sign of love for God.

Nehemiah endured plot after plot from his enemies—murder attempts, false rumors that he was conspiring to become king, efforts to disgrace him before the people. His blunt prayers for justice and protection punctuate his memoirs (which form most of the book of Nehemiah).

Once the city had a wall with gates and guards, Nehemiah addressed himself to populating it so that it would not be a shell, easily cracked when his back was turned. He was also concerned to help Ezra in his ongoing campaign to keep the people focused on Yahweh. So the two of them summoned the whole community to Jerusalem for the autumn festivals. For a solid six hours on the first day, Ezra read from the Book of the Law of Moses while the Levites interpreted the teaching so that the people could grasp it clearly. The people wept as they saw how far short they fell of this standard, but Nehemiah told them to go home and celebrate: the strength to move toward this holiness would come not from self-punishment but from joy in Yahweh.

The people cast lots for the one family out of ten who would move into the new city. Nehemiah's book carefully records the name of each of those families as a sign that this was an ordered people, a network of men and women with a past and a future. The community then held an elaborate festival to dedicate the wall—and hence the whole city—to Yahweh as his holy place. It was not the vast complex envisioned by Ezekiel, but it was the city of God for now.

MALACHI

The last prophet of the Old Testament may have been at work during the days of Ezra and Nehemiah or just afterwards. He addressed the same issues they faced: the Jews, disappointed that none of the great things Haggai and Zechariah had promised had happened, were settling into lukewarmness. They doubted Yahweh's love for them because he had not come to his temple in power nor liberated his people from their over-lords. They doubted his justice because the wicked were still prospering more than the good. So they continued to go through the motions of worship, but they cut corners, offering to Yahweh only what they didn't want. The priests set scandalous examples, and the people followed them in divorcing their first wives in order to make more socially advantageous marriages with pagans.

To this community who said it didn't matter what they did because Yahweh had gone on vacation, Malachi declared that Yahweh was going to send a messenger in the spirit of Elijah to prepare for his own coming to his people. Then they would find out that God's showing up was not as pleasant as they thought. He would come like a blazing sun—purifying and healing those who were willing to bear the heat of holiness but consuming in its fire all those who were only casually interested in religion.

THE SILENT YEARS

Most of the Jews completely ignored Malachi. So after his death the prophetic voice fell silent in Judah, and the land held its breath, awaiting the Elijah-messenger. Yet a handful of people here and there retained the fire in their hearts and continued to seek Yahweh's presence, not just his gifts. They fulfilled one of Yahweh's promises through the prophet Isaiah:

I have posted watchmen on your walls, Jerusalem;
    they will never be silent day or night.
You who call on Yahweh,
    give yourselves no rest,
and give him no rest till he establishes Jerusalem
    and makes her the praise of the earth. (Isaiah 62:6-7)

For four hundred years the hidden watchmen prayed.

Questions for Reflection and Discussion

1. What did Esther contribute to the ongoing story of Yahweh and his people? What do you most admire about her?

2. What character qualities made Nehemiah a good leader?

3. How does it affect you to think of the watchmen (male and female) praying for four hundred years?

23

THE SILENT YEARS

*P*ersia fell to Alexander the Great in 331 B.C. When Alexander died in 323, his generals dismembered his empire, and the next century and a half saw the Middle East shredded as two Greek empires sparred for control. Judah (now called Judea) played pawn and trophy in this game but was largely able to govern herself as one of the many sacred temple-states in the Greek domain.

But around 190 B.C., Daniel's fourth beast—Rome—began to prowl eastward. Two Jewish priests took advantage of their Greek overlord's terror by taking turns offering bribes for the high priesthood. (The high priest was effectively the ruler of Judea.) Patriotic and godly Jews banded together in 168 B.C. behind the more legitimate of the two bribers, and their stance landed them in rebellion against their king. Guerrilla war and religious martyrdom followed for several years while the king, Antiochus IV, handed the Jewish temple over to the local cult of Zeus. A statue of Zeus (or rather his Syrian equivalent, Baal Shamem) was erected in the temple. To the distraught Jews this was a clear fulfillment of Daniel's prophecy that an "abomination of desolation" (*shiqquts me-shomem* in Hebrew, which sounds like a pun on Baal Shamem) would desecrate the temple.

Eventually, though, Antiochus could no longer afford to bog his armies down in a pointless war with Judea. The ban on Judaism was lifted, and the temple was cleansed in a ceremony celebrated thereafter as the Festival of Dedication, Hanukkah. As Daniel had predicted, Yahweh came through for his people.

However, the guerrillas had no intention of settling for religious freedom. They fought for twenty years until they won control of a free Jewish state. Politically free, at any rate. For in the meantime, the legitimate line of high priests had all fled to Egypt, and the new Jewish governor was popularly acclaimed the first of a new dynasty of high priests. His sons took the title "king" as well as high priest and mimicked Greek kings in their despotism without mimicking any of the redeeming features of their culture. At length two sons of this dynasty fell into civil war and left the door open to a non-Jewish politician named Antipater. Antipater cut a deal with the Roman general Pompey, and almost overnight in 63 B.C. Judea became a Roman sub-province.

Roman rule may have been no worse than what the graft-ridden Judeans deserved, but it was very bad indeed. Arrogant toward "inferior races" and gluttonous for plunder, the Romans did not endear themselves to their subjects. Antipater was assassinated in 43 B.C. for being Rome's toady, but his sons carried on his pro-Roman policy. They effectively ran Judea, the high priest having been reduced to a figurehead. After the elder son was killed in an invasion from Rome's enemies, the younger son, Herod, was named "king of the Jews" once he restored order. Herod was as good a friend to Rome as he was a stench in Jewish nostrils, so he retained his throne right through the transition from the Roman Republic to the Roman Empire under Augustus Caesar in 27 B.C.

When Augustus declared himself emperor, he ended decades of war and launched what his regime dubbed the Pax Romana, or Roman Peace. An altar of peace was set up in Rome. By the time he died, paid poets hailed him as the bringer of peace and savior of the world.

HASIDS AND PHARISEES

In Judea such titles were bitter irony, but there was no agreement on what to do about the Romans. Some Jews believed the best response was to obey God's laws, have as little to do with non-Jews as possible and wait for him to deal with the Romans in his own time. The Pharisees held this view.

As far back as the time of Malachi, bands of faithful Jews had started meeting together to support each other in resisting the general spiritual snooze. They called themselves Hasids because they maintained *hesed*—covenant faithfulness to Yahweh. Psalm 119 reflects their twin passions for Yahweh and his laws:

> I have sought your face with all my heart;
>> be gracious to me according to your promise. (Psalm 119:58)

> Oh, how I love your law!
>> I meditate on it all day long. (Psalm 119:97)

The Hasids strove in vain to keep their Jewish relatives from adopting Greek customs. They supported the guerrilla war against Antiochus but broke with the new Jewish kings when they proved to be no better than debauched Greeks. Those who broke away (around 145 B.C.) came to be called Pharisees, meaning "separatists." Their hallmark was ritual purity—strict adherence to the food laws, the Sabbath and other practices that made it difficult to have normal social contact with non-Jews. They invested incredible energy in studying the law of Moses, and in the process they developed a body of tradition about how to interpret and apply it. That tradition was eventually considered to be as sacred as the law itself.

In some ways the tradition made it easier for the average person to feel confident about obeying Yahweh. For instance, Exodus 16:29 said "no one is to go out" on the Sabbath. The Pharisees decided that Yahweh couldn't have meant to confine everyone to his or her house, so in light of Numbers 35:5 (which described the extent of pastureland around a town) they concluded that one could go two thousand cubits (about three-fourths of a mile) from wherever one designated as home for the day. If one wasn't sure what counted as work on the Sabbath, one could refer to the thirty-nine classes of work outlined by the Pharisees' rabbis.

But sometimes the interpretation pushed so far as to virtually nullify the original intent of a law. And often the tradition became so complicated that only an expert could remember it, let alone follow it. And the more one focused on getting all of the complex rules right, the less attention one might give to the other Hasid distinctive: "I have sought your face with all my heart."

One tradition that may date back to a time well before the Pharisees emerged had to do with Yahweh's name. Exodus 20:7 declared, "You shall not misuse the name of Yahweh your God." His name deserved honor because it expressed the essence of his character. It was not to be used flippantly and certainly not in false oaths, magic or fake prophecy. But the Jews came to feel that it was too holy to be used at all. So when reading the law and the prophets, they would substitute the title "Lord" for the name "Yahweh." They referred to him as "Lord" or "our Father in heaven."

As a result, when the Jews rendered their Scriptures into Greek, the translators used the Greek word for Lord, *Kyrios*, in place of the name Yahweh. As we now move into the part of our story that takes place in a Greek context, we will reflect that practice by saying "the Lord" or "God" as they did.

SADDUCEES AND COMMON PEOPLE

Over against the Pharisees stood the Sadducees, whose name probably comes from their having been members of the Sanhedrin, or ruling council. They were the favored party of the Jewish kings, so although they comprised only a few of the richest priestly families, they held great political power. They controlled the high priesthood and the temple with its lucrative treasury. On the religious side, they rejected the Pharisees' tradition and claimed to hold the old, pure doctrine. They accused the Pharisees of getting many beliefs—such as bodily resurrection, rewards and punishments after death, predestination, and angels and demons—from Persian religion. They had a much more tolerant, expedient attitude toward pagan overlords than the Pharisees.

While the Sadducees dominated the temple and the ruling council, the people endorsed the Pharisees. This gave the Pharisees enormous influence beyond their numbers. The quarrel could get hot. Around 90 B.C. one high priest-king was pelted with citrons (similar to lemons) on the Festival of Tabernacles because he poured the holy water on the ground next to the altar like a Sadducee instead of on the altar as the Pharisees taught. He later dealt with the opposition by having eight hundred of the rebellious rabbis crucified.

However, the Pharisees and Sadducees were forced to tolerate each other when both sat on the Sanhedrin, the national ruling council. This was easier once Herod and Rome had reduced both to carving out turf under foreign rule. And Pharisees and Sadducees could agree on one thing: the common mob of artisans and peasants were barely Jews, either because they were disgustingly lax about keeping the laws and traditions or just because they were rabble. This rabble, who formed the largest segment of the population, had neither time nor education for doctrinal debates. They were just trying to survive under a crushing load of taxes levied by Rome and priestly Jerusalem.

ESSENES, QUMRAN AND THE ZEALOTS

Three other groups filled out the Jewish landscape at the turn of the first century A.D. The Essenes were like monks—they lived in male-only communities, avoided sex and other forms of physical indulgence and maintained their devotion to the Lord through strict separation from the world. Their brotherhoods grew because families would give them sons to raise. Even Herod held them in high esteem because they had the only prophets whose words came true.

A similar community, or network of communities, is best known by its main settlement at Qumran. This group was dedicated to the study of and adherence to prophetic writings, especially the book of Daniel. They went to the desert to prepare to be the Lord's instrument when he would come to judge the earth in a bloody war. Their mandate was Isaiah 40:3: "In the desert prepare the way for the Lord; make straight in the wilderness a highway for our God."

Purity, common property, menial labor, self-denial and ritual cleansing were key features. The Qumranites criticized the Pharisees for supporting the Jerusalem temple, even though the high priest there was no longer of the branch of Aaron's family to whom King David had assigned the high priesthood. In fact, they considered the Pharisees generally lax about the law of Moses. These were serious spiritual Green Berets.

The Zealots turned up as a formal party around 6 B.C. just after Herod's death. They held that it was against God's law to submit to a non-Jewish ruler. They adhered to most of the Pharisees' doctrines, but while the Pharisees were content to let the Lord break the foreign yoke in his own time, the Zealots felt called to be the instruments by which he would accomplish that purpose. Depending on your point of view, they were freedom fighters, guerrillas or bandits.

Questions for Reflection and Discussion

1. What can be said for and against the Pharisees and their traditions about God's law?

2. What are the pros and cons of calling Yahweh "the Lord" instead of speaking his name?

3. If these were your only choices, would you want to be a Hasid, Pharisee, Sadducee, Essene, Qumran member, Zealot or common person? Why?

Part Four

The Coming
of the King

∞∞∞∞∞∞∞∞∞∞∞∞∞∞∞∞∞∞∞∞∞∞∞∞∞∞∞∞∞∞∞∞∞∞∞∞∞∞∞

24

THE SILENCE BREAKS

Matthew 1:1–4:11; Mark 1:1-13;
Luke 1:1–4:13; John 1:1-51

*E*arth's great disaster had taken place in Eden, when Eve and Adam chose to disobey God. But on the evening of that day the Lord had promised that a son of Eve would someday crush the snake who had led humankind into misery. As time went on, the son of Eve was revealed to be a son of Abraham, son of Judah, son of David. Isaiah saw him as a warrior king, full of the Spirit of God. But he also gave him titles no mere human could claim: Mighty God, Everlasting Father, Prince of Peace.

Isaiah had also glimpsed someone whom he dubbed "the servant of the Lord." Like the son of David, he would establish a regime of justice. It would be not just a Jewish nation, for he would also bring the Gentiles the same deliverance from darkness. Yet before he attained his glory he would suffer unspeakably, bearing in his body

> *As time went on, the son of Eve was revealed to be a son of Abraham, son of Judah, son of David. Isaiah saw him as a warrior king, full of the Spirit of God. But he also gave him titles no mere human could claim: Mighty God, Everlasting Father, Prince of Peace.*

the full cost of his people's crimes. He would die and yet reign—a paradox.

Daniel saw another kingly figure: "one like a son of man" who would receive dominion over the whole earth forever. He even heard a timetable that might pinpoint the king's arrival within a decade or so. Micah learned the king would be born in Bethlehem. Zechariah implied that the deliverer would be priest as well as king, staining his holiness with the people's corruption in order to cleanse it away.

And yet God had told several prophets that he would not share his glory with anyone else. He himself would come to deliver his people: "Then suddenly the Lord you are seeking will come to his temple" (Malachi 3:1). There was also that odd bit in Zechariah about God apparently sending God.

But the fine points of these prophecies were largely lost on a nation staggering under the weight of Rome. The people had long pinned their hopes on the Anointed One (*mashiach*, or Messiah), the anointed king of David's line who would come to liberate them. The sufferings, the promises to the Gentiles, the inscrutable titles—these perplexities blurred amid the shining vision of Someone Who Will Get Us Out of This Mess.

God Becomes Flesh

Perhaps the most fantastic dream a Jewish woman could entertain was that of mothering the Messiah. She would have to consummate a marriage with a man of David's line, of course. How else did one have babies?

But God had never done anything the way humans expected, and he wasn't changing that pattern in the last years of Herod the Great, king of the Jews. Adolescent, virgin Mary lacked the only requirement for motherhood history has ever known. She had, however, all of the qualities God required: the right lineage and the same attitude of total trust and devotion that had won Abraham titles like "righteous" and "friend of God."

The stump of David had run into hard times since noble Zerubbabel led his compatriots back from Babylon more than five centuries earlier. But peasant Mary's blood was royal enough, and she was engaged to a man with comparable pedigree. So the Spirit of God came upon her and completed what was lacking in her egg's twenty-three chromosomes for the making of a child. It was that simple.

Simple. All it required was for that Person of divinity who had eternally been joined as a Son to a Father to empty himself of his infinity and pour himself into a single human cell. It required nothing but a divine self-humiliation that made heaven gasp.

It was God's joke on the wisdom of men. Greek philosophers had recently defined God as an unmoved mover, utterly detached from the base material world, utterly beyond feelings or any touch from the earth at all. For their part, the Jews had walled their God off behind multiple layers of temple courts and fully expected that if they slit the throats of the right animals every day, God would stay in line. But the Lord who had thundered to Moses, whispered to Elijah and wept with Hosea was not about to be banished to some hygienic spiritual plane where he wouldn't interfere with human plans. And while some were watching the skies, waiting for him to ride in on a cloud, he sneaked into their midst incognito, in a teenager's womb.

> *The Lord who had thundered to Moses, whispered to Elijah and wept with Hosea was not about to be banished to some hygienic spiritual plane where he wouldn't interfere with human plans.*

One of the baby's biographers, a man named John, called him "the Word"—God's self-expression, revealing in human form everything the Unpronounceable One had ever been. In a day when his people had grown afraid to utter his name, God chose a new one.

Jesus was the Greek version of that name. The Hebrew equivalent was Joshua, "Yahweh saves." The baby's namesakes were the general who led Israel to possess the Promised Land and Zechariah's high priest. Another name lingered in the background, for the impossible birth recalled one of Isaiah's more obscure predictions: "The virgin will conceive and give birth to a son, and will call him Immanuel"—God with us (Isaiah 7:14).

By rights, this Jesus was in every way a king. Son of David and Son of

God—who could dispute his claim? But the road to his throne would be the thorny one of a God who had always preferred to woo rather than ravish. A certain Matthew, another of Jesus' biographers, said it all in the genealogy that opens his book. The women he chose to mention in Jesus' ancestry were Tamar (who seduced her father-in-law because she saw no other hope of gaining her rights), Rahab the prostitute, Ruth (who came from an explicitly blacklisted foreign nation), Uriah's wife (Bathsheba, whom David seduced and whose husband he subsequently murdered) and Mary (whose neighbors were all certain she was a slut). Surely this boy bore in his bloodline all the worst that men and women could do to each other. He was a true son of Adam, and "Son of Man" was the title he chose for himself.

To drive the point home, God had the baby born in a stable. It was indeed in Bethlehem, but the only people who showed up to mark the occasion were a mob of shepherds (who ranked extremely low on the Pharisees' list of law-abiding servants of God) and some Persian astrologers. The prominent priestly families were notified but declined to attend. Herod responded to the news by decreeing that all unweaned boys in Bethlehem be slaughtered. His only interest in a Davidic king was to stamp out a rival. Herod was a snake's pawn, and the snake knew well enough who Jesus was.

It was pathetic. Haggai and Malachi had both extolled the glory of the day when "the desired of all nations" would come to his temple. But when Mary brought her newborn baby to the temple to fulfill the proper rites, only an elderly saint and a closet prophetess noticed. The priests were busy elsewhere. Jesus made hardly a ripple in the human world when he arrived, but behind the scenes heaven and hell were holding their breath.

JOHN THE BAPTIZER

A few months before Jesus' birth, God had given a son to a cousin of Mary's in one of those postmenopausal conceptions he had made famous with Sarah. This child may have been raised in one of the monastic communities scattered around Judea, for he emerged from the desert twenty-something years later as an ascetic firebrand. But whereas the folks at

Qumran were preparing for the day of the Lord by walling themselves off, John intended to prepare for it by slapping his countrymen into line.

He was in fact the first true prophet the nation had seen for four hundred years, and it was his business to summon every man, woman and child to prepare. His chosen piece of theater was baptism, a ritual washing that people who converted from paganism usually underwent as a sign of being cleansed from their idolatrous past. John insisted that even good Jews needed this bath. He hugely impressed the common people with his wild appearance and hellfire sermons on the banks of the Jordan River. The religious leaders rolled their eyes.

Perhaps the first and last time John was ever stopped in his tracks was when his cousin Jesus arrived to be baptized. John had been warning everybody that someone was coming who would baptize them with fire rather than mere water, and here was the Coming One looking at him serenely, waiting to be dunked. John tried to refuse. Jesus did not deny that he had no need to be cleansed, but he maintained that he needed to identify fully with the people to whom he was sent. Furthermore, his father had chosen this occasion to publicly declare that Jesus was the Son of God and was empowered by the Spirit of God. It was the first time in history that God publicly paraded his strange nature: there were three of him who related to each other as Father, Son and Spirit; yet he was one indivisible God.

ENTRANCE EXAMS

Before he had lifted a finger in his Father's service, Jesus emerged from his bath in the Jordan mantled in his Father's approval: "This is my Son, whom I love; with him I am well pleased" (Matthew 3:17). This conviction would be the bedrock of his life. In a whirlpool of popular acclaim and rejection, he would have one relationship to stand on. For it was his job to relive the trials of Adam and Israel and prove faithful where they had failed.

First the ancient snake met Jesus in the desert and coaxed him to make Adam's choice: Take by force what the Father could give by grace. Be a Messiah of your own making. Choose physical comfort, pride or personal glory. And always the refrain: "If you are [really] the Son of God . . ."

Doubt your sonship. Doubt your Father's love and wisdom.

Jesus faced this assault not with his divine strength but with only the weapons available to all people. He quoted from Moses' sermons about what Israel should have learned during her forty years in the desert. What Israel never did learn, Jesus clung to at the core of his being.

Those long desert days were his last test before his real work began. He was about thirty years old and had never yet done anything that anyone had taken special notice of. But now Jesus headed back to where John was still preaching and baptizing, and he did more nothing. The baptizer, however, told his followers that Jesus was "the Lamb of God, who takes away the sin of the world!" (John 1:29). In other words, follow that one instead. Somehow he is the fulfillment of all that the temple system represents. John probably didn't even know what he was saying when he pushed his own followers to abandon him. Yet five of them ended up accompanying Jesus on the eighty-mile walk north to the Sea of Galilee, where Jesus had been raised and where he was still based. They got far more than they bargained for.

Questions for Reflection and Discussion

1. In what ways was the fulfillment of God's promise surprising?

2. What can we learn about God from his decision to become fully human (not just a god disguised as a human)?

3. Why was it so important for Jesus to be confident in his identity as the beloved Son?

THE KINGDOM

Matthew 4:12–20:34; Mark 1:14–10:52;
Luke 4:14–18:43; John 2:1–10:42

The Son of God yielded his divine power when he confined himself to humanness. But at his baptism, Jesus received the power of God's Spirit, just as the prophets before him had done. And his total surrender to the Father made him more open to the Spirit than any prophet. For the first time ever a human walked in the full authority of the Holy Spirit. What God had intended for Adam, this second Adam lived.

His first public use of this power was to supply wine for a wedding feast. It was an appropriate debut. God liked parties. He had told Isaiah that his kingdom was going to be like one immense party with the best food and the finest wine. And weddings were his favorite, since they reminded him of the union he would one day have with his bride, the people he loved.

> *Weddings were his favorite, since they reminded him of the union he would one day have with his bride, the people he loved.*

So Jesus selected six huge stone jars, slimy with the scum of ceremonial Jewish washing, and ordered them filled with water. To the wedding guests who drank the water-become-wine, the miracle may have meant little. But to the five men who had followed Jesus from the Jordan, this was a hint. The King who had commanded the Jewish law for a season and a purpose was about to change stagnant water into fresh wine for a royal feast. It was time for men and women to be washed in fire and drink the new wine of God's kingdom.

THE KINGDOM AT HAND

This was Jesus' message as he began to visit synagogues and preach in the streets: "Repent"—reverse course, change your thinking and your lives—"for the kingdom of God has come near." The King has arrived.

But he faced a challenge: the people's idea of the kingdom was different from his. They thought the son of David would be a general leading a supernaturally equipped Jewish army to victory against Rome and bringing the people into an earthly golden age. They wanted peace and prosperity, lower taxes, a higher standard of living, the freedom to follow their customs their way.

For Jesus, though, God's kingdom was the realm in which what God wants done is done without resistance. Most of the cosmos does joyfully what God made it to do and thus is part of his kingdom. The stars, the other planets, they obey their Maker. Here on earth, though, humans resist God. We want our way. Our emotions and actions reflect that core goal. Defeating the Romans and the corrupt officials in Jerusalem at the point of a sword wouldn't change that. The Romans, the officials and the Jewish people would still strive to get their way as much as they could manage, and such a kingdom would be no more devoted to God than Israel had ever been.

So instead of forcing people to submit, Jesus invited them to choose: Renounce your resistance to what God wants done. Choose God's kingdom voluntarily. His invitation involved both words and actions. He told stories to help people picture what the kingdom was like. He described the way citizens of the kingdom treat each other and outsiders. And he demonstrated how the King behaves.

He declared himself the fulfillment of Isaiah 61:1-2:

> The Spirit of the Lord is on me,
>   because he has anointed me
>   to proclaim good news to the poor.

He has sent me to proclaim freedom for the prisoners
and recovery of sight for the blind,
to set the oppressed free,
to proclaim the year of the Lord's favor. (Luke 4:18-19)

Then from village to village in Galilee he healed the sick, gave sight to the blind, freed people from demons and taught the good news of the kingdom. The freedom he offered was freedom from the snake and from the madness that had gripped Adam's kin since the beginning. Freedom from people's insane efforts to feed their spirits with work or sex or possessions or power. Freedom from old bitterness and senseless grief and the compulsion to be in control. But the people persisted in not understanding what they needed to be free from, and what they needed to be free for.

STORIES, OBJECTS

To bridge this misunderstanding, Jesus sometimes used abstract discourse, but most of the time he communicated concretely, through stories and vivid images. He understood why the Bible is mostly stories and poetic imagery: life's most important truths are best conveyed that way. "A man was going down from Jerusalem to Jericho, when he fell into the hands of robbers," he said. "In a certain town there was a judge who neither feared God nor cared what people thought." Seed, tree, vine, pearl, light, darkness, water, bread, wine—material things pointed to truths about the kingdom and the King.

God created the material world. The Son of God made it holy by taking on a body and entering the world's story in the flesh. His teaching was full of stories about people and material things, stories that were easy to ignore but hard to forget. The unspoken punch line was always: So what are you going to do about it?

"The kingdom of heaven is like treasure hidden in a field. When a man found it, he hid it again, and then in his joy went and sold all he had and bought that field" (Matthew 13:44). How much is God's kingdom worth to you? What would you be willing to give up to gain it? How serious are you about seeking God?

THE SENSIBLE WAY TO LIVE

Jesus spoke and lived as if the most sensible thing to do was to seek the kingdom above everything else and to live as a kingdom citizen does, to treat others with love and not seek their harm:

> If someone slaps you on one cheek, turn to them the other also. If someone takes your coat, do not withhold your shirt from them. Give to everyone who asks you, and if anyone takes what belongs to you, do not demand it back.
>
> If . . . you do good to those who are good to you, what credit is that to you? Even sinners do that. . . . But love your enemies, do good to them, and lend to them without expecting to get anything back. Then your reward will be great, and you will be children of the Most High, because he is kind to the ungrateful and wicked. (Luke 6:29-30, 32, 35)

This wasn't ivory tower theory, and Jesus wasn't talking to people whose "enemies" were just annoying family members and coworkers. He was talking to people who had foreign soldiers marching in their streets, overlords taxing them to the point of starvation, bandits raiding their villages. He himself had enemies who plotted his death. Former neighbors in his hometown hurled abuse and tried to lynch him. His relatives thought he was out of his mind and tried to take charge of him.

In response he wasn't passive, and he could dish out sharp rebuke, but he always sought the good of even his harshest foes. The Qumran sect wanted the leaders in Jerusalem replaced. The Zealots wanted the Romans crushed. Jesus wanted them all reborn. This didn't make sense if your goal was to have your own way, to make money, to be popular, to lead a comfortable life. But it made perfect sense if your goal was to accomplish what God wants done in the world.

Jesus' priorities may surprise us. For instance, in pointing out the things that distract people from God's kingdom, he had far more to say about greed, corruption, anxiety and other sins related to money than he did about sins related to sex. He observed that it was often easier for people without great resources of their own to rely on God's resources. He wasn't prejudiced against rich people, but he recognized how powerful an idol money often is.

BE HOLY AS I AM HOLY

This startling teaching brought him into conflict with the Pharisees. He claimed the authority to interpret and even update the law of Moses, while they were committed to their long tradition of interpreting the law. To accept Jesus' teaching would have been to accept him as a new Moses. He said, "You have heard [from the rabbis] . . . but I tell you . . . " The law forbade murder and adultery; Jesus said those included even hatred and lust (the inner attitudes behind the actions).

A person could conceivably keep the law as the Pharisees understood it, but Jesus' standard was so high that it was unattainable without supernatural help. "For I tell you that unless your righteousness surpasses that of the Pharisees and the teachers of the law, you will certainly not enter the kingdom of heaven" (Matthew 5:20).

God had said through Moses, "Be holy, for I am holy." For the Pharisees, "be holy" meant "be separate from sinners." They stressed purity through separation, because they saw defilement as contagious. Leprosy, a contagious skin disease, was a symbol for sin, so lepers were outcasts. But God's goal in making Israel holy had always been to attract and transform those who didn't know him. So while most rabbis carefully avoided lepers, Jesus deliberately touched a leper when he healed him. He used the law's picture of holiness to say, Nothing defiles me. I've come to take away defilement and stigma, to make holiness and compassion contagious. Whoever I touch becomes holy as I am holy. Will you let me touch you?

He told his followers they were like a lamp set on a lampstand so that everyone could see the light of God and be drawn to it. "Let your light shine before others, that they may see your good deeds and glorify your Father in heaven" (Matthew 5:16). What good deeds? Deeds like prayer, fasting and giving to the poor weren't meant to be done publicly. Those were personal disciplines to strengthen one's intimacy with God and should be done secretly (Matthew 6:1-8). No, the good deeds that would make a world sit up and take notice would be forgiveness when people expected vengeance, humility when anyone else would be arrogant, welcome to those whom others ignore, honest dealing when swindling was standard in the Mediterranean world.

After setting this impossible standard, Jesus added promises to his invitation: "Come to me, all you who are weary and burdened, and I will give you rest. Take my yoke upon you and learn from me, for I am gentle and humble in heart, and you will find rest for your souls. For my yoke is easy and my burden is light" (Matthew 11:28-30). Those who committed themselves to the King would find him enabling them to do what was otherwise beyond them, living the truly good life.

In a word, what Jesus sought when he healed or taught was faith—trust in him personally, trust that expressed itself through surrender and action. "Your faith has saved/healed you; go in peace," he said to more than one supplicant. The kingdom and its way of life were freely available to anyone who had faith.

Jesus called out to people; the Father drew them; the Holy Spirit made faith possible. It was up to each person to say yes.

THE INNER CIRCLE

Few in the crowd who mobbed Jesus in search of healings and miracles were prepared to offer that kind of response. So Jesus increasingly focused his attention on the smaller group of people who really wanted to understand what he was saying. Every rabbi had disciples; Jesus was unusual in that he persistently weeded them out with statements like, "Foxes have dens and birds have nests, but the Son of Man has no place to lay his head" (Luke 9:58) and "Unless you eat the flesh of the Son of Man and drink his blood, you have no life in you" (John 6:53). Anybody who hung around for comments like these was seeing more in Jesus than just a miracle worker or a potential military commander.

There were at least seventy of these fairly serious disciples. From among them, he selected twelve men to be his inner circle—his confidants and crack trainees. They were known as *apostoloi* in Greek (this is where the English word apostle comes from) and as *shaluchim* in Aramaic, the language of Jewish Palestine. (The term is also *shaluchim* in Hebrew; we saw earlier how it was applied to Moses, Samuel and Elijah.) These words meant "sent ones," but in Jewish legalese they referred to a special representative, a proxy or ambassador. One could send a *shaliach*, or apostle, to collect religious taxes, deliver a certificate of divorce or even stand in for the bridegroom in a betrothal. Jesus was the official *shaliach* from the Father, and he was grooming these twelve men to carry on that task.

His selection gives one pause. He stayed up all night praying to discern which twelve were the right ones, and here is the group he chose:

- Simon (also known as Peter), a well-meaning if hotheaded fisherman who persistently rushed in where angels feared to tread.

- Simon's brother, Andrew, a disciple of John the Baptizer.

- James and John, fishermen brothers who bore the nickname "Sons of Thunder" because of their tempers.

- Simon the Zealot, a revolutionary with violent anti-Roman leanings.

- Matthew, a tax collector for Herod—the kind of person guys like Simon usually spat at when they met them in the street.

- Philip, Bartholomew, Thomas, another James, Thaddaeus—we know almost nothing about these five; were they so unremarkable?

- Then there was Judas Iscariot, the only man from Judea (the rest were backcountry types from Galilee). Being the sharpest with finances, Judas was in charge of the money, but he dipped into it for his own purposes.

All were rough diamonds at best. They followed Jesus from village to village, watching, listening, reaching their conclusions about who he was. After a while he sent them out to teach as he taught, heal as he healed, and then he gathered them back to debrief the experience. He gave them problems to solve, like the feeding of five thousand people, and he trained them even through their inadequacy and failure. "You of little faith, why are you so afraid?" he asked when they panicked.

But as weak as their faith and understanding were, they stuck with him as he traveled month after month for several years. Jesus and the Twelve were accompanied by several women who paid their bills out of gratitude because Jesus had healed them.

ACTING LIKE GOD

In a culture where even chaste women were considered instruments of the devil sent to corrupt nice Jewish boys, Jesus' decision to have women in his entourage was a move guaranteed to raise eyebrows. Rabbis were taught to speak to women (including their own wives) as little as possible, but Jesus freely chatted with women both alone and in public. He even taught them as disciples. At the home of a family in Bethany, for instance, Jesus allowed Mary of Bethany to sit at his feet as a male disciple would, even when her sister Martha protested that she should be doing the woman's role of preparing the food. No other rabbi would have dreamed of accepting female disciples.

In fact, if Jesus had intended to endear himself to his kinsmen, he was going about it the wrong way. He declared God's pleasure with the faith of a Roman soldier, one of the hated occupiers. He attended rowdy parties at the homes of the first-century equivalent of loan sharks and shady businessmen. He talked about humility but was constantly coming out with outrageous statements. He called himself "Lord of the Sabbath" and said that gave him the right to ignore the rules for that holy day. His followers did not fast, he said, because one should celebrate when he was present. He even claimed the right to forgive sins, which only God could do, and backed up the claim with miracles.

One day when he was at a Pharisee's home for dinner, a woman of the streets entered the house (homes were fairly public in that culture). She drenched Jesus' feet with her tears, kissed his feet, wiped them with her hair and finally poured wildly expensive perfume over them. Jesus acted as though this were a perfectly acceptable way for a woman to treat him in public. He had the gall to declare all her sins forgiven because of this shocking display. His host was speechless at a supposed great prophet acting as if he thought he was God.

The Sons of the Snake

And Jesus didn't stop there. The Pharisees seethed at him for breaking the no-work rule by healing people on the Sabbath and in general for implying that he was God's equal. They didn't like the familiar way he called God "my Father" instead of "the Father" or "our Father in heaven." So they spread a rumor that he was casting out demons by the power of the chief demon himself. Jesus pointed out the absurdity of this idea. Why would the devil cast out the devil?

Time after time Jesus faced off against his foes. He didn't mince words about their hypocrisy, pride and greed: "Woe to you, because you are like unmarked graves, which people walk over without knowing it" (Luke 11:44). It incensed him that they had reduced his Father's commands to a set of customs that one could practice while sidestepping matters like deceit, pride, malice and lack of compassion for people.

Many of his parables were arrows aimed at the Pharisees. When they complained that he treated the dregs of society like friends, he told a story about a father with two sons. The older son stayed home to serve his father obediently, while the younger left home with his inheritance, squandered it in wild living, lived hand to mouth for a while and finally crawled home, hoping for a job on his dad's farm. He was now willing to accept the humiliation he had coming, but the father welcomed him home, restored him to the full privileges of a son, and threw a party. The older son was irate:

> "Look!" [he said.] "All these years I've been slaving for you and never disobeyed your orders. Yet you never gave me even a young goat so I could celebrate with my friends. But when this son of yours who has squandered your property with prostitutes comes home, you kill the fattened calf for him!"
>
> "My son," the father said, "you are always with me, and everything I have is yours. But we had to celebrate and be glad, because this brother of yours was dead and is alive again; he was lost and is found." (Luke 15:29-32)

Jesus had come to welcome despairing younger brothers home to a Father who longed to throw his arms around them. It broke his heart to see the bitter elder brothers wasting their lives serving a Father they resented because they could not understand his love.

He grieved that their spite had blinded them beyond repair. Although

It broke his heart to see the bitter elder brothers wasting their lives serving a Father they resented because they could not understand his love.

he was not given to name-calling, he had a title for them: "You brood of vipers!" (Matthew 12:34; 23:33). After long ages the son of Eve had come, and the sons of the snake were waiting. The serpent had spawned not just among the pagan Romans who taxed Judea to support their decadence, nor only among the thieves and extortioners of the Jewish underclass, but among the religious leaders whose real gods were security, comfort, tradition and respectability.

Jesus knew exactly who stood behind the malice in these men's eyes. He told his apostles, "The Son of Man must suffer many things and be rejected by the elders, chief priests and teachers of the law, and he must be killed and on the third day be raised to life" (Luke 9:22). The Twelve were stunned. He was at the height of his popularity, and they were riding a cresting wave to Jerusalem with the anointed son of David. It was only a matter of time before he directed his power against Rome, and then God's kingdom would begin in earnest. But Jesus knew better. Luke, another of Jesus' earliest biographers, writes, "When Jesus went outside, the Pharisees and the teachers of the law began to oppose him fiercely and to besiege him with questions, waiting to catch him in something he might say" (Luke 11:53-54).

Knowing what lay ahead, "As the time approached for him to be taken up to heaven, Jesus resolutely set out for Jerusalem" (Luke 9:51).

Questions for Reflection and Discussion

1. What is the kingdom of God? How is it different from what people expected?

2. What are some of the ways you're inclined to resist what God wants done?

3. Why do people think living in the way of the kingdom isn't sensible? Why is it in fact sensible?

26

JERUSALEM'S LAST CHANCE

Matthew 21:1–26:56; Mark 11:1–14:52;
Luke 19:1–22:53; John 11:1–18:11

Jesus traveled to certain death, refusing either to fight or flee. It was so dangerous for him in Jerusalem that for a time he and his disciples stayed on the far side of the Jordan River. But he wasn't hiding; he was waiting until the appointed time.

A message from his friends Mary and Martha of Bethany set events into motion. Their brother Lazarus was sick. They were sure Jesus would hurry to heal him, even though Bethany was less than two miles from Jerusalem. But Jesus waited two days. By the time he crossed the Jordan, Lazarus was dead. Thomas, one of Jesus' apostles, said going to Bethany would seal all their death warrants (John 11:16).

Lazarus had been in his tomb four days when Jesus and his apostles arrived. Jesus had displayed his authority over disease, evil spirits, weather and even food, feeding thousands of people on a few fish and loaves of bread. Now he displayed his authority over death by reviving Lazarus. For some of those who watched Lazarus walk out of his tomb still wrapped in grave clothes, this was proof that he was the Messiah. For the leaders in Jerusalem, though, this was proof that if they didn't kill him, the people would proclaim him Messiah and the Romans would reduce their land to scorched earth. To save the Jewish people, he would have to die.

I AM

It was a loyal but motley band who followed Jesus from Bethany on the last two miles into Jerusalem for Passover. The apostles knew he was the Messiah; they just didn't have a clue what that meant. Knowing they could only make things worse, Jesus had strictly forbidden them to discuss his title in public. Peter had argued with him about predicting betrayal and death instead of victory. And one of the apostles' favorite pastimes was debating the pecking order that would go into effect among them once they took charge of the nation. All Jesus needed was these guys explaining his kingship to people.

The way they saw it, Jesus was mystifying the whole thing. He had fed five thousand leaderless insurgents with miraculous bread, then instead of accepting their offer to follow him in a march on Jerusalem, he alienated everybody by claiming, "I am the bread of life." He had shown up at the temple at the end of the Feast of Tabernacles, the biggest festival of the year, after the priests had spent a week doing rites of prayer for rain, and announced at the top of his lungs, "Let anyone who is thirsty come to me and drink" (John 7:37). When the festival recalled God leading the Israelites in a cloud of fire, Jesus had declared, "I am the light of the world."

"I am the good shepherd." "I am the door." "I am the resurrection and the life." I am . . . I am . . . I am. He drove the authorities nuts by echoing Exodus 3:14: "God said to Moses, 'I AM WHO I AM.'" But direct questions such as, "If you are the Anointed One, tell us plainly," he sidestepped. Look at my actions, he said. What do you think?

After all, what good would it have done to claim the title? It was the same as in the garden with mad Adam: if his people refused to see him clearly and choose him for who he was, then he let their choice stand.

And after three years of nonstop contact with Jesus, the Twelve still didn't get it. They had watched him heal and teach and drive out demons. They had thrilled to actually do those same things themselves. They had been part of the feeding of the five thousand. They had asked him endless questions. They had seen more than anybody, but they still understood almost nothing.

ROYAL PARADE

So if even the Twelve were blinded by their preconceptions of who the son of David ought to be, it was no surprise that the crowds approaching Jerusalem for the Passover were entirely in the dark. And for maybe the first and last time, Jesus did exactly what they expected.

About two miles from Jerusalem, the summit of the Mount of Olives reaches twenty-seven hundred feet above sea level, some three hundred feet above Jerusalem. (See map, page 351.) The road from Jericho crests that peak, then descends steeply toward Jerusalem. Near the top lay the villages of Bethany and Bethphage. There Jesus told his disciples to fetch an unridden donkey colt. Such a mount was ritually clean, suitable for sacred or royal use. His disciples knew at once what he was indicating by mounting this colt. He was claiming to be the fulfillment of Zechariah's promise that Jerusalem's king would come "righteous and victorious, lowly and riding on a donkey." He was announcing that he was coming to the capital as its king.

The disciples were ecstatic. They could see it all: Jesus would ride in amid popular acclaim, ascend the temple steps, march into the inner court and grasp the horns at the corners of the altar. That would signify that he was declaring his kingship. The people would rise against the Romans, and with the power of God behind them they would quickly oust the pagans and institute the kingdom. The disciples' job was to get the crowd behind their nominee. So they shouted royal acclamations based on Psalm 118, such as "Blessed is the king who comes in the name of the Lord!" (Luke 19:38). They threw their cloaks on the ground in front of the donkey, a proper regal welcome.

The local villagers and probably lots of pilgrims from Galilee who had seen Jesus' miracles soon responded to the revelry. They cut branches from the trees to add to the royal carpet and joined in shouting "Hosanna," a cry from Psalm 118 for God to save his people through the king. By the time the entourage reached Jerusalem, it had swelled to a rollicking mob ready to follow their king into battle.

Some Pharisees in the crowd rebuked Jesus for encouraging this riot, but he retorted, "If they keep quiet, the stones will cry out" (Luke 19:40).

LAST CHANCE

Then, with the crowd in his grasp, he let them drop. As he gazed down over Jerusalem from the Mount of Olives, he wept. He knew what her choice today was going to cost her. He knew how she would look forty years hence, surrounded by Roman armies quelling exactly the armed rebellion the people wanted now. The citizens would be slaughtered and their temple burned because they would not yield their demand for a military deliverance. They wanted liberty on their terms, under their control. They would not humble themselves before a God who wanted their hearts and the tough choices of self-sacrifice and love. And therefore, although they could quote every Scripture about the Lord coming to his temple, they did not recognize him when he came.

> *They would not humble themselves before a God who wanted their hearts and the tough choices of self-sacrifice and love.*

For he did ride up the temple steps and enter the outer court, the one called the Court of the Gentiles because it was supposed to be set aside for Gentiles to pray and perhaps encounter the true God. But he did not proceed to the altar to claim his throne. Instead, he stopped and grimaced at what had happened to the Gentiles' place of prayer. It was mobbed with people buying and selling animals for sacrifice (at stiff prices because there was no competition), or changing common currency for the coinage in which offerings had to be made (which was another monopoly). Only someone blind and deaf could pray in this bedlam. Either on that day, or on the next day after returning to Bethany overnight (the biblical accounts of Jesus' life don't always make it entirely clear in what order events occurred), Jesus pushed over the money changers' tables and singlehandedly drove the whole throng out the front door. Then he sat down to teach a stunned audience about God.

Until now he had clashed mainly with the lay leaders of Judaism—the Pharisees and teachers of the law. But now he was challenging the chief priests. Their families owned the businesses Jesus had just shut down.

And worse than that, if animals couldn't be bought, then sacrifices couldn't be offered. Jesus' action seemed to endorse the Essene view that the temple was defiled and invalid. But in truth, his message was far more radical: the sacrificial system had served its purpose and was now replaced. He was himself the fulfillment of all the festivals and sacrifices. He was the water and the light of the Feast of Tabernacles. He was the manna in the wilderness. He was the scapegoat for the Day of Atonement. He was the Passover lamb.

And he was dangerously close to bringing the wrath of Rome down on the people's heads. Yet the chief priests couldn't do a thing about him because the people applauded his behavior as a bold prophetic deed. The crowd was probably a little disappointed that Jesus hadn't claimed his crown, but they still doted on him and were convinced he had something up his sleeve. So the priests decided to lay aside their animosity toward the Pharisees in the face of a common enemy. Passover was only a few days away. They were determined to find a way to arrest Jesus as a political activist before he did whatever further intolerable prophetic antics he was planning.

Farewells

For three days Jesus taught as an ordinary rabbi in the temple courts, while the Pharisees and Sadducees tried to trap him with trick questions. But he was a master at turning their questions back on them and making them look like fools.

When their frustration was at its zenith, their golden opportunity appeared. Judas, the apostle who handled the finances for Jesus and the Twelve, came with a proposal. He had followed Jesus for three years, convinced that he had hitched his wagon to a rising star. But now it was clear that Jesus was throwing it all away in political blunders and spiritual nonsense, and Judas had had enough. For a price, he would reveal where they could find Jesus apart from the adoring crowds and arrest him. It was a deal.

That same Wednesday afternoon, Jesus spoke a veiled farewell to his gawking audience. He bore no ill will toward the many who had heard his words and disregarded them. Their indifference would be its own judge when those words returned to them on the day of the Lord.

On Thursday Jesus did not go to the temple. He spent a quiet day apart, then celebrated a Passover meal with his apostles in the evening, a day early. This would be their last night together, and he had an intense session planned to brief them for his departure.

As usual, the lesson was full of theater. He stripped like a slave and washed his followers' feet. His point: "Now that I, your Lord and Teacher, have washed your feet, you also should wash one another's feet. I have set you an example that you should do as I have done for you" (John 13:14-15). They had bickered and competed long enough. As Jesus' sent ones, they had to represent his character, one who would submit to the lowest self-abasement and sacrifice himself for the good of those he loved.

His other drama involved the food at the meal. The fare at a Passover supper was already symbolic: the unleavened bread represented the haste with which the Israelites left Egypt; the bitter herbs recalled their bondage. Cups of wine punctuated the dinner at intervals. There was supposed to be a roast lamb to signify the sacrifice whose blood protected Jewish homes from the destroyer. But the official lambs would not be sacrificed until Friday afternoon, and only by the temple priests. Jesus added two more symbols to this paramount meal of the old covenant. A Jewish dinner commenced when the host blessed and broke the bread. When Jesus did this, he added, "This is my body given for you; do this in remembrance of me" (Luke 22:19). Then he made each man eat a piece of the bread and remember his bizarre words about eating his flesh. Human sacrifice was unthinkable; this was getting scary.

The meal ended with the last Passover cup, over which Jesus declared, "This cup is the new covenant in my blood, which is poured out for you" (Luke 22:20). Here was Jeremiah's new covenant (Jeremiah 31:31-34), not ratified by the blood of bulls, as was the old covenant at Sinai, but by what—this rabbi's blood? Surely the meal ended in confusion, as each guest sipped the cup and wondered.

Along with this disturbing gesture of drinking blood came an equally disturbing lecture. Jesus tried to explain that he was leaving and that in his absence the apostles would face fierce opposition from the world around them. But they needn't feel fearful or abandoned, because the Spirit who had inspired the prophets and who empowered Jesus to do his works would aid them. All the disciples had to do was to remain connected to Jesus like branches to a vine, and everything would be fine. Exactly how they could remain connected to him when he was leaving was left unclear, but somehow it involved obeying his commands, especially the one to love each other.

The disciples were in no way encouraged by these promises and pressed for a better explanation. Where was Jesus going, and why couldn't they go too? Jesus replied with characteristic ambiguity. He knew his men were still woefully ill-equipped to face the next twenty-four hours, let alone the rest of their lives, so he closed the feast with a magnificent prayer for them and for those whose lives they would touch. Then he led them back to their camp site in a garden on the Mount of Olives.

ARREST

Judas had left the dinner early to summon the temple guards to that site. Jesus knew his betrayer's errand, so while his disciples fell asleep, still baffled, he kept vigil and steeled himself for the ordeal ahead. It was time to fulfill Isaiah's words: "He was despised and rejected by men, a man of sorrows, and familiar with suffering." It was time to do for real what Ezekiel did symbolically when he bore the sin of Jerusalem. It was time to give meaning to the death of every bull and goat whose blood had ever been spilled on the bronze altar for centuries. None of that blood and burning flesh had ever paid the cost for God's grief at his children's rejection of him. It had always been God absorbing the price into himself, paying the terrible cost in his own suffering. Now he was going to do before all the cosmos what

> It had always been God absorbing the price into himself, paying the terrible cost in his own suffering. Now he was going to do before all the cosmos what he had been doing all along.

he had been doing all along. And if human sacrifice was unthinkable because of the exquisite value of human life, what of God sacrifice?

Yet Jesus was human, too, and his every nerve cried out against the coming torture. He had faced his entrance exams in the wilderness of Judah; this was his final exam. In utter frankness he acknowledged that his will was to walk away from this ordeal. But what Adam had been unable to say, Jesus said to his Father: "Yet not my will, but yours be done."

On the Day of Atonement each year, the high priest sprinkled the blood of one goat on the throne of God as the price of the people's crimes. Then he laid his hands on a live goat and confessed those crimes over it, transferring the guilt to this innocent substitute. The scapegoat was driven into the desert. Here in this garden, Jesus began to live out what centuries of goats had symbolized. As high priest and victim in one, he took into himself the crimes of a planet. He had never before experienced evil within himself. The weight of it alone nearly killed him.

The soldiers arrived. It was a farce: they were armed to the teeth but quaking; he was defenseless yet in total control. They expected a dangerous revolutionary with an armed band and possibly miraculous powers. They were unprepared for a calm commanding presence who used the divine name "I AM" to identify himself. It was more a matter of Jesus giving himself to the soldiers than of their actually arresting him.

<hr />

Questions for Reflection and Discussion

1. Why didn't Jesus prove his divinity in ways nobody could deny?

2. How is Jesus the manna in the wilderness? How is he the Passover lamb? The goat from the Day of Atonement?

3. What is the drama of the bread and the cup about?

27

THE DEATH OF DEATH

Matthew 26:57–28:20; Mark 14:53–16:20;
Luke 22:54–24:53; John 18:12–21:25

Jesus' trial, too, was a charade. Roman soldiers had shared in Jesus' arrest on the grounds that he was a political revolutionary. Because such revolutionaries were a severe threat to order in the province, the governor's mandate was to maintain order even if it meant ruthless suppression. The Sanhedrin—the Jewish leaders—feared Jesus might spark an uprising, perhaps unintentionally, but they knew perfectly well he was no guerrilla leader.

The trouble was that they needed Rome to believe otherwise. Their real motive for getting rid of Jesus was that, like every prophet before him, he threatened their power, their lucrative businesses and their idea of God. But they couldn't execute him for being a prophet. They might possibly convict him for blasphemy, claiming to be the Son of God. But if they had him stoned for blasphemy, he might become something even worse than a live prophet: a martyred one. His disciples might launch a whole movement around him.

No, the only sensible move was to have Rome execute Jesus on political grounds. And so the Jewish leaders had to convince the governor that he was a threat to public peace, an insurrectionist claiming to be their rightful king.

So around three o'clock a.m. on Friday, Jesus was marched into the home of the godfather of the chief-priestly families: Annas. Annas had been high priest many years earlier, and since then Rome had appointed five of his sons to that office, probably on his advice. The current high priest was Caiaphas, Annas's son-in-law.

Annas intended to conduct a preliminary interrogation to gather evidence for the real trial. But Jewish legal procedure declared the accused innocent and not even on trial until at least two independent witnesses had given testimony that agreed. Accused people could not be asked to incriminate themselves. Knowing that Annas had no right to interrogate him, Jesus refused to answer his questions. He politely directed Annas to any of the dozens of people who had heard his teaching in the temple. Had anyone heard him say anything that could prove he was a false prophet?

An official lost his temper and slapped Jesus across the face. But the man who had said, "If someone slaps you on one cheek, turn to them the other also," put his own preaching into practice. Neither cringing nor spiteful, Jesus pointed out that this was one more illegality that Annas and company really ought to face up to. Exasperated, Annas summoned the entire Sanhedrin from their beds to give this upstart his trial.

Unfortunately, it wasn't legal to hold a capital trial in the middle of the night. Even after coaching the witnesses, the priests couldn't get them to agree except on a vague story that Jesus had said, "I am able to destroy the temple of God and rebuild it in three days." Jesus didn't bother to explain that he'd really said, "Destroy this temple [my body], and I will raise it again in three days." The trial was a show anyway.

Finally Caiaphas asked him point blank if he was the Messiah. Jesus responded with an expression that implied, yes, but you haven't a clue what that means. To really shake up his audience, he added an allusion to Daniel's prophecy about the divine Son of Man coming from heaven.

That was the last straw for the Sanhedrin. It never occurred to any of them that Jesus' claim might be true, so the outrageous apparent blasphemy disgusted them. Some began to hit him and spit on him. When dawn broke they held a quick official trial in which they got Jesus to repeat his claim to be the Messiah and promptly shuffled him off to the governor.

ROMAN TRIALS

The governor, Pontius Pilate, was less than thrilled to have this case on his morning docket. He knew his Jewish subjects detested him for his record of extortion, murder, atrocities and social blunders. He had recently provoked a riot by parading his soldiers with a portrait of the emperor on a Jewish holy day (the Jews regarded the portrait as an idol). Rome had disciplined Pilate for endangering public order, and Rome would fire him if there were riots about a supposed Messiah.

Pilate's first dodge was to suggest that the Sanhedrin execute Jesus on religious grounds, such as blasphemy. Roman subjects weren't allowed to inflict the death penalty, but Pilate promised to look the other way. But this offer wasn't good enough for the priests, so Pilate agreed to question Jesus about his kingship. When it became clear that Jesus' claim didn't challenge Roman rule, Pilate wanted to dismiss the whole case. He almost got out of it when he learned Jesus was a Galilean. Technically, that put him under the jurisdiction of Herod Antipas (son of Herod the Great), who ruled Galilee. But Herod, who was in town for Passover, found Jesus a bore and returned him to Pilate.

So back came Jesus to Pilate's office, dressed by Herod in a mock imperial robe. The governor's next sidestep was to have Jesus beaten within an inch of his life. Pilate hoped that would satisfy the Sanhedrin without getting him into serious trouble with this God Jesus claimed to serve. The prisoner's serenity in the face of his accusers was getting under Pilate's skin. Jesus was too lucid to be a madman and too confident to be safe.

It was customary for the governor to demonstrate his benevolence by freeing one Jewish prisoner at the Passover. When Pilate led Jesus out to the crowd, he expected them to beg him to show mercy on this teacher they so adored. But the sight of him dripping blood in a royal robe and wearing a crown of thorns changed their infatuation to contempt. The Sanhedrin had already coached the people to request another prisoner's release—Barabbas, a real guerrilla captain. Ironically, his name meant "son of the father."

The Sanhedrin led the cry, "Crucify!" for Jesus, and the people echoed it. This was the Roman execution for slaves and scum. To Romans it was a disgrace. To Jews the curse in the law of Moses against "anyone who is hung on a tree" (Deuteronomy 21:23) applied to criminals who were crucified. Such a death would silence any notion that Jesus was a prophet.

Pilate was beside himself. It terrified him to think of lifting his hand against one who might be divine (Romans were incredibly superstitious). He confronted Jesus: "Where do you come from? . . . Do you refuse to speak to me? Don't you realize I have power either to free you or to crucify you?"

Jesus replied, "You would have no power over me if it were not given to you from above. Therefore the one who handed me over to you is guilty of a greater sin."

The Sanhedrin threatened, "If you let this man go, you are no friend of Caesar. Anyone who claims to be a king opposes Caesar."

This was too much for Pilate. He feared the gods, but he feared Caesar more. He wanted this God to know that the man's blood was on the Jews' heads, though.

"Shall I crucify your king?" Pilate asked. "We have no king but Caesar," the chief priests answered. It was true. The snake laughed.

CRUCIFIXION

It was a grisly way to kill, even by the standards of the day. The Romans' law forbade crucifying one of their own citizens. The victim was nailed (or tied) by hands and feet to wooden crosspieces shaped like a T, Y, I or ✝. He straddled a hornlike projection, which took some of the weight and kept the flesh from tearing away from the nails. It usually took hours for the blood loss from beating, exposure to sun, and restricted circulation and breathing to produce heart failure.

Jesus was half-dead from flogging before he reached the site. But he was aware enough to deliver a mournful prophecy to the women who followed his escort. He felt no bitterness, not even toward those who had plotted his death and now mocked him as he hung. It had always been so since the first rebellion; his executioners were only carrying out what humans had ever longed to do: kill God so that they could rule their lives themselves. He said, "Father, forgive them, for they do not know what they are doing" (Luke 23:34).

As Isaiah had foreseen, he was executed among criminals. The two thieves crucified with him provided an object lesson on the choice being offered an entire planet. One cared only for self and let himself be devoured by his hatred of God and others. The second thief saw past Jesus' humiliation and acknowledged his kingship. Hatred or humility. Bitterness or faith.

Of the Twelve, only John dared attend the execution. Proud Peter had said he was willing to die for Jesus, but something broke inside him when Jesus refused to let him fight the soldiers who arrested him. Despair clutched him, and outside Annas's house he denied three times that he even knew Jesus. Then he remembered that Jesus had predicted this betrayal, and Peter could hardly believe he was capable of stooping so low. Too late, he knew himself.

So while John stood watch at the cross, Peter wept in hiding. Judas had killed himself in too-tardy remorse for his treachery. But Jesus had prayed that Peter's faith would not utterly fail, and in the desperate hours a thread held Peter back from choosing Judas's despair.

However, the women of Jesus' entourage were not afraid to show their faces at the cross. Perhaps it was safer for them; no one paid attention to women. Perhaps they had more faith, or more guts, than the men. Certainly Jesus' mother didn't care whether the Sanhedrin boiled her in oil now that they were killing her son. But Jesus cared, so he asked John to take her into his household.

That was his last piece of business. Ever since the previous night he had been carrying in his body the guilt of an entire world of warped humans. Now the full cost of that burden suffocated him. Evil dug an impassible gulf between the evil person and God. Yet now the Son of God was full to overflowing with the evil of the ages. For the first time in his existence, that dark gulf yawned between him and his Father. From eternity they had always been intimately one; now the Father was nowhere to be felt.

In the agony of abandonment Jesus found the energy to wail the first verse of Psalm 22: "My God, my God, why have you forsaken me?" It was a song of grief under persecution and divine rejection, yet it ended in a victory to which Jesus clung fiercely:

Posterity will serve him;
>   future generations will be told about the Lord.
They will proclaim his righteousness,
>   declaring to a people yet unborn:
>   He has done it! (Psalm 22:30-31)

"He has done it!" The hour had come. It was about three o'clock on Friday afternoon, and the temple priests were getting ready to slaughter the Passover lambs. That night the Jews of Jerusalem would feast on roast lamb to celebrate their deliverance from slavery. A thin column of smoke rose from the temple as a signal that the lambs were about to die. Jesus asked for a sip of wine to rinse his parched mouth. He had one last word to say, and he wanted it to ring.

Tetelestai! Greek accountants scrawled this word across invoices every day. It literally meant "It is finished," but the point was "Paid in full."

It was over. Peaceful at last, Jesus prayed in the words of Psalm 31, a song Jews often sang before going to bed, "Father, into your hands I commit my spirit."

The earth shook when its King died, and the heavy curtain that divided God's throne room from the rest of the temple tore in two from top to bottom.

REVERSAL

Although he was a member of the Sanhedrin, Joseph of Arimathea was conveniently absent from the meeting that condemned Jesus. Perhaps he was not notified because he was known to be a follower of Jesus. At any rate, he and a Pharisee named Nicodemus risked the chief priests' ire by asking Pilate to let them bury Jesus' body. Joseph was well-off and spent a small fortune preparing the body as for a royal burial and interring it in his own rock-hewn tomb. The men had to rush the job because both Passover and the Sabbath started at sunset.

The Sanhedrin remembered that Jesus had predicted he would rise from death on the third day, so they asked Pilate to post a guard at the tomb. He did.

It was a bleak Sabbath for the Eleven. They spent it huddled in a house, expecting that the moment the sun set they would hear the heavy feet of soldiers at the door. But Saturday night fell, and nothing. They were awakened at dawn, however, by the women disciples wailing that Jesus' body had been stolen. Peter and John ran to the tomb and found it empty except for the burial cloths. This was astounding, since the ointments with which the body was wrapped included resins that, when hardened, would have cemented the cloths to the corpse. It would have taken strange robbers to spend the time to painstakingly— and with marginal success—peel the grave clothes off the body and carefully fold them.

The guards were nowhere to be found. They had run to the chief priests with a wild story about an earthquake at the tomb and an angel who rolled the heavy stone from the mouth of the cave. The priest bribed them to say they fell asleep and the disciples stole the body, and the soldiers agreed because they knew the priests could have them executed for failing in a mission.

Some hours later, one of the women returned to the disciples' hideout claiming she had seen Jesus risen from the dead, and others said they had seen angels. The men ridiculed this nonsense, but that evening two disciples ran in claiming to have met Jesus on the road northwest of town.

At that very moment Jesus walked into their locked apartment. He demonstrated that he was not a ghost by eating in front of them. He also showed them his nail wounds, the evidence he would carry into eternity that he had entered the depths of human pain and triumphed in it. Then he began to explain why he had to be killed and raised from the dead. Finally, he kept the first installment of his promise about the Spirit.

Again Jesus said, "Peace be with you! As the Father has sent me, I am sending you." And with that he breathed on them and said, "Receive the Holy Spirit. If you forgive anyone's sins, their sins are forgiven; if you do not forgive them, they are not forgiven" (John 20:21-23).

The Spirit had empowered Jesus to do amazing miracles. It was even by the Spirit's power that the Father had raised Jesus from death. But the first power these people needed as ambassadors of the true King was the ability to forgive.

Questions for Reflection and Discussion

1. Do you think it was easy for Jesus to respond to Annas without either rage or terror? Explain. What do you think helped him?

2. What was Jesus' attitude toward Pilate's power?

3. Why do you think one of the first things Jesus did after rising from the dead was give his disciples the power to forgive?

Part Five

MESSENGERS
TO THE
NATIONS

28

A MOVEMENT EXPLODES

Acts 1:1–8:40; 9:32–11:30

*D*uring the forty days after his return from death, Jesus appeared frequently to groups of his followers. He also appeared to his brother James. Many of his friends and relatives had found it difficult to believe he was the King during his former life, but seeing him back from the dead sure convinced them. He appeared and disappeared like a ghost, but he was too solidly physical to seem like anything other than a live person.

He did not do what one might have expected: materialize in the high priest's office or the temple courts and demonstrate his resurrection beyond any doubt. That would have been coercion. If he'd done that, the leaders and people would have been forced to bow to him even though their inner commitments were unchanged. They still would not love him. If blatant power displays had not won the generations who saw Moses on Sinai and Elijah on Carmel, they would not win this granite-hearted bunch.

Instead, Jesus trained his followers to present the evidence about him in a way that would invite a change of heart. Like the prophets before them, these apostles would be the King's friends sent to woo a bride on his behalf. One day he would come to claim his realm by force, but in the meantime his disciples would infiltrate enemy territory and seek recruits.

Then he vanished for the last time, warning his troops not to take action until the Spirit of God came on them to equip them for the job. They already had the Spirit's power to forgive; they still needed his power to testify.

> *If blatant power displays had not won the generations who saw Moses on Sinai and Elijah on Carmel, they would not win this granite-hearted bunch.*
>
> *Instead, Jesus trained his followers to present the evidence about him in a way that would invite a change of heart.*

For the next ten days, the 120 of Jesus' followers who were residing in Jerusalem spent their time almost constantly in prayer. The one thing we know they did was select a replacement for Judas. If there had been twelve tribes of Israel with twelve patriarchs, the group reasoned, there had to be twelve apostles to lead the new Israel.

The other way they probably passed that time was in dealing with unfinished business among them, and between them and God—putting that power of forgiveness into practice. Jesus had shown them how it was done. After Jesus was arrested, Peter had three times denied he knew Jesus. So during one of his post-resurrection appearances, Jesus drew Peter aside and asked him three times, "Do you love me?" Peter, no longer the macho freedom fighter who had sworn to stick by Jesus to the death, three times replied that, yes, he loved Jesus to the best of his human ability, but not perfectly. In no way perfectly. Yet each time Jesus reaffirmed his confidence in Peter by commissioning him, "Feed my lambs."

Peter didn't deserve to be trusted as head of the team, but Jesus' forgiveness had the ability to transform anyone who let it touch him or her. Jesus' trust made Peter trustworthy.

Perhaps it was like that for the rest of the 120, as Simon the Zealot and Matthew the tax collector let supernatural forgiveness weld them together when they could not naturally love each other. Jesus' brothers were welcomed into the community they had ridiculed. Everyone forgot the old debates about which of them would be the greatest in the kingdom. And at least one of the Sons of Thunder, John, became an impassioned proponent of spiritual love and unity.

PENTECOST

Ten days after Jesus' final disappearance came the Festival of Weeks. It had originally celebrated the beginning of the wheat harvest, but of late it had come to commemorate God's covenants. Greek-speaking Jews called the day Pentecost because it was fifty days after the Passover Sabbath (*pentēkostē* means "fiftieth" in Greek). The biblical historian Luke (we've already met him as one of Jesus' earliest biographers) tells us, using redundancy for emphasis, that the 120 followers of Jesus "were all together in one place" (Acts 2:1). They were together spiritually as well as physically, for the power of forgiveness had done its work.

Into that place of unity the Spirit of God burst as wind and fire. The power of testimony came upon the believers, and they proclaimed the news about Jesus in the dozens of languages of the known world. At Babel God had confused human languages so as to crush the threat of unified evil. Now he gave a token that he was beginning to reverse that process. A true unity of those filled with his Spirit would reknit for good what God had unraveled to prevent evil.

A hundred and twenty people shouting in different languages at the top of their lungs attracted attention. Pentecost had brought pilgrims to Jerusalem from all the places where Babylonian and Greek conquests had scattered the Jews. These pilgrims were astonished to hear, amid what was otherwise gibberish, voices declaring "the wonders of God" in their own obscure local dialects.

A crowd gathered, some snickering that the babblers were drunk. Eventually Peter made himself heard in Greek over the tumult. Jesus had said that the Spirit's power to drive out demons was evidence that the kingdom was in Israel's midst (Matthew 12:28). Now Peter announced that this further display was nothing other than the fulfillment of Joel's prophecy of the day of the Lord:

> I will pour out my Spirit on all people.
> Your sons and daughters will prophesy,
>> your young men will see visions,
>> your old men will dream dreams. (Acts 2:17)

Peter went on to explain how David had predicted that the son of

David would be recognized by his resurrection from death. The supernatural languages were evidence that Israel should believe the apostles'
testimony that Jesus had in fact risen and was the long-awaited King.
Peter pleaded with his audience to be baptized as a public sign that they
were turning their allegiance to Jesus the King. This, Peter told them,
was their only hope of survival.

About three thousand people took up Peter's offer. Most of them were
just visiting for the feast, and within days they carried their news and
their revolutionized lives back to their far-flung homes.

THE COMMUNITY IN JERUSALEM

Those who remained in Jerusalem carried on the apostles' custom of
living as family. They ate, prayed and learned together daily. They relived
the drama of bread and cup, body and blood, that Jesus had told them to
repeat in his memory. They saw to it that all of their group was ade-
quately fed and housed. Some thought nothing of selling their possessions to provide for the rest. All Jerusalem held them in awe because of
the power and love in their midst.

Peter healed a man who had been lame from birth. And he did it on
the front steps of the temple, where he then announced to the amazed
onlookers that this was a sign that Jesus, whom they had crucified as a
criminal, was in fact "the author of life," the rightful King. The Sadducees were irate. They didn't believe resurrection was possible, and
these apostles claimed it had happened to a criminal the Sanhedrin had
condemned. Peter was accusing them of killing the Messiah. If the
people believed that, how would they feel about their leaders?

It was ominously close to blasphemy for Peter to say of Jesus things
like, "Salvation is found in no one else, for there is no other name under
heaven given to mankind by which we must be saved" (Acts 4:12). To a
Jew, the one name by which one might be saved from anything was the
unpronounceable name of God.

But the whole city had seen Peter heal the beggar, so the Sanhedrin
could do no more than threaten him. Their hostility only roused the
little community of believers to pray aggressively that God would enable
them to proclaim Jesus with even more boldness.

AWE

The next event that gave the citizens of Jerusalem pause was the sudden death of two members of the new sect. There was no hint of foul play; the couple dropped dead in public for lying to Peter (and God) about money they had promised to give for the community's poor. Members were free to keep their possessions if they chose to do so, but lying to the Holy Spirit brought instant death. With God so palpably in their midst, deceit was impossible.

That incident put an end to all but serious converts joining the community. People carried their sick relatives into the streets when Peter passed, hoping his shadow would fall on them and heal them. But they wouldn't undergo baptism just for thrills and free food. It was too dangerous.

Some in the Sanhedrin wanted to stamp out the new sect by executing the apostles. Peter answered them boldly despite the danger. He would certainly have gone the way of Jesus if Gamaliel, a rabbi respected for his great learning who was the leading Pharisee on the council, had not intervened. Gamaliel reasoned that if the sect was merely of human origin it would be a flash in the pan. But if it was from God, then nothing could or should stop it.

THE HELLENISTS

The Twelve might have gone on indefinitely maintaining a little Jewish community in Jerusalem. Except for their unconventional ideas about Jesus, they were scrupulously observant Jews. They were content to pray and teach among their fellow Jews in Jerusalem, enjoying the goodwill of their neighbors. But God had other plans. So he let this ground-laying party go on for a few years, then brought it crashing down.

There were two distinct groups in Jerusalem's Jewish community at this time. So-called Hebraic Jews retained their traditional culture and still spoke Aramaic, a language related to Hebrew. The group known as Hellenistic Jews had adopted Greek as their primary language and embraced much of Greek culture. (*Hellas* is the Greek name for Greece.) Within the community of Jesus' followers, a dispute arose between the Hebraists and the Hellenists. The apostles were all Hebraic, so to keep peace they urged the Hellenistic believers to choose leaders from among themselves. The apostles would still take responsibility for teaching, but the Hellenistic leaders would see to it that their people's needs were not overlooked.

At least one of the Hellenistic leaders soon began showing the same signs of miraculous power as the apostles. But this man, Stephen, was not one to sit quietly in the temple week after week. Many Jews believed that the age of the Messiah would displace the age of the law of Moses. Moreover, God had said repeatedly through the prophets that he was not bound to a building. So Stephen reasoned that if Jesus had come, then the age of the law was past and the whole temple system might as well be dispensed with. Stephen hadn't quite worked out how Jesus' death had fulfilled the sacrificial system, but he had a gut feeling that there was no point to the system anymore.

When he said this to the other Jews in his synagogue, he met with fury. Nobody but the Sanhedrin much minded these guys claiming Jesus had risen from the dead and was the Messiah. But when they started speaking against the temple and the law, they were blaspheming. Stephen was dragged before the Sanhedrin, and when he called them stiff-necked murderers, the mob stoned him to death.

THE COMMUNITY'S WALLS EXPAND

This lynching triggered a general uprising of traditional Jews against the followers of Jesus. All of the Hellenistic and most of the Hebraic be-lievers had to flee Jerusalem, although the apostles managed to stay be-cause of their impeccable reputations. But this flight, which appeared to be the community's destruction, was actually a godsend. Jesus had told the apostles, "You will be my witnesses in Jerusalem, and in all Judea and Samaria, and to the ends of the earth" (Acts 1:8). The community had been too comfortable to venture out on the next stage of its as-signment, but now it had no choice.

Once again the Hellenists led the mission. Philip, another Hellenistic leader, had success proclaiming Jesus in Samaria, especially since he backed up his claims with the apostolic signs of healing and casting out demons. Even so, Philip acknowledged the apostles' authority to ap-prove his ministry. After all, these new believers were not Jews, but the hated Samaritans. So Peter and John came and inspected the situation, decided it was in line with what Jesus had taught them, and gave the Samaritan believers their blessing. As public proof that the Samaritans were full members of the community, God gave them the Pentecost signs of the Holy Spirit's presence.

From Samaria Philip went on to bring the news of Jesus to an official of an African kingdom who was already sympathetic to Judaism—yet another radical move for a religious group that had come to define itself by its ethnic purity. Philip finally settled in Caesarea, the seat of Roman government in Judea and hence a largely Gentile city. Proclaiming the good news in that region kept him busy for the next twenty years.

TO THE GENTILES

But God knew that if a Hellenist launched the mission to the Gentiles, the Hebraic Jews would never accept it. So he gave Peter a vision and sent him to Caesarea to tell a prominent Roman military commander about Jesus. This man had long been praying to and serving the Jewish God, but to the Jews he was still a dirty pagan. Peter broke with deeply ingrained taboos by actually entering this man's house and eating with him and his household, in addition to welcoming them into the community of Jesus.

The signs of Pentecost fell on these Gentiles when they committed themselves to Jesus, so what could Peter do? This was his defense when the Hebraic believers back in Jerusalem demanded an explanation. And after hearing his story, they had to admit he was right. As incredible as it seemed, they had to admit that God wanted people they considered "unclean" in his kingdom.

It was a good thing they admitted this, for the Hellenists were launching full steam ahead into Gentile territory. When the persecution drove them from Jerusalem, some of them had settled in Antioch, the third-largest city in the empire and the capital of the Roman province of Syria. Before long, crowds of Antiochene Gentiles were dedicating themselves to this Savior called Jesus Christos. With no Jewish background, Christos (Messiah) meant nothing to them as a title (the Oiled One?), so they treated it as part of his name. Unbelievers in Antioch soon nicknamed them *Christianoi*, followers of this guy Christos.

If Philip's work in Samaria had been radical for the Hebraic believers, this new Gentile community in Antioch was off the page. The half-million residents of Antioch were a cosmopolitan bunch, and people in such large trading centers tended to assemble their own approaches to spirituality from the smorgasbord of available religious options. A little Greek philosophy, a little Persian dualism, a little from the ancestral cult, a little Judaism, or maybe something from one of the other newer, fashionable cults. Antioch's priestesses of Daphne were famed ritual prostitutes. There was no telling what the pagans of Antioch might do with the teachings of Christ.

Accordingly, the apostles sent one of their trusted leaders, Barnabas, to inspect the Antiochene work. Barnabas was so impressed that he not only conveyed his approval to Jerusalem, he decided to settle in Antioch. People were converting right and left; there wasn't enough leadership to keep up with them. Eventually Barnabas thought of a fellow Hebraic believer who would be an ideal partner in getting this Gentile community into shape. His name was Saul.

Questions for Reflection and Discussion

1. After he returned from death, why didn't Jesus appear to those who had rejected him?

2. How did Jesus' resurrection prove that he was the long-awaited Son of David?

3. What key roles did each of these men play in spreading the movement?
   - Peter
   - Stephen
   - Philip

THE ADVENTURES
OF PAUL

Acts 9:1-31; 12:1–14:27

When Stephen was raising the hair on the back of Jewish necks in Jerusalem, Saul was a student of Gamaliel, the influential member of the Sanhedrin whom we met a moment ago. Saul was passionately attached to the law and already influential among the young rabbis. The law asserted that anyone hanged on a tree (this included crucifixion) was under God's curse. By this logic it seemed that Jesus could not be the Messiah and that it was blasphemy to say he was. This reasoning led to Stephen's stoning, an act that Saul approved and supported. After that, Saul got himself appointed as a leader in stamping out the Jesus blasphemy, arresting and executing dozens of believers. Having all but exterminated the plague in Jerusalem, Saul took an official delegation to nip it in the bud in Damascus. (See map, page 351.) As he neared the city, a flash of light knocked him to the ground. He heard a voice: "Saul, Saul, why do you persecute me?" The voice identified itself as Jesus.

Saul's clever reasoning was undone. Blinded and shattered, he let himself be taken to Damascus, where he fasted for three days. He groped to make sense of his world. If the voice was Jesus, then Jesus was the Messiah. If Jesus was the Messiah, then somehow the curse of crucifixion had been overcome. But why would the Messiah deliberately let himself bear a curse? Moreover, if the Messiah had come, then was the age of the law over? How could one live without the law?

After three days of this, a believer named Ananias arrived at Saul's lodging to lay hands on him. Jesus had appeared to Ananias in a vision and ordered him to restore Saul's sight and impart the Holy Spirit to him. Nothing short of a vision would have moved Ananias to approach enemy number one, and even so Ananias argued with Jesus about the wisdom of this move.

But Jesus insisted that this persecutor would become one of his chief ambassadors: "I will show him how much he must suffer for my name" (Acts 9:16). Not a very encouraging promise, perhaps, but by this time Saul was a broken man, ready for anything.

SAUL IN ACTION

The first thing Saul did after recovering his strength was make the rounds of the synagogues proclaiming Jesus as the Son of God. This claim from the man notorious for leading the Jerusalem persecution was electrifying. First electrifying, then infuriating. Saul knew the Jewish Scriptures backwards and forwards and could argue for Jesus' messiahship from any passage his opponents chose. He did this for more than two years in Damascus and the surrounding district of Arabia until the Jews were at last so enraged that they plotted to kill him. His followers had to smuggle him out of the city.

Next he traveled to Jerusalem, where the believers who remembered their martyred friends would have nothing to do with him. Eventually Barnabas saw the potential in Saul and convinced the apostles to accept him. Once part of the community, Saul launched his confrontational tactics in the synagogues until murder plots started surfacing again. Again Saul was smuggled out of town, and this time the community told him to go back to his hometown of Tarsus and lie low. He was still too much the same arrogant hothead he had always been, and he needed his rough edges smoothed before he could accomplish anything useful. This training period went on for years until Barnabas arrived to invite him to Antioch.

ANTIOCH'S LEADERSHIP TEAM

The believers in Jerusalem were organized under the leadership of the twelve apostles plus some "elders." This was a natural system, because synagogues were run by teams of elders. It was unheard of to have a single elder in charge.

Antioch seems to have adopted a similar team approach. At one point we read of five men called "prophets and teachers" making decisions for the citywide believing community. As in Jerusalem, much of their teaching, worship and practice of life in Christ probably went on in homes and workplaces, but in some way the small cells were linked under their leadership team. Barnabas was a member—perhaps the most prominent one—of the Antiochene team. Saul became the fifth member when Barnabas brought him in to assist in teaching the Jewish Scriptures, the truths about Christ and the lifestyle of a believer.

When Saul had been in Antioch for several months, some prophets arrived from Jerusalem. Prophets evidently functioned as official emissaries from the apostles, as well as bearers of messages from God. Like the prophets of Israel, they spoke God's current word to the community on matters about the present and the future. But because the Holy Spirit now inhabited every believer, these new covenant prophets no longer bore the sole responsibility for hearing from God. Antioch's leadership team included prophets (Barnabas and/or Saul may have served that function); by contrast, Jerusalem's prophets seem to have served alongside the leadership team.

At any rate, one of the Jerusalem prophets, Agabus, told the Antiochene community that the empire was about to undergo famine. Judea was particularly at risk. The Antiochenes decided to show their love for their Judean fellow believers by sending aid. As Jews who had lived in Jerusalem, Barnabas and Saul were the natural choices for emissaries. (As it turned out, famine hit various parts of the empire successively during this decade. Judea suffered severely in A.D. 46 and 47.) Barnabas and Saul seized this chance to report to the Jerusalem leadership on the work in Antioch.

Everyone agreed that it was crucial to prevent two distinct branches of the faith from developing, a Jewish one based in Jerusalem and a

Gentile one based in Antioch. So they came to an agreement about the essentials of their message. They used a Greek word that meant "good news" as the word for this essential message. In English it's known as the "gospel," from an older way of saying "good news" in that language. The leadership also agreed that while there was only one community and one message of Christ, the Antiochene team (especially Saul) would be responsible for getting the message to the Gentiles, while the Jerusalem team (headed by Peter) would take responsibility for the Jews, particularly in and around Palestine.

AN APOSTOLIC TEAM

This idea of getting the message to the Gentiles burned in the hearts of the Antiochene group. Their approach to strategic planning was to spend extended periods of time fasting, praying and worshiping God. In the midst of one such session, one or more of the prophets received instructions from the Holy Spirit. Barnabas and Saul were to be set apart for a new task: to take a mobile team westward into areas where the gospel had never been proclaimed.

The two of them set out with Barnabas's cousin John Mark. Their plan was to go to the cities where the Holy Spirit led them and to find a synagogue in each one. Up to this point the gospel had been most successful among Gentiles who sympathized with Jewish beliefs but had not yet undergone the rites of conversion. Also, God had laid down a principle that the truth must be offered to the chosen race first before it was proclaimed among the nations. The Jews still deserved a chance to take up their ancient assignment to be lights to the Gentiles.

Saul had the rare privilege of being a Jew born with Roman citizenship. His family must have had some standing in his hometown to have won that right. As a citizen, he had a Roman name as well as his Jewish one. His Roman surname was Paulus, and when he left Antioch to proclaim Jesus to the Gentiles, he decided to use that name rather than one that advertised his Jewishness. One of his basic principles of ministry was to adapt in every way possible to the culture he wanted to reach. He wouldn't compromise his morals, of course, but in nonessentials like food, clothing, customs and even his name he was committed to adopting local ways in order not to obscure his message.

A curious shift occurred as Barnabas, Paul and Mark traveled from city to city. When they left Antioch, Barnabas was the ranking team member. But it soon became clear that Paul was the more gifted spokesman and that God was choosing to work more miracles through Paul than Barnabas. Paul became the senior partner.

Moreover, during this trip the biblical account shifts from calling the partners "prophets" or "teachers" to labeling them "apostles." Paul and Barnabas began to realize God had given them a commission parallel to one the Twelve apostles had. The two of them would be apostles to the Gentiles. No one would challenge the special status of the Twelve, because they had actually been with Jesus, but Paul and Barnabas were now serving as "sent ones" themselves. They had apostolic authority and even showed signs of power—blinding a sorcerer and healing a lame man—to back it up.

So the local team in Antioch had spawned something new: a mobile apostolic team for spreading the gospel to places it had never touched. The threesome journeyed to the island of Cyprus, then sailed to the coast of Asia Minor. Young Mark had had enough of the grueling missionary lifestyle by that time and he took a boat to Jerusalem. But Paul and Barnabas hiked inland to and around the region of Phrygian Galatia. (See map, page 350.)

Every Sabbath they visited a synagogue, and as learned Jews from Jerusalem, they were naturally invited to speak on the passage of Scripture for the day. Invariably Paul used the passage as a springboard to announce the Messiah. He consistently won over Gentile converts and sympathizers, but the Jews were usually furious and ran the team out of town. However, the expulsion normally didn't take place until a tiny new community of believers had been established.

HOMEWARD BOUND

After planting seeds in seven towns, the pair retraced their steps to visit each of these communities. Along with impressing on the new disciples the basic truths they needed to remember, the team had a word of tough encouragement: "We must go through many hardships to enter the kingdom of God" (Acts 14:22). It was not going to be easy to follow Christ in towns where the community of faith numbered maybe a dozen, where the Gentiles scorned people who accepted only one God and where the Jews viewed the new sect as a wicked heresy.

In each city, Paul and Barnabas selected a few of the most responsible new believers to serve as elders. It wasn't ideal to put raw recruits in charge of a platoon, but there weren't any alternatives. And these people had the Holy Spirit just like every other disciple, so the apostles trusted him to mature the new plants however he chose.

What with the snail's pace of ancient travel and the time needed to establish new cells, this trip probably took a couple of years. But sometime in A.D. 48, the mobile team arrived back in Antioch, flush with victory, to report to their home community. There they stayed for probably more than a year.

No doubt they needed the rest. Road life in the ancient world was harsh. A very rich person might rent a carriage, but exactly two means of travel were available to anyone else: a ship by sea or one's two feet by land. (Horses were extremely hard to ride because stirrups and real saddles had not yet been invented.)

The Roman roads were good and relatively safe; at least there were no pillaging armies, although bandits were inevitable. And about every twenty-two miles was an inn. But twenty-two miles a day is a stiff pace on foot. If the road was hilly, the weather wet or muddy, or the morning start delayed, Paul and Barnabas no doubt camped in the open. Heat or illness could weaken them; snow could block a mountain pass; hail, flooding or wild animals could be life-threatening. The road across Asia Minor (modern Turkey) crosses a plateau that averages three thousand feet of elevation and is twice that in some sections. Temperatures rise and plummet dramatically.

Furthermore, the inns were not exactly the Ritz. Most were bare courtyards surrounded by rooms. Baggage and animals shared the courtyard with livestock drivers, who slept around dried dung fires. If Paul and Barnabas were low on funds, they probably slept with them. If they had more money, they could rent a bed in a room along with several strangers who snored or who might steal their possessions while they slept. There was also the inevitable colony of bedbugs.

If a traveler wanted food from a local peasant, he had to pay for it. Paul was trained as a maker of tents from leather or wool, but it took time to ply the trade. Yet Paul preferred to avoid asking for money from the people he was introducing to Christ, so the team probably spent stretches of time working to earn money to finance the next leg of their trip.

With land travel so slow and hazardous, one might think people traveled by sea whenever possible. But because ships of the day were at the mercy of prevailing winds, east-to-west sailing was exasperatingly slow. Paul preferred to walk west and sail east. Further, passenger ships were rare, and cargo ships took passengers only when they had room. Paul and Barnabas would have to find one going in their direction, haggle with the owner over the fee, then wait until the captain had judged both winds and omens to be favorable. (Sailors were even more superstitious than land lubbers.)

On board, passengers took turns cooking their own food in the galley after the crew was fed. The captain generously furnished water. A stray splash or rough seas might mean no fire for the evening. There was no way to refrigerate meat, so ships planned to dock at least every few nights. But if a storm or long voyage delayed docking, only grain was edible.

Few ships had cabins, so passengers lived on deck with only the sail for shade and shelter. Experienced travelers brought tents for nights when the ship docked at a port with no inn.

Shipwreck and damage were common. Violent storms made winter sailing suicidal, but even in spring and fall sailing was a risk. Yet Paul was willing to take this risk. In the course of his life, in addition to trudging about eighteen hundred miles overland on missionary journeys, he also logged about thirteen hundred miles by sea.

In a letter some years later, Paul mentioned that an illness first brought him to preach in Galatia (Galatians 4:13). This may have been a pre-existing condition, but it was certainly aggravated on the road. Weeks of exposure, hunger, thirst, sea sickness and hard hiking might make even strong travelers drop in their tracks.

Questions for Reflection and Discussion

1. Crucifixion was associated with God's curse. How was this a central issue for Saul?

2. What was a mobile apostolic team? How was it important to the spread of the story about Jesus?

3. What impresses you most about Saul/Paul?

BREAKING THE
CULTURE BARRIER

Acts 15:1–16:5, Galatians

*T*he community at Antioch was no doubt honored to receive such a
visitor as the apostle Peter. And Peter was as pleased with the work in
Antioch as Paul and Barnabas knew he would be. The leadership team
had done an amazing job of translating the gospel without distorting the
essential message into terms Gentiles could understand even though
they lacked the Jewish background to understand terms like Messiah
and kingdom of God. The Way of Jesus had not degenerated into one
more Greek cult that promised immortality through contact with the
divine. And Peter, who had received a vision from Christ repealing the
kosher laws, was comfortable socializing with Gentile believers. If Jesus
himself said so, then the longstanding Jewish prejudice against people
they considered filthy pagans was null and void.

But then a delegation arrived claiming the authority of James, the
ranking member of Jerusalem's leadership team. These visitors bore a
new policy: One could not belong to the people of God unless one adhered to all of the law, including circumcision. One had to be a Jew to be
a disciple of Jesus.

Further, they told Peter privately that his behavior in Antioch was
threatening efforts to spread the gospel back home. The apostles had
been enjoying great favor among their Jewish kinsmen because they

were known to be faithful observers of the law. Peter was undercutting that reputation by openly flouting the kosher laws. Would he please rein in his own freedom for the sake of reaching the Jews?

Certainly Peter would do that, and immediately he withdrew from sharing meals with Gentiles. Under pressure from the delegation, the rest of the Jewish believers in Antioch followed suit. Even Barnabas. But not Paul. He was incensed.

Peter may have been the chief apostle, but in Paul's eyes he was not above reproof. And since his fault was public and influencing many, his reproof had to be public too. For by bowing to Jewish scruples—even in order to draw them to Christ—Peter was compromising an essential point of the gospel and endangering efforts to reach Gentiles. Peter's withdrawal implied that Gentiles were second-class believers. It suggested that Peter supported the delegation's whole position about having to become a Jew in order to be a child of God.

FAITH OR RELIGIOUS SUBCULTURE

Barnabas and the rest hadn't thought through the implications of this position, but Paul had been thinking about the law for a long time. His message to Peter can be summarized like this: If you won't even eat with these Gentiles, you're pretty much saying that they're not part of the family. Therefore you're saying that something in addition to committing one's life to Christ is necessary to join God's family. You're saying we need Christ plus the law of Moses as interpreted by the rabbis in Jerusalem.

But we've already admitted that keeping the law never won us God's acceptance. We could never keep it well enough. That was why Christ died for us lawbreakers. He fulfilled the whole law—the meaning of the festivals, the sacrifices, the separation between holy and common. In doing so he began a new era in which living by the Jewish subculture's traditions is optional. We live with his life, obeying God by the power of the Spirit within us. By all means, let's pursue the moral character to which the Spirit draws us—love, joy, self-control. But the ritual laws of circumcision and diet are optional. At best they're an ethnic tradition we value as our heritage, but they don't make us more like

Jesus, and at worst they divide the community and deny that Christ's mercy alone is sufficient.

What got to Paul was that Peter and the rest already knew all this. They were just afraid to come out and say that belief in and commitment to Christ alone—not keeping the rules of an ethnic group or subculture—were what God required. And they were afraid because part of them cared more about what people thought than what God thought.

But the part of them that cared about God was stung by Paul's rebuke. Peter, Barnabas and the other Antiochenes immediately saw the truth. However, the delegation from Jerusalem did not. Hot debates got nowhere, so at last it was decided to send Paul and Barnabas to Jerusalem to sort the issue out.

CONFERENCE AT JERUSALEM

The Jerusalem community of Christ gathered to weigh a matter with huge implications. The bulk of opinion leaned toward the law party. But Paul's accounts of the miracles God had done among the Gentiles were powerful, and Peter redeemed himself by siding with Paul. He reminded the assembly of his visit with the Roman commander in Caesarea and concluded his speech with a question: Why put a yoke on the Gentiles that we have never been able to bear? Both we and they are saved by Christ's unearned work in our lives. Period.

When James—a man known to be zealous in observing the law—was convinced, his influence swayed the assembly to consensus. James proposed that the council circulate a letter to avoid any confusion or misrepresentation. That letter would free the Gentiles from Jewish rules but would ask them to avoid three practices that Jews found especially difficult to tolerate. Paul himself didn't see anything immoral in two of the practices (eating meat used in pagan sacrifices and eating meat from which the blood had not been fully drained), but he agreed that Gentile believers could go that far in restraining their freedom for love of their Jewish fellow believers. The third requirement—avoiding sexual immorality—Paul agreed was a moral absolute, not a cultural preference.

This landmark conference gave the transcultural Christian community two bedrock principles. First, the religious rules of one group, no matter how hallowed by time, must not hinder another group's freedom to serve Christ by the Spirit. But second, it may sometimes be appropriate for a group to voluntarily limit its freedom out of love for another group.

PAUL ON THE MOVE AGAIN

The Jerusalem community dispatched two of its own prophets to accompany Paul and Barnabas as they delivered the letter to Antioch. Paul got on so well with one of those prophets, Silas, that a few months later he invited Silas to join him as a new partner. Paul and Barnabas had been planning to revisit the communities they had founded, but a disagreement told them it was time to part ways. So now there were two apostolic teams sent out from Antioch: Barnabas and his nephew Mark, and Paul and Silas.

We know little about Barnabas's movements during the following years, but we know a great deal about Paul's. First he revisited each of his plantings to see if knowing Christ was having the desired effect upon the people's lives. Considering that the fledgling communities had had no one but the Holy Spirit to nurture them for at least eighteen months, it was remarkable how healthy they were.

In the town of Lystra Paul found a teenage believer eager to join the traveling team. As an uncircumcised half-Jew, Timothy had faced identity crises all his life—he was not fully welcome among either Jews or Gentiles. Now for the first time he belonged to someone—Jesus—and despite his shyness he longed to leave his hometown behind to serve his new Master. Paul was glad to have him. But in order to solve Timothy's neither-fish-nor-fowl problem, Paul circumcised him. For Paul the rite no longer had a major spiritual significance, but he was all for anything that would dissolve social barriers to the gospel. If Timothy would be more effective as a full Jew, fine. Circumcising Gentiles, of course, was another matter.

LETTER TO GALATIA

The Jerusalem council didn't end the debate about Christ-plus-Moses. Several years later Paul had to hit the issue head on in Timothy's hometown and the other Galatian communities. The same sorts of law promoters who misled Peter in Antioch confused Gentile believers in Galatia. (See map, page 350.) These Judaizers even questioned whether Paul was an apostle at all.

Paul was of course furious when he heard that Gentile believers were being told to adhere to Jewish religious rules. In a scathing letter he defended his apostleship, rebuked the Galatians for listening to hogwash and laid down the essence of his view of the gospel. The Spirit of God is active in your lives, he told the Galatians, because you believed in Christ, not because you kept religious rules. Christ bore the lawbreaker's curse for you so that you could live freely by the Spirit. Therefore the Spirit will continue to work in you, making you more loving as you actively yield to the Spirit's influence and say no to the impulses of your selfish nature. Persistently obeying the Spirit will accomplish what nitpicking about rules cannot possibly do.

He continued, "As for those agitators [urging circumcision], I wish they would go the whole way and emasculate themselves!" (Galatians 5:12). Paul was on most matters incredibly humble and gentle, but he pulled no punches with people who corrupted the essentials of God's message.

> *He wasn't interested in adapting them to the religious culture he found comfortable. He was interested in renovating their hearts.*

Paul understood what God had been doing ever since Eden. God had chosen a people not to huddle together in their cultural superiority, but to be a lamp in the darkness of paganism. He'd had a purpose in separating Israel geographically, ethnically and culturally. He had to protect a group long enough for some basic concepts (one God, holiness, the Messiah) to take root. Now the time had come to scatter the people of God, to send them equipped with the message of Christ and with the Holy Spirit into the streets and the nations. Just as Jesus had sought out the sick over the healthy, the rough over the nice people, so Paul was committed to the Gentiles with all their unpleasant habits. And he wasn't interested in adapting them to the religious culture he found comfortable. He was interested in renovating their hearts.

~~~~~~

Questions for Reflection and Discussion

1. Why was it so important to stop seeing the message as Jesus-plus-the-Jewish-way-of-life?

2. Was it bad to continue to live by the law of Moses? Explain.

3. What are some ways we today sometimes ask people to adapt to the religious culture we find comfortable rather than focusing on the renovation of their hearts?

31

STRATEGIC BASES

Acts 16:6–19:41;
1 and 2 Thessalonians

*P*aul's mission strategy was a combination of shrewd planning and careful listening to the Holy Spirit. For some weeks Paul, Silas and Timothy plodded uncertainly across Asia Minor as the Spirit kept saying, "Not here" and "Not that way." At last clarity came in a vision: Macedonia.

So they sailed for the rugged land north of Greece and a few days later found themselves in the Roman colony of Philippi. (See map, page 350.) "Roman colony" meant that the town was wall-to-wall Italian war veterans thoroughly bigoted against Jews. There wasn't even a synagogue in town, only a spot outside the gates where a few women gathered to pray.

That was good enough for Paul. He found the prayer spot, and it wasn't long before one of the gathering, a wealthy businesswoman named Lydia, believed the message and invited the team to stay in her home. Her entire extensive household followed her lead. Overnight Philippi had a Christian community.

The biblical account of how the gospel spread from Jerusalem to Rome is called the Acts of the Apostles. It is the second of a two-volume history by a doctor named Luke who became a biblical historian. As you've seen, his first volume—the Gospel of Luke—recounts the good news of Jesus from just before his birth to his resurrection. The trajectory of the story is toward the climactic events in Jerusalem. Acts picks up the story after the resurrection, and its trajectory is outward from Jerusalem.

In that second volume Luke focused on Paul's work because he was a colleague and sometime companion of Paul. He may have been from Antioch, or perhaps the seaport of Troas, or even Philippi. At the point where he describes the sea voyage from Troas to Macedonia, Luke begins to speak of "we" instead of "they." He was an eyewitness to the events at Philippi as well as later events in his book, and it was probably through watching Paul that Luke came to appreciate how the Holy Spirit operated.

In fact, Acts could equally be called the Acts of the Holy Spirit. Luke's first volume describes how Jesus fulfilled his mission to proclaim the good news of the kingdom by the power of the Holy Spirit. His second volume recounts how the Holy Spirit continued that job after Jesus' departure.

Paul was one of the people through whom the Spirit worked. In Philippi, a day's work for Paul included a lynch mob, an arrest on a charge of anti-Roman proselytizing, a merciless flogging and a miraculous escape from prison. Hounded out of that town, Paul and his team hiked another hundred miles to Thessalonica, the capital of Macedonia, where another mob attacked them after a mere three weeks. (See map, page 350.) The seedling community smuggled the team fifty miles away, but some Thessalonian Jews pursued them until Paul had to flee Macedonia entirely.

GREECE

Paul sailed south to Athens while Silas and Timothy stayed in Berea to solidify the work there as best they could. Beautiful Athens held a mystique won five centuries earlier by a generation of brilliant poets, artists, philosophers and statesmen. But now the city's laurels were faded: the best philosophy students sought other universities; the best artists worked elsewhere. Yet second-rate scholars abounded, and what they lacked in creative thinking they more than made up for in pride. They could tell in a minute that Paul lacked the genteel accents of a cultured gentleman and that his doctrines were backwater notions far from the fashionable views of educated men. They were much less concerned with whether his ideas were true than with whether they were "in."

When Silas and Timothy arrived eventually, Paul's mind was on the believers in Macedonia. It was a lot to expect of people who had known

Christ for bare weeks to withstand contempt and even outright violence from their neighbors. Paul grieved to think his children might have collapsed under pressure. So he immediately dispatched Timothy to check on the Thessalonian community and Silas to visit Philippi. He himself set off down the Greek peninsula to Corinth. (See map, page 350.)

Corinth was Greece's political and economic hub, as it commanded both the land route through Greece and the sea route from Italy to anywhere east. Its population of some 250,000 free persons plus 400,000 slaves included every nationality in the known world crowded into a few square miles. The temple of Aphrodite attracted tourists and sailors to its sacred prostitutes, who catered to any taste.

Paul was overjoyed to meet some Jewish believers in Corinth. A couple named Priscilla and Aquila had left Rome a year or so earlier when Emperor Claudius expelled all Jews from that city because of riots instigated by someone named "Chrestus." At least, that was the way the Romans understood it. It's possible that Jewish followers of Christ had reached Rome and caused the same tumult there that Stephen had raised in Jerusalem and that Paul had generated in nearly every city he visited. The Romans could make nothing of this Jewish dispute; all they cared about was public order.

So here in Corinth were some seasoned troops for Paul to ally with. Amazingly, Priscilla and Aquila were leatherworkers just as he was. For a while the new team supported themselves making tents and other leather goods. Their business was an ideal forum for exposing customers and neighbors to Christ, and they could spend their Sabbaths discussing Jesus in the synagogue.

LETTERS TO THESSALONICA

Eventually Silas and Timothy returned from Macedonia with good news and money. The good news was that both Thessalonica and Philippi were standing firm against bitter hostility. The money came from Philippi; the Philippian community wanted to be full partners with Paul in the work of spreading the gospel. They knew their main task was to attract their neighbors to Christ by the way they lived. Paul carried the message across cultural and geographical lines, converted whoever was ready to respond and moved on. Then the local group continued to expand in its sphere of influence. That was the standard strategy. But the Philippians also wanted to support Paul's work with prayer and money. They were his first planting to think of that.

Paul must have been overjoyed to receive this financial gift. For one thing, it meant that the Philippian group was healthy enough to be caring about God's wider purposes, not just personal needs. For another, it meant Paul could devote himself full time to talking about Christ instead of spending long hours at leatherworking.

He may have sent Silas back to Philippi with a thank-you note, but if he did, it no longer exists. We do, however, have two letters Paul sent to Thessalonica about this time; Timothy played courier for the next six months or so.

Those letters gush with Paul's pride over his spiritual children and his longing to see them again. Evidently, news of the Thessalonians' tough faith in the face of suffering had spread in unexpected directions around the empire, for Thessalonica was a busy seaport. In a world full of cults, this group stood out for its love and commitment.

The letters also stress the model Paul tried to set. In 1 Thessalonians he wrote, "We are not trying to please people but God"; "We could have asserted our authority, but we were like young children among you"; "Because we loved you so much, we were delighted to share with you not only the gospel of God but our lives as well"; and "We worked night and day in order not to be a burden to anyone" (1 Thessalonians 2:4, 6-7, 8, 9). Such attitudes, along with the courage to face persecution, would give the Thessalonian believers credibility among their skeptical neighbors. Paul knew preaching like his could not touch those leathery hearts, but the changed life of a kinsman or coworker would gain Christ a hearing. So "how to live in order to please God" (1 Thessalonians 4:1)—an ethical, loving lifestyle—was his theme.

What undergirded that lifestyle was the hope that set the believers apart from the pagans around them. Their response to a loved one's death, for instance, could be confidence rather than despairing grief because they knew Jesus' promises about the future. Some unknown day Jesus would return for his own, the dead ones would be raised to life, and all believers would be caught up to be with Jesus forever. God's people need never say permanent goodbyes. This certainty of resurrection could enable the Thessalonians to resist futile sensuality, face martyrdom calmly and handle tragedy in ways that would make the pagans take notice.

In his second letter, Paul also responded to a prophecy or letter that was supposed to have come from him. Paul was reputedly saying that the day of the Lord—the day of Jesus' return—had already come. No, said Paul, that would not happen until "the man of lawlessness" appeared, proclaimed himself God and convinced many by working miracles. Paul's comments about this man of lawlessness (an evil world leader?) seem cryptic because in his letter he was simply alluding to things he'd said at length in person.

That's the hardest thing about interpreting the letters in the Bible. They were written to specific groups in specific situations, and all we have in each case is a small slice of an ongoing two-way discussion. It's like listening to part of one side of a telephone conversation and trying to figure out what's going on.

Legal Precedent

Compared with his stops in other towns up to this point, Paul spent an unusually long time in Corinth: a year and a half. Perhaps his (or God's) reasoning was that Corinth should become the kind of base for regional outreach that Antioch was in Syria. Trading hubs like these made ideal bases because people and information flowed through them so rapidly.

Paul's success in drawing key members of the Jewish community to Christ (including an important synagogue official and a wealthy Gentile sympathizer) made him a stench in the Jews' nostrils, but they were unable to stage the kind of lynch mob that had been so effective in Thessalonica. Their plan B was to bring charges against Paul in the Roman court. Freedom of religion was not an automatic right. A religion had to be explicitly authorized to be legal. Judaism was legal, and the Way of Jesus had always been seen as a Jewish sect. However, the Corinthian Jews insisted it was not Judaism at all and therefore was not legal.

But to the Roman governor it seemed that both Paul and his accusers were Jews, and their argument had to do with Jewish doctrines. In refusing to try the case, he unknowingly set a precedent. For almost a decade more—a crucial period—the messengers of Christ had a precious legal umbrella. Had Gallio ruled against Paul, Christianity might have become immediately outlawed throughout the empire while it was still possibly too young to survive statewide persecution. A decade later, the fire would be too big to stamp out.

PERSONAL BUSINESS

Although Paul protested imposing Jewish rules on Gentiles, he himself did not turn his back on the customs he grew up with. Toward the end of his stay in Corinth, he made a vow as an act of thanksgiving and devotion to God, as prescribed in Numbers 6:1-21. The vow required that he visit Jerusalem to offer a sacrifice in the temple. Paul evidently saw nothing wrong with such Jewish rites. So he spent the spring and summer of A.D. 52 sailing to Jerusalem, visiting his friends in Antioch, hiking across Asia Minor with stops at the communities he'd planted and finally arriving in Ephesus perhaps as winter was shutting down travel for the year.

EPHESUS

Ephesus promised to be another strategic base for outreach, like Antioch and Corinth. It was the queen of the rich Roman province of Asia. Through her port passed goods from China and the eastern provinces bound for Italy. Wide avenues, huge public buildings and squares and luxurious private homes were all designed to impress tourists. A hundred local aristocrats owned most of the land around Ephesus and controlled the city government. However, the strength of the city was its large class of merchants, business owners and artisans. These people might be barely better fed than day laborers, nearly as wealthy as aristocrats or somewhere in between, but none of them had any say in the government except those who were "clients" of one of the ruling hundred.

The business/working class tended to be politically dissatisfied and interested in any kind of new religion, so it was a fertile field for the messengers of Christ. Back in the spring, Paul had left Priscilla and Aquila in Ephesus on his way east, and by the time he returned in the fall they were already hard at work with their leather business as a base for contacting their target group.

They had met a sophisticated Egyptian Jew who had learned some distorted version of the gospel in his hometown of Alexandria (where one of the empire's premier universities was always churning out the latest in esoteric philosophy). Once Priscilla and Aquila set him straight, Apollos turned out to be a gifted spokesman. He eventually moved on to Corinth to assist in teaching believers and debating unbelieving Jews.

A CITY IN TURMOIL

Paul spent three months appealing to the Ephesian Jews until their hostility drove him to shift his base from the synagogue to a lecture hall. He spent the normal working hours making tents with his partners, and the siesta time of eleven a.m. to four p.m. teaching about Christ. He attracted a great following among the working class for his teaching, backing it up by miraculous healings and exorcisms. Ephesus was a hotbed of the occult, and Paul's miracle working was just what many Ephesians needed to draw their attention. Supernatural power was something they took seriously. New converts burned books of sorcery worth a small fortune (more than two hundred years' wages for a laborer), and news about Christ spread throughout the metropolis and the surrounding area.

In fact, Paul's team was so successful during its two-year stay in this strategic city that its efforts rocked the local economy. In a fragile system like Ephesus, this nearly spelled political disaster. Here's how it went.

Nearly everyone in the business/working class belonged to a club with others of the same profession. Although these were social clubs, not political parties, Rome sometimes outlawed them because they encouraged sedition. The shipwrights or the weavers often rioted when they felt their interests were threatened, for there was no peaceful, legal means of petitioning the government. One day a silversmith named Demetrius decided that his business was slumping because people weren't buying as many silver shrines of Artemis as they used to. He blamed the decline on Paul, who claimed the goddess Artemis was no goddess at all. Demetrius got the members of his club stirred up about this, and soon others in related trades joined them.

The issue wasn't just silverworking. It was a matter of civic pride that touched the number-one industry: tourism. Of the dozens of gaudy temples in Ephesus, the greatest was dedicated to Artemis. It was the biggest tourist attraction in half the empire: resplendent with 127 marble pillars inlaid with gold, crammed with works by the world's leading artists, mobbed with sightseers, especially during the May fertility festival. Idolatry was big business, and Paul's preaching threatened it.

As happens in an already discontented community, it took almost no time for a riot to erupt. Crowds chanted, "Great is Artemis of the Ephesians!" in the streets, and one of Paul's team members was identified, seized and carried bodily into the open-air theater. Paul wanted to address the mob, but he had a friend or two among the city's ruling aristocrats, and they begged him not to enter the theater. In the end, one of the top city officials managed to silence the crowd, but only with threats of Roman intervention. This was no idle warning. Rome was known to suppress riots ruthlessly.

Murder was averted, but Paul knew he had reached the end of his welcome in Ephesus. He and his team had launched a fine, healthy community. It could carry on spreading the gospel to neighbors and co-workers, while the mobile team moved on to untouched ground.

Questions for Reflection and Discussion

1. Paul's strategy was to plant churches in strategic cities and then let those believers spread the story of Jesus among their neighbors. What do you think it was like for those believers once Paul and his team left town?

2. How did Paul expect those believers to draw their neighbors toward Jesus?

3. To what extent does firm hope (or the lack of it) affect the way you think, feel and live?

Part Six

LETTERS
TO THE
CHURCHES

32

◇◇

CRISIS IN CORINTH

Acts 20:1-3; 1 and 2 Corinthians

*I*f Paul had had nothing else to do in Ephesus but make a living and nurture former occultists in the ways of Jesus, he would have had his hands full. But he was also keeping tabs on affairs in the other cities where he'd worked. Most of his seedlings were flourishing, despite hostile soil. But the Corinthian group became a nuisance during his last year in Ephesus.

First came news that a member of the community had a sexual alliance with his father's wife (presumably not his mother). Paul wrote to Corinth with instructions not to associate with someone like that. Blatant incest of a kind that shocked even pagans brought disgrace on the people of God. (This letter from Paul has not survived; we know about it only because he mentions it in 1 Corinthians 5:9.)

Sometime later a believer named Chloe visited Paul in Ephesus and brought more discouraging news. The Corinthian group was splitting into factions, each of which claimed some prominent Christian leader as its authority. Several of the factions expressed contempt for Paul and his instructions. Then three Corinthians brought Paul a letter from the whole community. This letter was full of questions about various issues, but the messengers also reported that the incest was continuing, and class snobbery and other cancers were infecting the church. In response to these ills, Paul dictated a second and very long letter—the one we call 1 Corinthians.

Corinth may have had a reputation for loose morals, but it was also known for money and intellectual pride. It was rich in commerce and prostitution, and its upper classes had pretensions of philosophy. Wealth, loose morals and intellectual pride lay at the root of the troubles in the Corinthian church.

WISDOM AND FOOLISHNESS

Paul tackled the pride first. The anti-Paul factions regarded him as an inferior apostle compared with Peter and Apollos. Paul agreed that both of these men were honorable apostles, but the Corinthians entirely misunderstood what that job implied. To them, an apostle held the community's highest rank, and the members decided who should be accepted as one. The criteria included an air of authority, talent at public speaking, philosophical sophistication and an impressive appearance. Paul's sin was that he lacked stage presence.

He scoffed at this attitude. God turned up his nose at sophistication. He had always deliberately chosen the weak and foolish to fulfill his plan so that nobody would try to take credit. Anybody who thought his brains or talents were earning a place in God's front office needed to go back to sweeping floors.

It wasn't that God's truth was so simple that any fool could understand it. It was that the kind of wisdom necessary to understand it was not intellectual. IQ made no difference. God's truth required the wisdom of humility. Apostleship wasn't some grand rank that one could lord over everybody else. It meant one had to excel at unselfish service, refuse to draw comparisons with others, take no interest in a pecking order and accept weakness, dishonor, hunger, homelessness and slander. In God's upside-down system, the ranking office was to be "scum of the earth" (1 Corinthians 4:13). When the Corinthians understood that, they would be ready to be taught some of God's "sophisticated" truths.

DISCIPLINE

Next Paul explained his views on handling immorality. These people who were so proud of their religious knowledge were still unmoved by a case of open incest. Paul repeated that they should expel the offender from their group until he stopped his offense. This wasn't a matter of a besetting sin that someone was struggling against and occasionally giving in to. It was a coolly chosen lifestyle. The community needed to withdraw its spiritual protection so that Satan could have free access to inflict the natural consequences of flagrant evil. The Corinthians would be doing the man a favor since suffering might be the only thing that would bring him to his senses.

Furthermore, excising the cancer would keep it from infecting others in the group. Paul clarified that when he talked about avoiding immoral people, he didn't mean avoiding immoral pagans. All pagans were immoral, and God's people were called to reach out to them. Rather, he meant avoiding believers (or those who claimed to believe) who practiced gross sin without a blush.

The community needed to be serious about exercising discipline. Paul was shocked that people had to take fellow believers to court to get justice because the community wouldn't even discipline swindlers. He wasn't saying the group should correct every deviation from its norms. Almost always, God was the trainer and judge, not people. But in glaring cases like adultery, idolatry, theft and slander, the community needed to step in.

SEX AND MARRIAGE

Corinthian society made it hard to have healthy views on sex. Visiting prostitutes was standard recreation. Nobody thought twice about it. So Paul had to explain why God forbade something as apparently harmless and fun as extramarital sex.

Free sex isn't harmless, he said. Intercourse isn't just a physical act. It forges a powerful link between the partners. But believers' bodies and spirits are united with Christ. The Holy Spirit permeates not just their spirits but also their bodies. So to take that which belongs to God and join it to a prostitute makes real intimacy with Christ impossible. Physical acts have spiritual consequences. Paul's bottom line: "You are not your own; you were bought at a price. Therefore honor God with your bodies" (1 Corinthians 6:19-20).

However, side by side with those who regarded sex as morally neutral were some in Corinth who considered it base. Greeks considered spirit good and matter evil. Thus, according to them, the human spirit was divine but the body was corrupt. Some people concluded that spiritual persons could therefore do anything they liked with their bodies (the free-sex faction), while others concluded that spiritual persons should deny their bodies' desires, especially those for food and sex. These same two pagan points of view were apparently rife in the Corinthian community. Some people were evidently saying that believers should avoid not only sex outside marriage but also sex within marriage, and even marriage itself. Since Paul was himself unmarried and celibate, they pointed to him as an example of the truly spiritual man. In reply, Paul explained why he recommended his own lifestyle to those who could handle it, but unhesitatingly advised marriage to everyone else.

RIGHTS AND RESPONSIBILITIES

Paul gave these judgments on sex and marriage in response to questions brought by his three visitors. Another question had to do with eating meat sacrificed to idols. Was it okay or not? The issue was important because it was hard to avoid such meat in Corinth. For one thing, nearly all dinner parties, trade association meetings and other social occasions included some dedication to the patron deity of the gathering. Many parties and meetings were actually held in temples.

Furthermore, nearly all butchers (except Jewish ones) sold sacrificed meat. Many were even attached to temples. When an animal was offered in a temple, a small portion was burnt for the god, the worshipers got some (they usually ate it right there in a dinner party) and the priests got the rest. What the priests couldn't use they sold to the butchers. Since only the best animals could be offered to the gods, the best meat was more than likely from a sacrifice.

In order to avoid idol meat, one would have to shop only at Jewish butchers (or Christian ones if there were any) and never attend any social occasions with pagans. For anyone whose livelihood depended in part on business dinners or trade association meetings, this was out of the question. For anyone who cared about social standing, it was absurd.

Some of the Corinthian Christians reasoned that because the idols were not real gods there was no reason to sabotage their businesses, their social standing and their diets. These enlightened ones may have been the wealthy and educated who were used to eating meat daily in ordinary, nonreligious situations. However, others found it hard to shake the idea that the idols they had been worshiping all their lives were real, powerful entities who somehow contaminated the meat offered to them. Among this group were probably the poorer members of the community whose daily diet was vegetarian and who normally saw meat only in temple feasts. For them, the association between meat and idolatry was strong. This group couldn't help feeling that by eating meat offered to idols they were defiling themselves, and by attending parties in temples they were countenancing the worship there.

Paul went to great lengths to outline the principles behind eating or not eating idol meat. He wanted to leave his readers not just with a yes-or-no rule, but with standards they could apply widely.

First, love is more important than knowledge. Yes, idols are nothing, and Paul himself usually wouldn't hesitate to eat idol meat. But if somebody doesn't know what we know, we shouldn't just sneer at that person, he said. We should voluntarily limit our freedom out of love for weak believers who would be tempted to violate their consciences and imitate us. Encouraging them to do this would be very harmful. On the other hand, we should refuse to give in to pressure from arrogant people who are tempted not to imitate, but to complain and judge.

Second, serving God is more important than exercising rights. As an apostle, Paul had the right to financial support from the people he converted and trained. But he voluntarily declined that right and worked to support himself so that money matters wouldn't keep people from coming to Christ. Paul was always ready to forgo his own preferences in order to draw someone to Jesus. He ate meat with the meat eaters and vegetables with the vegetarians. Moral standards he would not sacrifice, but with social customs he was flexible.

Third, purity is more important than comfort, and self-deception is easy. In the midst of liberty, Paul exercised self-discipline so that he wouldn't be overtaken by addictions. Paul lived constantly like an athlete in training, keeping his body and spirit in shape for serving God. He pointed to Israel's history as proof that sharing in idol feasts led easily to idolatry, loose sex and coldness toward God. Those strong Corinthians who were so sure they could attend dinner parties at temples and not be tempted to share in the worship, drunkenness and sex that took place at these parties should think again. Were they really as strong as they thought? For if they crossed the line and dabbled in paganism, they had better be clear on the implications: they were worshiping demons.

CORPORATE WORSHIP

Paul also rebuked the rich members of the community for making a mockery of the Lord's Supper. At that time, believers commemorated Jesus' last meal with his disciples by eating a full meal together, which the community came to call its "love feast" (Jude 12). The meal was supposed to be like a potluck dinner, with each member bringing something to share. But in Corinth, the rich were arriving early with the fine meats and wines they were used to and going ahead without the rest. The slaves and artisans arrived later when they had gotten off work. They had to make do with the scanty food they were able to bring.

When pagan aristocrats gave feasts, they usually invited their entire households. The slaves and servants received smaller portions and cheaper wine than the higher-class guests. Evidently the rich members of the church considered this appropriate in the love feast as well. Paul considered it sacrilege. The love feast was a holy celebration, a foretaste of the kingdom wedding banquet, a profound sharing in the very blood and body Jesus offered for humankind. It was sitting down to dinner with God himself. Like the meal Israel's elders shared to seal the old covenant, this meal bound those who ate it in union with each other and Christ. To treat it lightly was to

> *The love feast was a holy celebration, a foretaste of the kingdom wedding banquet, a profound sharing in the very blood and body Jesus offered for humankind. It was sitting down to dinner with God himself.*

spit in God's face, and Paul attributed some of the illnesses and deaths among the Corinthians to this travesty.

SPIRITUAL GIFTS

Another knotty problem had to do with the way people treated abilities they received from the Holy Spirit. People with certain spectacular gifts were claiming higher status than those who lacked them. Paul came up with an analogy to explain what God was really doing.

The community of believers, he said, is like a human body. Each person is a limb or organ of the body. No organ is unnecessary, even those that seem to have less glorious functions. God's Spirit works through each member to fulfill the function he or she is designed for.

When the Spirit enables someone to do something useful for the body, it is not so that the person can be exalted. It is so that a necessary job can get done. Bringing the presence of Christ to a dark world requires some supernatural activities. Believers should do the activities they are equipped for without comparing themselves to others. Everybody needs everybody else if the whole job is going to get done. Love, not flashiness, is the standard by which to measure every gift.

RESURRECTION

The last big issue Paul addressed in this long letter was resurrection. When Christ returns, his people will be raised from death to live with him forever. Some in Corinth were denying that physical resurrection was possible or even desirable. After all, if bodies are nasty and corrupt, as most Greeks believed, wouldn't it be much more spiritual to be a disembodied immortal soul? And how could a body that gets sick and old be suitable for eternal life?

First of all, said Paul, if there's no resurrection, then Jesus wasn't resurrected either and we might as well be pagans. Physical resurrection is a cornerstone of the gospel.

Second, there's no need to dismiss resurrection because of crude ideas of what it would be like. It's not a matter of coming back to life in the body you had when you died, old or crippled. Like a seed that is buried in one physical form and sprouts into a startlingly different one, so we die in one form and will be raised in another: imperishable, glorious, a "spiritual body" (1 Corinthians 15:44).

Death is the great terror behind every human fear. But for Christians, death holds no threat. Paul wrote,

> When the perishable has been clothed with the imperishable, and the mortal with immortality, then the saying that is written will come true: "Death has been swallowed up in victory."
>
> "Where, O death, is your victory?
>   Where, O death, is your sting?" (1 Corinthians 15:54-55)

The one who clings to the resurrected Christ can face anything.

A GIFT FOR THE MOTHER COMMUNITY

Paul closed with some personal business. Years earlier, he had promised the apostles in Jerusalem that he would "continue to remember the poor" (Galatians 2:10). He had brought a contribution from the Gentile churches to the Jerusalem church during a famine, and the apostles wanted him to continue to do this. Jerusalem was a poor city. The Jews there were supported partly by contributions from Jews living abroad, but the followers of Jesus had no access to those funds. They needed help from their spiritual offspring, and Paul was glad to aid them.

Paul had decided to take up a collection among his communities in order to acknowledge the debt the Gentiles owed the mother community in Jerusalem, to show that these Gentiles were genuine believers and to knit the Jewish and Gentile groups together. He planned to visit Corinth on his way from Ephesus to Macedonia, so he asked the Corinthians to have their contribution ready when he arrived. There was no set fee. It was between them and God what they wanted to give.

AMBASSADORS OF RECONCILIATION

Paul dispatched this lengthy message and asked Timothy to drop in at Corinth on his way back from Macedonia to see how his letter was received. Timothy was rudely rebuffed, and when Paul himself visited Corinth briefly, the defiant factions humiliated him. Paul wrote a severe letter "out of great distress and anguish of heart" (2 Corinthians 2:4) and sent it with Titus, another of his young associates. This anguished letter is now lost.

Paul left Ephesus with the issue still unresolved, so, contrary to his former plan, he went to Macedonia to gather the contribution for Jerusalem while Corinth hopefully cooled down. There Titus met him with good news: the Corinthians had repented of their rebellion. Paul quickly sent Titus back with a letter that was full of affection but also contained a stern warning—the letter we call 2 Corinthians.

Not that there wasn't still tension. Paul's adversaries were still saying that by changing his itinerary, Paul proved that he couldn't be trusted. And they still hinted that he wasn't a genuine apostle and was probably pocketing the money he was supposedly gathering for the people in Jerusalem.

In response, Paul defended at length his trustworthiness and genuineness. But his defense was much less self-centered than Christ-centered. Paul exalted "the God of all comfort" who rescued his team from life-threatening pressures in Ephesus, the God who had commissioned and equipped him for his job and who continued to set the agenda and take care of his needs. Paul saw himself as a common clay pot holding a priceless treasure: the message of Christ, who transforms those who behold him into glorious beings like himself.

Paul wanted the Corinthians to taste his passion for Jesus and his mission. "Christ's love compels us," he wrote (2 Corinthians 5:14). If Jesus truly did die for humankind and was really raised from death, then there is no longer any need for people to devote their lives to self-seeking ends. On the contrary, it makes no sense to do anything other than serve Christ in relieved gratitude. All of the reasons for self-focus—fear of death, of failure, of rejection; craving for love, for security, for mattering in the universe—all have been rendered pointless by the Cross.

The hope of resurrection transfixed Paul and made him capable of anything:

> Therefore we do not lose heart. Though outwardly we are wasting away, yet inwardly we are being renewed day by day. For our light and momentary troubles are achieving for us an eternal glory that far outweighs them all. So we fix our eyes not on what is seen, but on what is unseen,

since what is seen is temporary, but what is unseen is eternal. (2 Corinthians 4:16-18)

PAUL IN CORINTH

Titus and two other well-respected believers carried this letter to Corinth, so that when Paul and the delegation to Jerusalem arrived, the Corinthians would be ready to receive them and to turn over the funds they had raised for the poor. He didn't want the Corinthians to look unprepared, selfish or in disarray in front of other believers they had never met. Titus's mission was apparently successful, for Paul's group stayed three months in Corinth until some Jews plotted to kill him and forced him to leave.

◇◇

Questions for Reflection and Discussion

1. Which of the issues the Corinthian church struggled with are ones that you or your church struggles with? Choose one to focus on, and see if you can put Paul's views into your own words.

2. What does Paul say about how we should use our freedom?

3. Why does it matter that we are raised from the dead with bodies, not just disembodied souls?

33

PAUL'S MANIFESTO

Romans

*E*ven as Paul was heading east to Jerusalem, his thoughts were already turning westward. He had been serving as an apostle for a decade, and he felt his work in the eastern half of the empire was fulfilled. He had planted strategic bases from which central Asia Minor, western Asia Minor, Macedonia and Greece could be reached. (See map, page 350.) Local leaders were equipped to spearhead internal care and outreach. So Paul looked to a region that had never heard the gospel: Spain, the farthest end of the empire.

On the way to Spain, Paul hoped to satisfy a longing to visit Rome. Although legally a citizen, he had never seen the famed imperial capital. A stay there would be a chance to meet members of the sizable network of home-based communities of believers already flourishing there. He hoped the Roman believers would help provide funds and a base of operations for his mission to Spain.

However, he had met only a few of the hundreds of believers living in Rome. They were most interested in spreading faith in Jesus among Jews, and Paul was the famous apostle to the Gentiles. Why should they support his work in Spain? Also, he could not journey westward until he finished his errand in Jerusalem. So during his three-month sojourn in Corinth in the spring of A.D. 57, he dictated a long letter introducing himself to the Roman communities. It turned out to be his greatest treatise on his understanding of the gospel.

ROME

The first followers of Jesus in Rome were probably Jews. Business, religious pilgrimage and pleasure carried Jews back and forth between Rome, Jerusalem, Antioch and other cities. There may even have been Roman Jews among the first Pentecost converts. Priscilla and Aquila had belonged to the Roman community of believers before Paul met them in Corinth.

All Jews were expelled from Rome in A.D. 49 because of the riots caused by "Chrestus." But a few years later they were back, and by 57 there were also a substantial number of Gentile believers in Rome. Predictably, the multiethnic composition of the communities of Jesus was causing tension.

Paul's understanding of the gospel was only one of many circulating around the empire. Only a very few of the Roman believers had ever heard from Paul what he believed. Others had presumably heard rumors of his ideas, probably with certain distortions. But like believers everywhere, the Romans were working out a view of the gospel as well as they could, with the Holy Spirit and the Old Testament to guide them. Some approached their relationship with Jesus from an orthodox Jewish point of view, others from an idolatrous past and others from one of the many Jewish sects with various interpretations of the Old Testament and Jewish tradition.

Consequently, Paul decided that the best way to introduce himself was to explain carefully what he actually believed. This would clear up any confusing rumors and bring any crucial disagreements to the surface. His readers would get a chance to chew on his ideas and even discard some of their false ones before they saw him in person. When they read how he handled some of the personal issues they were facing, they would get to evaluate what they thought of him as an apostle. After all, they were not automatically obliged to recognize his authority. He had been appointed by nobody but God, and unless the Holy Spirit showed them who he was, they had no reason to back him.

THE RIGHTEOUSNESS OF GOD

Paul chose as his theme the righteousness of God. Righteousness was an old biblical concept: the state of being in right relationship with someone, fulfilling one's covenant responsibilities. It also meant legally in the right, or declared "not guilty." The gospel, said Paul, reveals how a person can be restored to a reconciled, intimate, covenant relationship with God. It tells how one can become God's loyal subject, adopted child, spouse and friend.

Paul laid out his explanation with his eye on both Gentile and Jewish believers in Rome. First he defined why both Jews and Gentiles had broken relationships with God. On the one hand, by choosing the delusion of idolatry over gratitude to their Creator, the pagans had mired themselves in sexual perversion, greed, murder and every other vice. It was a fair portrait of life on the streets of Rome. On the other hand, by trusting in their performance of religious duties, the Jews had entangled themselves in a subtler trap: pride. They thought themselves better than the pagans because they not only abstained from debauchery but also lived the lifestyle prescribed by Moses.

Now to Paul, there was nothing wrong with living according to the law of Moses. It was a cultural form given by God to shape a nation, and it had its advantages. But the primary covenant responsibility to God had always been to trust him, even when it is confusing or costly. To trust him to keep his promises. To trust that his standard of right and wrong is true and good, not based on his selfish interests. To trust that his wisdom is greater than ours. This was the faith for which God had declared Abraham righteous long before the law was given to Moses. This was the faith Jesus had praised in the humble people he healed and forgave. This, not conformity to Jewish subculture, was the key to a right covenant standing before God.

Praying, keeping the Sabbath, performing the rites, eating the right foods—these weren't wrong ways to live, but they weren't the essence of a right relationship with God. You could recognize a real friend of God by inner transformation, what Moses called a circumcised heart (Deuteronomy 30:6; Romans 2:29).

Here was the mistake too many Jews made. They thought the proper response of gratitude for God's love was to keep Moses' rules. But the response God wanted went much deeper.

So the law had served its primary purpose: It was an objective standard by which one could see plainly that both Jew and Gentile were falling short. With that fact clear, God had provided a way to restore the broken relationship. Jesus had borne the full weight of human evil, so there were no outstanding debts for a person who chose to accept Jesus' sacrifice. By swearing allegiance to Jesus, one changed sides in the war between God and Satan. Adam had chosen Satan's side, so his children were all born into rebellion. But anyone who changed sides by choosing Jesus received the same standing with God that Jesus had: God became Father and friend.

> *They thought the proper response of gratitude for God's love was to keep Moses' rules. But the response God wanted went much deeper.*

LIVING BY THE SPIRIT

Okay, so God is happy when we bet our lives on Christ rather than on a religious system. Does that mean we can do whatever we want? No, Paul insisted. Remember the slime the pagans live in. They're in bondage to all sorts of addictions and delusions. Doing whatever you want turns out to be a prison. Obeying God is freedom. You can choose evil freely once, even twice, but before you know it, evil has wrapped its tentacles around you and you've lost the power to say no.

Furthermore, consider what it means to bet your life on Christ. The public ceremony by which a person declared allegiance to Jesus was baptism. It was like a funeral: a public declaration that someone was dead. In this case, one was joining Christ in his death. Symbolically, baptism was death by drowning—death to one's past evil, self-centered life. When one came up out of that water, one was choosing to be joined to Christ in his resurrection, choosing to pursue freedom from compulsions, idolatries and other slaveries. Not freedom to do whatever one's lowest nature craved (that was a fast route back to bondage), but freedom to serve the God of life.

Under the old covenant, the only way ordinary people could serve God was by keeping the law by their own effort. A few prophets and leaders had the power of the Spirit for service, but they were rare. The trouble was, the law set that inner standard: not only must we not steal, but we must not even covet. And the natural rebelliousness of humans responded by going crazy with covetousness. People who really wanted to please God could manage the external rules—they could be model religious persons—but they'd shipwreck every time on those inner attitudes. They were utterly enslaved to covetousness, or pride or anger.

Thank God, said Paul, that Christ's death made possible not only a restored relationship, but also the process of inner transformation. Friends of God are able to have God's Spirit actually live inside of them. The Spirit's power is constantly available to help them choose what God wants; all they must do is set their minds and wills on Christ, to make a moment-by-moment choice to be united with, directed toward and impelled by the Spirit of God. In the beginning it can be a gut-wrenching choice, but bondage slowly releases its claws with each decision. It's not just that the Spirit adds that extra bit of grit that was lacking in the willpower of believers; it's that the Spirit makes what was utterly impossible fully possible (though not necessarily easy).

Paul couldn't get over the honor of the relationship with God that the Spirit made possible. He was overwhelmed that he could call the Lord of the universe Abba—Papa. When the kingdom appeared in its fullness, Paul looked forward to a share in it alongside his brother Jesus. He longed, he groaned with the cosmos to be freed from bondage to decay. The hope of resurrection gripped him. And more than resurrection: the goal of the Spirit's work in God's children was nothing less than to make them like the Son of God in perfect moral beauty.

GOD'S FAITHFULNESS

A question lingered: If the gospel is the culmination of God's work among the Israelites, why have so few Jews responded, while Gentiles have responded in large numbers? Has God abandoned his chosen people, broken his promises to them?

No. Paul pointed out that there had always been many in Israel who disregarded God and a few who truly trusted him. There had always been a remnant who clung to God while the rest wandered. That remnant persisted in Paul's day, and God stuck by his promises to Israel through them. Paul and other Jewish believers like him were proof that a faithful remnant still lived to inherit the promise. They inherited it not because of their ethnicity or their devotion to Jewish customs, but because of God's free kindness. And as for the many Jews who rejected Christ, God was bringing good even out of that. For if most Jews had recognized Jesus as Messiah in Paul's day, the people of God would have been over-whelmingly Jewish and it would have been much harder for Gentiles to retain their Gentile culture while becoming believers. The gospel would have had a much harder time penetrating Gentile society. Amazingly, Jewish unbelief inadvertently opened the gospel to pagans. But Paul warned Gentile believers not to look down on the Jews. He foresaw a day when Jewish unbelief would have served its purpose, and God would turn Israel's heart back to himself.

Israel's calling had always been for the sake not just of Israel but the nations. They had preserved the Scriptures and produced the Messiah. And God had a future planned for them too.

LIVING SACRIFICES

So much for God's supposed promise-breaking. Paul concluded his discourse by outlining how one should live in light of God's mercy. If Jewish subculture wasn't the standard, what exactly were the qualities that the Holy Spirit wanted to instill in God's people?

Rather than offering the right temple sacrifices, Paul wanted his readers to be like temple sacrifices. Like the animal on Moses' bronze altar, lay out your life as an offering to God. Live with sacrificial, open-hearted, wildly generous and joyful love for friend and enemy alike.

Such love includes mundane duties like obeying the civil government and maintaining sexual and emotional discipline. It also includes working out the tensions of a diverse community. Believers in Rome didn't all have the same convictions about whether to be vegetarian, keep Sabbaths and holy days, abstain from wine and so on. Paul's counsel was much like what he told the Corinthians: Know what you personally can and can't handle. Know what God's written Word says about moral standards. Based on these facts, form your own convictions. Don't look down on the weak, but let love for them limit your freedom. Don't judge those who disagree with you or impose your standards on them.

It was a heavy letter for an introduction. And Paul was straightforward about his agenda—his hope that the Romans would be his partners in ministry. He also begged their prayers for protection on his trip to Jerusalem. Something told him that trouble awaited him there.

Questions for Reflection and Discussion

1. What is righteousness?

2. Paul claimed that the primary response God had always wanted from people was faith or trust: trust in God even when it's costly, trust in his wisdom and his commands. Where do you see that in God's dealings with Adam, Noah, Abraham, Moses, David?

3. What does it mean to obey God in the power of the Holy Spirit?

34

PAUL IN PRISON

Acts 20:4–28:31, Philippians,
Colossians, Philemon, Ephesians

Paul was an international pariah in his ethnic group. That spring of A.D. 57 he fled Corinth because they were trying to murder him. On his way east he visited with the elders of the Ephesian community to say goodbye; he expected never to see them again because of trouble awaiting him in Jerusalem. Each time Paul's ship docked at a port where disciples of Jesus lived, the Holy Spirit warned them that danger awaited him in Jerusalem, and they begged him not to go. But he insisted the Spirit wanted him to go, even if it meant death.

The elders of the Jerusalem community greeted Paul's Gentile delegation warmly. But however much they appreciated the money he brought, they were more concerned with how Paul's arrival would affect their work. It was rumored that Paul was teaching Jews not to keep the law. This was probably false—he had said only that keeping the law's rituals didn't affect their standing with God. Unless they were trying to reach Gentiles, he didn't mind their cultural preferences. But Paul's own freedom to ignore the law had undoubtedly affected Jewish believers who knew him. In any case, the Jerusalem elders asked Paul to finance an expensive sacrificial rite for some men as a sign that he was still a practicing Jew.

He was glad to do that. But one day some Jews who had seen him in Ephesus noticed him in the temple. They incited a riot, accusing him of bringing Gentiles into the sacred temple precincts. The penalty for that was death. Only the intervention of the Roman troop commander saved Paul from a lynching.

The commander granted Paul's request to address the crowd, and they listened with fascination as he described his encounter with Jesus on the Damascus road. But when he got to the part where Jesus sent him to the Gentiles, they went wild. The commander had no idea what was going on, so he had Paul dragged off for questioning. He tried to get the Sanhedrin to make a coherent charge, but Paul threw the Jewish council into confusion by saying, "My brothers, I am a Pharisee, descended from Pharisees. I stand on trial because of the hope of the resurrection of the dead" (Acts 23:6). The Pharisees on the council began to defend him staunchly (they had a longstanding dispute with the Sadducees about resurrection).

The dispute degenerated into a brawl, and the commander was obliged to have Paul carried out to keep the Sadducees and Pharisees from tearing him apart between them. The next day Paul's nephew informed the commander of a Jewish plot to assassinate Paul, so the commander had this perplexing but important prisoner moved to the Roman governor's headquarters in Caesarea.

Waiting in Caesarea

Governor Felix was the first former slave ever to become governor of a Roman province. His brother was an imperial toady. Felix kept Paul under house arrest for two years without settling his case. He didn't want to release Paul, even though he knew the charges were absurd, because he feared upsetting the Sanhedrin. Also, he hoped Paul would offer him a bribe. But Felix wouldn't condemn Paul to death because something about his message scared and fascinated him. Occasionally the governor sent for Paul to hear him talk about Jesus, but statements about self-control and judgment for wrongdoers made Felix too uncomfortable to face what he feared was true.

When Felix's brother finally fell from favor in A.D. 59 and could no longer protect him, Felix was recalled to Rome for mishandling riots, overusing violence and other acts of incompetence and corruption. Because he couldn't afford to make the Jews any madder than they already were, he left Paul in prison.

Felix was replaced by Governor Festus. Three days after he arrived in the province, representatives of the Sanhedrin arrived to press charges against Paul and ask that he be transferred to Jerusalem for trial. But Paul, knowing that a trial in Jerusalem meant death and that God wanted him to testify in Rome, appealed for trial before Caesar. It was his right as a Roman citizen, so Festus agreed.

To ROME

Sailing westward was tedious because the prevailing winds blew eastward and rudders hadn't been invented. It was already October before Paul, two companions and his guard reached Crete. Sailing in autumn was hazardous bordering on insane, and Paul prophesied trouble, but the harbor into which the ship had limped was unsuitable for wintering over. When a gentle south wind blew in, the pilot thought he had a prime chance of reaching a better harbor. Suddenly a northeaster swept through and enveloped the ship in a two-week virtual hurricane. The crew threw the cargo overboard and rationed the food. Nothing helped. At last Paul coolly added a second prophecy that everyone would survive because his God wanted him to testify before Caesar.

A few days later the crew was able to ram the ship aground on the island of Malta. There Paul further amazed his guards. He sustained no ill effect from the deadly bite of a viper. He healed sick Maltese by laying his hands on them and praying for them. In response the Maltese entertained Paul and the others from the ship generously all winter. But Paul's guard took the first vessel that left harbor the next March, and in a few weeks Paul was under house arrest in Rome.

The first thing Paul did was contact the local Jewish leaders to give them their chance at accepting Jesus as their Messiah. As usual, few heeded him, but he now felt free to turn to the Gentiles. For two years Paul worked at full steam while under arrest in a house he had to rent with contributions from friends.

LETTER TO PHILIPPI

Under house arrest Paul had to pay rent and buy food. But the believers in Rome were likely reluctant to support a missionary accused of an imperial crime. It was not illegal to be a disciple of Jesus, but it was dangerous to be associated with enemies of the state, so prudent people kept at arm's length from someone Rome suspected of agitation and treason.

The believers in Philippi had sent financial support when Paul planted the community in Thessalonica (Philippians 4:16) and again in Corinth. They were Paul's most loyal financial supporters. At some point, however, they lost track of him, perhaps after he set off for Jerusalem with their gift for the poor. But when they heard that Paul was in financial straits, they dispatched one of their members, Epaphroditus, to bring Paul some cash and take care of him while he was under arrest. Sadly, Epaphroditus became so severely ill that Paul felt he should send him back to Philippi to finish recovering. He sent Epaphroditus with a letter explaining the unexpected return, thanking the Philippians for their gift, informing them about his circumstances and exhorting them to respond to their none-too-pleasant situation in a way befitting servants of Christ.

PARTNERS

The way these friends were always there when Paul needed them, always eager to support him with prayer and money, always avidly serving Christ in their own sphere as Paul was in his—all this told Paul they understood what partnership or community was supposed to be about. The affection between them and Paul had deep roots born of time and shared commitments.

He reassured them that his imprisonment was actually advancing the gospel because as soldiers took shifts guarding him, they were forced to observe the community of Christ in action. By now the whole imperial guard had heard the gospel. Likewise, Paul urged the Philippians to use their shaky situation to the best advantage. If the hyperpatriotic Roman colonists of Philippi made life rough for followers of an obscure Jewish cult, the believers' very response to this mistreatment would make the pagans sit up and take notice. The attitude that would grab attention most would be the selfless, humble unity that was possible only among those who were letting the Holy Spirit change them into the likeness of Jesus.

Only people who understood that Jesus had emptied himself of his rights for the sake of the humans he loved could "do nothing out of

STORY OF STORIES

selfish ambition or vain conceit." "Rather," he told them, "in humility value others above yourselves" (Philippians 2:3). Paul wasn't urging people to be doormats but to exercise the same tough-minded unself-ishness Jesus had displayed. When unbelievers saw a group of people free of complaining and arguing, that would be positive proof that Christ was more than just another god.

JOY

Another attitude that would attract the pagans was joy. How many of those hard-bitten colonists knew joy? But the people of God had every reason to rejoice because they could release their anxieties to one who had the love and power to take care of his own. In frank prayer born of genuine trust, God's people could find peace in the midst of danger as well as the daily grind of life's hassles.

Paul added a warning against listening to the circumcision party, who urged believers to substitute rules for relationship. His years of flawlessly obeying religious rules had never given him anything of value. All of his self-powered achievements were worthless compared to the "surpassing worth of knowing Christ Jesus my Lord, for whose sake I have lost all things" (Philippians 3:8).

In fact, as much as Paul appreciated his friends' gift, he wanted them to know that he valued it more as a love token than as survival funds. Life was hard in Philippi for someone who allied with Jesus, and Paul hoped to set an example of contentment in the face of hardship. He wrote, "I know what it is to be in need, and I know what it is to have plenty. I have learned the secret of being content in any and every situation, whether well fed or hungry, whether living in plenty or in want. I can do all this through him who gives me strength" (Philippians 4:12-13). Strong words from a man who could have been a prosperous rabbi but who had chosen prison, lean living, even shipwreck and imminent execution.

CRISIS IN COLOSSE

Sometime during his imprisonment in either Caesarea or Rome, Paul received a visitor from the believing community in the town of Colosse.

Colosse was a small cosmopolitan city in Asia, less than a hundred miles from Ephesus. Originally known for its wool industry, the town had declined and had been surpassed by Laodicea, ten miles to the west, and Hierapolis, twelve miles to the northwest.

The community at Colosse was probably planted by Epaphras, one of Paul's converts at Ephesus. Paul had never been to Colosse, but Epaphras apparently felt that the town fell under Paul's apostolic jurisdiction. When trouble brewed, Epaphras sought Paul's advice.

The gospel had been flourishing in Colosse until some false teachers arrived and confused the young believers by mixing ideas from pagan cults with the gospel. Unable to combat this cancer alone, Epaphras appealed to Paul for help. Paul did the only thing he could: write a letter to help the Colossian believers see the truth.

First, the false teachers claimed that Christ was less than God, on the level of a created angel. Paul stressed that Jesus "is the image of the invisible God. . . . For in him all things were created. . . . For God was pleased to have all his fullness dwell in him" (Colossians 1:15-19).

Second, the teachers said true enlightenment required knowledge of certain secrets. Paul countered that the only secret anybody needed to know was God's plan to place Christ's life in anybody who welcomed it, Gentiles included.

Third, the troublemakers taught believers to practice ascetic rules about food, sex and an amalgam of Jewish ritual. "Do not handle! Do not taste! Do not touch!" (Colossians 2:21), they said. Those rules had something to do with the worship of angels or spirit beings—they were perhaps based on a belief that rituals and physical self-denial put a person in harmony with or appeased the spiritual forces. In Greek culture, it was commonly believed that the material world was essentially evil, or at best indifferent. Therefore, the body was evil and had to be controlled. Also, between matter and the pure divine essence there supposedly lay a host of spiritual powers that ruled the world. Religion was largely aimed at pleasing those powers.

Against these ideas Paul insisted that the only thing necessary for intimacy with God was commitment to the crucified and resurrected Jesus. On the cross Jesus defeated all the anti-God spirit beings, so the Colossians had nothing to fear from them. As for rules to control the body, too often they failed to affect what really counted: lust, greed and selfishness in the heart.

The real key to holy living, said Paul, is to set your mind on the agenda and activities of God's kingdom. Invest your energy in putting to death real evil in yourself: lust and sexual immorality, evil desires and greed, malice and lying and slander. Invest in seeking Christlike qualities such as compassion, forgiveness and peace. Paul believed these were attainable qualities (though not overnight) for people filled with Christ, in love with Christ, drawing on Christ's power.

Paul did lay down a few rules for the Colossians. They had to do with how to run a household, and they were remarkable in that strict hierarchical society. Not only should wives submit to husbands, but husbands should love their wives and not be harsh with them. Not only should children obey their parents, but fathers should take care not to embitter their children. Not only should slaves obey and work diligently, but masters should be fair. Compared to the practice in most pagan homes where wives, children and slaves were mere property, this was radical thinking.

A lifestyle that fit the society but treated everyone with dignity was important for two reasons. First, it encouraged harmony in the community. But second, it made the gospel attractive to outsiders. Paul commissioned the Colossians not only to pray for his ministry but also to keep reaching out to their pagan neighbors: "Be wise in the way you act toward outsiders; make the most of every opportunity. Let your conversation be always full of grace, seasoned with salt, so that you may know how to answer everyone" (Colossians 4:5-6).

A PERSONAL INTERVENTION

One of Paul's team members, Tychicus, carried this letter from Rome (or Caesarea) to Colosse. With him went a new believer named Onesimus. This Onesimus was a slave of another Colossian believer, Philemon. Onesimus had apparently stolen something from Philemon, then had run away—crimes punishable by death. However, somehow he had found his way to Paul and, under his influence, become a follower of Jesus.

Onesimus wanted to stay with Paul and feared returning to Colosse to face his master. But Paul wanted to give Philemon the chance to do something Godlike. So he sent Onesimus back with a letter for Philemon, asking him to do what God had done: free Onesimus from slavery and accept him as family rather than as a servant.

How could Philemon say no? He owed Paul his own life (a fact that Paul did not blush to point out), and Onesimus was a brother now. God himself had freed Philemon from slavery and an unpayable debt; could he hold Onesimus to the letter of the law? Paul didn't attack slavery as an immoral institution on humanistic grounds. He merely laid the situation out in plain colors and let Philemon judge for himself: is it even conceivable for one child of God to treat another as unforgivable or inferior?

IN CHRIST

Tychicus and Onesimus carried another letter from Paul besides the ones to Philemon and the Colossians. This one reads more formally than Paul's often ironic and blunt personal notes. Although his letter is addressed to the community in Ephesus, Paul writes as though many of his readers are strangers to him (he says he's heard of their faith, not seen it). Probably this letter was meant to circulate among communities throughout western Asia Minor, many of which Paul had never visited. In musical phrases, it sketches the glorious place believers have in God's eternal purposes and the lives they should live in light of their identity.

Ever since he decided to create, God had one overarching plan, Paul said: "to bring unity to all things in heaven and on earth under Christ" (Ephesians 1:10). His idea was a choreographed dance with the Son of God as center and leader—the source from whom would flow the patterns and rhythms of relationships.

But some of God's spirit creatures followed the snake in rebellion and ensnared men and women into their corruption. Instead of a grand ball there was war. Hostility devoured souls. Yet God was not thwarted. All along his plan had been to teach his creatures—especially those without bodies who inhabited the heavens—something about him they could never otherwise understand. They knew his power and holiness, but certain areas of his wisdom eluded them. Above all, his love was a mystery.

> *They knew his power and holiness, but certain areas of his wisdom eluded them. Above all, his love was a mystery.*

The cosmos watched as God painstakingly groomed a family generation after generation: Seth, Noah, Shem, Abraham, Isaac, Jacob . . . Jesus. The line had survived by a hairsbreadth more than once. But when the time was ripe, the King invaded earth to begin reversing the process of hostility. First he reconciled humans to God by taking their penalty upon himself. Then he reconciled these freed ones to each other by dissolving the barriers between them. Even pagans were now welcomed into this realm that Paul called "in Christ." Christ united warring factions into one body, one community, with himself as its head.

The spirit beings who well knew human hearts must have gaped. Who would have thought Christ could weld such selfish renegades together? This is the primary reason the community exists on earth: God's "intent was that now, through the church, the manifold wisdom of God should be made known to the rulers and authorities in the heavenly realms" (Ephesians 3:10).

Therefore, Paul went on, it is crucial that we live up to our noble calling. Not only is the pagan world looking on to judge Christ by the quality of our love and unity, but so are the heavenly beings. Our reason for existence is not only to be ambassadors of reconciliation, drawing unbelievers to Christ through the quality of our lives, it is also to display God's greatness to the universe through that same quality of living. God has raised us from the sludge and made us joint heirs of Christ's wealth. How can we not respond?

Paul prayed that God "may strengthen you with power through his Spirit in your inner being . . . that you, being rooted and established in love, may have power . . . to grasp . . . the love of Christ" (Ephesians 3:16-18). Only a person who is experiencing Christ's love and the Spirit's work has what it takes to live this calling.

This "unity of the Spirit" (Ephesians 4:3) isn't uniformity in which everyone thinks the same thoughts, lives the same lifestyle, does the same things, enjoys the same activities. It's a body, a living organism in which each part has function and responsibility. The body doesn't work as long as some members are mature but the rest are infants living off their leaders and believing whatever new ideas drift by. Each member needs to be mature, connected to Christ, drawing strength from him to do unique tasks and interconnected with other believers like the cells of a body. As in an orchestra, wide diversity weaves together in harmony.

Paul closes this letter in a way unusual for him: with an open reference to war. Usually he only alludes to the cosmic conflict and focuses his readers' attention on their earthly job. But this time he stresses that his readers are not in a struggle against the Roman authorities, malicious neighbors or irritating relatives. Rather, they are engaged in a violent wrestling match with evil spiritual beings. Those beings are committed to corrupting love and mutual submission in the body. They will use every trick to encourage domination, manipulation, selfishness and hostility. The defense against such deception is to armor oneself with Christ's nature: his truth, righteousness, salvation, faith, a solid understanding of the gospel and God's written Word.

These are offensive weapons when employed in prayer. In giving humans the freedom to make real choices in their world, God has committed himself not to do certain things unless humans invite him. The rebel spirits think God weak for yielding some of his authority to paltry humans. That he loves the dust creatures enough to become one with them is inconceivable.

But God's joke is this: He doesn't esteem the traitors even so much as to defeat them with his ungloved power. He vanquished them decisively

> *The rebel spirits think God weak for yielding some of his authority to paltry humans. That he loves the dust creatures enough to become one with them is inconceivable.*

through the humiliation of the cross, and now he is handling the cleanup through the prayers and love works of this very community of humans.

~~~~~~

Questions for Reflection and Discussion

1. What impresses you about the way Paul dealt with imprisonment?

2. Why is living unselfishly an important part of spreading the gospel?

3. What seems significant to you in Paul's counsel about unseen spiritual beings?

35

<<<<<<<<<<<<<<<<<<<<<<<<<<<<<<<<<<<<<<<<<<<<<<<<<<<<<<<<<<<<<<<<

FAREWELLS

1 and 2 Timothy; Titus

*L*uke's book of Acts ended with Paul spending two years in Rome under house arrest awaiting trial. What happened then? Was Paul convicted of anti-Roman agitation and executed? Or was he acquitted and allowed to pursue his plans, either westward to Spain or back east to his existing communities?

We don't know. Tradition has it that he was acquitted in A.D. 62 but rearrested and executed two to five years later in a general persecution of Christians. In A.D. 64, a fire broke out in Rome, raged for five days, consumed three of the city's fourteen districts (including the imperial palace) and ravaged seven others. Emperor Nero worked overtime to help the homeless, but rumors flew that he had arranged arson in order to rebuild the city to his taste. (It was true that the reconstruction he financed was far more elegantly planned than the old irregular blocks of tenements, but the new approach was partly aimed at fire prevention.)

As the whispers grew louder, Nero became desperate for scapegoats. He fastened on a controversial sect: the Christians. Some said they were cannibals (they supposedly ate somebody's flesh and blood in a secret rite). They were certainly atheists and antisocial, for they refused to worship the Roman gods or participate in public functions that they called debauched and idolatrous.

So the Christians were charged with arson, and anyone fingered as a member of the sect was rounded up. "A huge crowd" of those who ad-

mitted being followers of Christ were convicted, as a Roman writer put
it a few decades later, "not so much of arson as of hatred of the human
race." Anti-humanists.

Nero had perverse tastes in fun. He opened his gardens for the mass
executions. Believers were crucified, sewn in animal skins and hunted
by dogs, doused in pitch and lighted, raped in reenactments of Greek
myths. Even the jaded Roman populace thought Nero went too far.
Nonetheless, sporadic arrests and killings continued for several years.

Paul may have been one of the early casualties, or he may have been
imprisoned and killed as late as A.D. 68. Rome was the only city that
claimed to hold Paul's tomb in the early centuries after his death, so it's
a safe guess that he was tried and executed there. But all we know for
sure is that three more of his letters survived to be included in the New
Testament. They seem to date from the last years of his life, and they
share certain themes in common.

First Timothy

At some point late in his career, Paul sent Timothy to handle some
problems in Ephesus while he himself continued on to Macedonia.
When he realized that he would not soon get back to Ephesus, he dispatched a letter to Timothy with his instructions. This letter was read
aloud to the community to remove all doubt that Paul's authority lay
behind what Timothy was trying to accomplish.

Timothy's main assignment was to silence certain leaders who were
teaching falsehood and to make sure that qualified people were in leadership roles. The troublesome teachers were provoking useless contro-
versy by inventing doctrines that had nothing to do with the essence of
the gospel.

That essence, for Paul, was simple: "Christ Jesus came into the world
to save sinners—of whom I am the worst" (1 Timothy 1:15). In all his
years of passionately serving Christ, Paul had never lost his amazement
that God had shown so much kindness, and even honor, to someone
who had actually murdered his people. Wide-eyed gratitude had always
shielded Paul from pride, and he wanted to set that example before the
leaders in Ephesus, especially Timothy.

Beyond that example, Paul had specific criteria for assessing candidates for leadership in the community. Integrity, proven ability to govern one's own family, and experience in serving Christ figured prominently. An overfondness for money was something to watch out for.

He also had instructions for what should happen in community gatherings. Believers should pray for the pagan civil authorities (whom, despite his own experiences in prison, Paul treated as a gift from God). Disputes should be reconciled before the group gathered to pray. Women should dress modestly, gaining their self-esteem not from being the best dressed but from the quality of their service to others. They should also not compete with the men for control.

The community should take responsibility to care for widows who were truly in need. In fact, one of the things that impressed pagans the most about the followers of Christ was the way they took care of poor members. But Paul insisted that the group as a whole should not have to support elderly people who had family, for families should take responsibility to care for their own. Also, there was no sponging off the community; those people on support had to be too old to work and known for their past service. Paul counseled younger widows not to make vows of chastity because eventually they might want to get married. As happy as Paul was in the single life, he was ever practical.

He encouraged Timothy to believe the prophecies spoken about him years earlier and not to let anyone look down on him for being barely thirty years old. Love, faithfulness and God's commission were his qualifications for leadership, not age. (Timothy seems to have been persistently inclined to self-doubt.) Paul viewed Timothy as his son in a special way, and he pulled out all the stops to offer the support of an affectionate coach.

TITUS

Titus, another of Paul's longtime team members, was probably not much older than Timothy but had a tougher personality. At some point Paul worked briefly in Crete and then left Titus to remain as his representative until another team member could replace him.

Crete was no easy assignment. The laziness, wickedness and dishonesty of its people were proverbial, even among pagans. When Apollos and a lawyer named Zenas happened to pass through Crete, Paul asked them to carry a letter to Titus so that, like Timothy, he would have his authorization from Paul in writing. His instructions were much like those Timothy received: evaluate the character of potential leaders, silence factions who had unethical motives and who threatened to seriously sidetrack the group, teach and model a lifestyle consistent with a believer's mission in the world. "Doing what is good" became a refrain in this letter sent to a community who apparently found this a challenge.

SECOND TIMOTHY

Paul's second letter to Timothy was the farewell of a man who knew he was about to die. He was no longer under house arrest but sat chained in a cold damp dungeon somewhere in the bowels of Rome. One of his friends even had trouble finding out where he was being kept. He was lonely—some colleagues had deserted him, others were away on assignment, and only Luke remained. Paul wrote to Timothy partly to ask him to come and be with him during his last days. Of Timothy, Paul had told the Philippians, "I have no one else like him" (Philippians 2:20).

Personal desires never overshadowed Paul's sense of ministry, however. Many of the original apostles were dead, and all were aging. It was time to pass the baton to the next generation, people like Titus and Timothy and the leaders in local communities. Paul's chief concern was that this generation understand the gospel accurately and thoroughly and that they pass it on the same way to those who came after them. There were many teachers traveling from town to town with concoctions of the gospel and pagan mysticism. Paul had devoted his life to keeping the gospel pure, not so that it could be set in concrete, but so that it would remain unencumbered by cultural trappings or falsehood. A Jewish gospel or a Greek gospel would be impotent to renew lives in Spain or Africa.

Likewise, just as they had to keep the message pure, so the upcoming generation had to keep their lives pure. Corruption would forever lick at leaders' heels, and many would give in. Paul charged Timothy to set an example with his own life and not to shrink from confronting other leaders who might drag whole communities down with them. On the other hand, quarreling and resentment were absolutely to be avoided. Confrontation did not mean mudslinging.

Paul did not hide his personal pain from his friend, but he didn't want Timothy to be discouraged by it. Even trial and martyrdom could be used for God's agenda. Let the pagans watch how a believer handles suffering and death; let them wonder at his joy and hope; let them ask where this hope came from. He would tell them this:

> I have fought the good fight, I have finished the race, I have kept the faith. Now there is in store for me the crown of righteousness, which the Lord, the righteous Judge, will award to me on that day. (2 Timothy 4:7-8)

Questions for Reflection and Discussion

1. Given the hostility Christians (including Paul) faced from the surrounding society, why do you suppose Paul's writings emphasize godly living rather than the evils of the culture?

2. How does a believer handle death? Why?

36

INTERNATIONAL MAIL

Hebrews; James; 1 and 2 Peter;
Jude; 1, 2, and 3 John

*P*aul was not the only servant of Christ sending letters around the Mediterranean world. The Bible includes eight other letters that the early believers accepted as authoritative from God. Three were written by the apostle John, two by the apostle Peter, one each by James and Jude (two of Jesus' brothers) and one by an unknown author.

In this last letter the sender and addressees are not named, but it has become known traditionally as the "Letter to the Hebrews." It was apparently sent to a single community of Jewish believers living somewhere in the Roman Empire. Its author was someone with stature in the international network and a personal bond with its readers. Paul, Apollos, Barnabas and others have been proposed.

These Hebrew believers were facing two temptations to cool their passion for Jesus the Messiah. On one hand, they were still strongly attached to their Jewish ethnic identity and to the religious traditions of their people. They wanted to continue keeping the ceremonial laws, the festivals, the food laws and so on. In many ways, they felt more akin to other Jews than to Gentile followers of Christ.

At the same time they were facing persecution to abandon their commitment to Jesus. The pressure may have come from unbelieving Jews, who viewed them as traitors to God and true Judaism, as followers of a blasphemer. It was normal for Jews who announced faith in Jesus to be expelled from their synagogues, have their children barred from synagogue schools and lose their jobs in areas controlled by Jews. Stresses like these may have begun to cause these Hebrew believers to reconsider their pledge to Christ.

Or the tension may have come from the secular authorities. By A.D. 60, Rome was beginning to distinguish between Christianity and Judaism. The latter was a legal religion, but the former—if it was not just a Jewish sect—was not. As Judaism and Christianity diverged, it was becoming necessary for Hebrew believers to throw in their lot either with the people of Christ or with the Jews. To remain a Jew meant security; to identify with Christ meant legal and social limbo. The writer to the Hebrews observed that they had not yet had to shed their blood because of allegiance to Jesus, but we know that by A.D. 64 this was no longer true.

No matter what the precise date of the letter or the source of the recipients' conflict, one thing was certain: Serving Jesus Christ was costing these Hebrew believers more than they were comfortable paying. Their friend faced them with a burning question—Is Jesus worth it all?—and then tried to persuade them that the answer was yes.

The letter's message is that the way of Christ is better than any alternative, including Judaism. Jesus is greater than the angels, greater than Moses, a greater priest than Aaron, a greater sacrifice than those offered in the temple. He totally understands our weaknesses because he experienced life as a fully human person. He learned what it feels like to obey God amid terrible suffering. Yet he is a priest in the line not of Levi but of Melchizedek, whose name means "king of righteousness." David had foreseen the coming of an eternal priest-king in his line and had written, "You are a priest forever, in the order of Melchizedek" (Psalm 110:4). This priest offered one perfect sacrifice once for all humans, for all time. Therefore the butchering of animals day after futile day was obsolete. The sacrificial system had been theater to explain what Jesus would do, but now it was passé and would soon fade away.

The Hebrews needed to understand how suffering fit into the life of God's people. "It was fitting," their friend wrote, "that God . . . should make the pioneer of their salvation perfect through what he suffered" (Hebrews 2:10), because pain is the hallmark of life after Eden. Thus, "since the children have flesh and blood, he too shared in their humanity so that by his death he might break the power of him who holds the power of death—that is, the devil—and free those who all their lives were held in slavery by their fear of death" (Hebrews 2:14-15).

Death need hold no terror for Christ's servants. They can follow the example of God's people in every generation who have endured anguish with clear-eyed hope because they were convinced that God was telling them the truth, even with no material evidence to back it up. Noah built a landlocked boat and kept faith in it for half a year. Abraham went to his grave with only one son and a square yard of land. Isaac, Jacob and Joseph bet their lives on a kingdom they never saw. Moses gave up princedom. Rahab risked her neck for a God she'd only heard of. Generations of faithful Jews had faced death because they refused to settle for the easy compromise. Could this generation do less?

The choice was stark. Jesus' death had gained access for believers to the very throne room of God. They had the full rights of sons and daughters to stand before the Father and tell him anything. But if they retreated from this offer out of fear of what unbelievers might do, there was no other hope available to them. To know that Jesus was the Son of God and to reject him for self-protection was to choose death.

Jesus fulfilled the old covenant in every minute detail. Under the old covenant the blood of a sin offering was brought to God's throne in the temple, but the body was burned outside the camp or city because it was corrupt—stained with the evil of the people for whom it substituted. "And so Jesus also suffered outside the city gate to make the people holy through his own blood. Let us, then, go to him outside the camp, bearing the disgrace he bore. For here we do not have an enduring city, but we are looking for the city that is to come" (Hebrews 13:12-14). The holy city of Ezekiel's vision. A new Jerusalem. The kingdom of God.

JAMES

The letter to the Hebrews is written in more elegant Greek than any other New Testament book. It is also the New Testament's finest overall commentary on the Old. Its author was a person of remarkable learning and culture.

The book of James, by contrast, is the plain talk of a Jew who probably knew little of the world outside Palestine. The author identifies himself simply as "James, a servant of God and of the Lord Jesus Christ" (James 1:1). Of the three followers of Jesus named James (the English equivalent of Jacob), this one was probably the eldest of Jesus' four brothers. However, he based his authority not on legal kinship to Jesus but on having been forgiven by him.

During Jesus' earthly lifetime James thought he was a bit crazy. But when Jesus appeared to him after the resurrection, James changed his mind. He became a leader of the Jerusalem community; Paul even called him a "pillar" of the wider community of Jesus' followers. James's judgment of the Gentile question carried the day at the first Jerusalem council.

James was known as "James the Just" by the people of Jerusalem, both followers of Christ and others. He was scrupulous in observing the law and had a reputation for holiness and asceticism. However, the Jewish historian Josephus recorded that James was stoned by the Jews in A.D. 62 for violating the law.

James did try to make the way of Christ more appealing to Jews by encouraging Jewish believers to keep the law and avoid eating with Gentiles. But there is no evidence that he claimed the law was necessary for pleasing God, and he supported outreach to Gentiles that did not bind them to the law.

Although his book is framed as a letter, it's less like Paul's letters than like the books of the Jewish wisdom tradition, like Proverbs and Ecclesiastes. James's theme is practical daily living, and his method is a series of brief responses to questions or situations.

> Who is wise and understanding among you? Let them show it by their good life, by deeds done in the humility that comes from wisdom. But if you harbor bitter envy and selfish ambition in your hearts, do not boast about it or deny the truth. Such "wisdom" does not come down from heaven but is earthly, unspiritual, demonic. For where you have envy and selfish ambition, there you find disorder and every evil practice.
>
> But the wisdom that comes from heaven is first of all pure; then peace-loving, considerate, submissive, full of mercy and good fruit, impartial and sincere. Peacemakers who sow in peace reap a harvest of righteousness. (James 3:13-18)

Because of its very Jewish flavor, James's letter has caused Gentile believers some confusion. It rarely mentions Jesus and never his death and resurrection. Some readers have felt it contradicts Paul's teaching that one can do nothing to earn God's favor. But in fact James shows no sign of ever having read Paul's letters to the Romans or Galatians, so he is not intentionally contradicting them. He simply uses some of the same words differently.

James wasn't against faith, but he felt as strongly as Paul did that one couldn't remain a spiritual baby forever. "Believing" or "faith" was not just a mental assent. It was the kind of active trust that moved Abraham to tie his son to an altar, that prompted Rahab to put her life on the line. Even demons believe intellectually, said James. Real faith can be seen in actions like caring for the poor and avoiding moral corruption.

James was writing to people who knew the gospel, so he didn't rhapsodize on mystical union with Christ or the meaning of the crucifixion. Instead he got down and practical about how to live in light of the gospel.

He called his readers to a tested, mature commitment. He was blunt. Don't blame God when you are tempted to do evil; blame the slime in your soul and deal with it. Don't call yourself the community of God and then treat well-dressed people better than shabby ones. Don't claim to be a teacher of the gospel when you can't control your mouth. Don't imagine you're wise if envy and ambition are poisoning your heart. Don't just read the Bible; do what it says.

James may have been committed to the outward rules of the law, but he was no legalist. He understood human psychology surprisingly well. The reason you have conflicts with people, he said, is not because of those rules. It's because you have desires in your heart, and you want to make people fulfill them. Your desires aren't met because (1) you refuse to depend on God for them, or (2) they are selfish. James's solution: First, just decide that God is in charge and you are not. Second, stop listening to what you know is demonic deception. Third, go to God with your desires, trusting that he'll welcome you. Stop pretending and face the damage your self-centeredness is doing. Grieve over it. When you really want God more than your selfish desires, he will be able to change your heart and satisfy your longings.

FIRST PETER

We know much less about Peter's activities than Paul's because he didn't have a friend like Luke following him around taking notes. Tradition has it that Barnabas's nephew John Mark took notes on Peter's memories of Jesus and that those notes were the basis of the Gospel of Mark. But what Peter did after the book of Acts leaves him in Jerusalem around A.D. 50 is unknown.

Early sources are unanimous that he was executed in Rome under Nero's persecution, either in the pogrom immediately after the fire or a year or two later, around A.D. 65. He had evidently been in Rome for some time nurturing the communities there. Mark's Gospel reflects a Roman audience, and it repeatedly emphasizes that disciples must be willing to suffer for their commitment to Jesus. Peter dodged that suffering on the eve of Jesus' death, but after Jesus forgave him, Peter never made that mistake again.

Of Peter's two surviving letters, the first says he wrote it (along with Paul's former colleague Silas) from "Babylon" (1 Peter 5:13). Early believers sometimes used that name to symbolize the ultimate corrupt pagan city, so Peter may have been referring to Rome. Alternatively, he may have been in literal Babylon (which at that time was a small town on the Euphrates River) or in an Egyptian military outpost by that name.

He sent this letter to believers in several provinces of Asia Minor. They were suffering harassment by pagan neighbors and the normal hassles of life, and Peter wanted to help them live up to their calling in the midst of the stress. He addressed them as "foreigners and exiles" (1 Peter 2:11)—citizens of another kingdom who should not be surprised that the people of this world find them confusing, unnerving, even threatening. He also named them "a chosen people, a royal priesthood, a holy nation, God's special possession" (1 Peter 2:9). Their mission: to praise their Master not only with their lips but with their lives.

He wrote, "Live such good lives among the pagans that, though they accuse you of doing wrong, they may see your good deeds and glorify God on the day he visits us" (1 Peter 2:12). How does a pagan glorify God? By turning away from rebellion and toward God. The behavior of a royal priest draws unbelievers to God. Peter tells his readers to explain their hope in Christ "with gentleness and respect." Don't be alarmed if a coworker or a city official ridicules or interrogates you. See it as an opportunity to offer life to that person.

Like Paul, Peter saw daily life as an ideal chance to make Christ attractive. A slave who did excellent work and endured abuse without bitterness would stand out in the crowd. A wife who glowed with inner contentment would make a pagan husband take notice. A husband who treated his wife with respect would be noteworthy. A community where the leaders were not in it for the money or the prestige and where the young respected instruction from the old—that would be something for the pagans to think twice about.

When Peter was a young man and Jesus told him he would have to suffer in his service to God, Peter said, "Never, Lord!" (Matthew 16:22). He wanted a pain-free faith. Now as an old man he told his readers never to be surprised by suffering, but to be faithful in the midst of it as their brothers and sisters everywhere were doing.

SECOND PETER

In his first letter Peter dealt with how to respond to persecution from outside the community. In his second he addressed the other main problem that plagued the body: fraudulent teachers distorting the gospel for their own gain. Peter was evidently furious when he dictated this letter, for it rings with comments like, "These people are springs without water and mists driven by a storm. Blackest darkness is reserved for them" (2 Peter 2:17).

The community to which Peter wrote had been thrown into confusion by false teachers who distorted the gospel so badly that they even justified drunken orgies in broad daylight. They may have been forerunners of the full-blown cults of the next century who said nothing a spiritual person did with the body mattered. They preyed upon people who had just converted to Christ from paganism and were struggling to give up wild sex and drinking. According to Peter, these false teachers "promise them freedom, while they themselves are slaves of depravity—for 'people are slaves to whatever has mastered them'" (2 Peter 2:19).

Also, the charlatans claimed to have some secret knowledge beyond the gospel that one needed to know in order to be secure about one's life after death. Against this notion, Peter insisted that God had already given believers "everything we need for life and godliness through our knowledge of him" (2 Peter 1:3). It is knowing Jesus personally and intimately, not knowing some esoteric body of information, that enables a person to live the spiritual life.

Finally, the false teachers ridiculed the idea that Jesus would ever return and usher in the end of this age. It had been decades since his departure, and a lot of believers were getting impatient. They hadn't expected to live their whole lives waiting. But Peter said that God's slowness allowed more people to have a chance to respond to his invitation.

It was indeed looking like the whole first generation of believers might die out before Christ's return. That was not at all what Peter and his colleagues had expected thirty years earlier when they ate and talked with the resurrected Jesus. They expected the end of the world any day. But in looking back, Peter understood that Jesus had said nothing that guaranteed he would return within Peter's lifetime, or even within the century. Like Abraham, Peter and his readers had to keep looking forward with hope. Peter assured his readers that he himself had seen Jesus transfigured in glory on a mountaintop (Mark 9:2-8), the glory he would have when he returned.

JUDE

Much like his brother, Jude called himself "a servant of Jesus Christ," but he also emphasized that he was "a brother of James" (Jude 1). He claimed kinship with a leader in the Jerusalem community rather than with Jesus himself, because every one of his readers could claim to be a brother of Jesus in the only way that really counted.

Jude's letter is a short warning about frauds that shares some language with 2 Peter. Peter may have first heard about the false teachers from Jude's letter and then added his own authority to Jude's.

Disagreement about precise understandings of the gospel was one thing—there was plenty of room in the body for that. But these frauds were claiming that God's free forgiveness meant they could commit any immorality they wanted and not fear God's anger. Paul had been accused of teaching that, and he had strongly denied it. Jude pulled out all the stops in condemning such an idea, which was a slap in God's face. As Paul had told the Romans, what person who really loved God enough to receive his grace would want to enslave themselves to activities that grieved God?

JOHN

The other apostles were all dead by A.D. 90, but the apostle John remained—the last person alive who had been intimate friends with Jesus during his life on earth. The Romans had leveled Jerusalem and burned its temple to the ground back in A.D. 70 to stamp out a Jewish revolt. That was the end of the Jerusalem community. Its members were now scattered. John ended up in Ephesus, where the believers received him with honor bordering on awe.

After all, John had been one of Jesus' closest friends. In his youth Jesus had dubbed him a "son of thunder" because of his temper. Now that intensity was channeled into a passion for his Lord and a talent for piercing to the core of an issue. His demeanor would have been alarming had he not placed such a high value on gentleness and love.

Ephesus and its environs had been Paul's assignment during his lifetime, but now John took responsibility for believers in every town for a hundred miles around. It was probably for them that he wrote his Gospel. And when a clique of pseudo-Christians began to wreak confusion in the area, John's response was a letter that circulated among the communities under his care.

ULTRAPLURALISM

The region around Ephesus was a cultural melting pot. Greeks, Egyptians, Syrians and Persians had immigrated over the generations and mixed their customs with whatever ancient ways still lingered. Few people thought it necessary to hold one school of thought rigorously. They thought there were many roads to truth, and people took what they liked from each—a pinch of Plato, a dash of Persian dualism and one's ancestral cult for tradition's sake.

In this environment, Jews and Christians were considered narrow-minded and even atheistic for showing respect to just one God. Most people acknowledged hundreds and favored several. Some hedged their bets by joining one or more "mystery" cults—groups with secret rites of initiation that promised encounters with the divine and bliss in the afterlife. There were sects that mixed Judaism with Plato or astrology or secret revelation. Thus it was inevitable that someone would try to add the teachings of Jesus to a Greek-Persian-occult casserole and challenge the apostles' gospel.

Fifty years after John's death these semi-Christian hybrids were as common, various and thorny as roses. The seeds were planted in John's lifetime. The full-blown systems are labeled Gnostic (from the Greek *gnōsis*, meaning "knowledge") because they all offered some secret knowledge by which a person could be saved. This knowledge was not available through study but only through revelation from some higher spiritual plane. It was basically self-knowledge; one recognized the divine spark that was the true self.

Most Gnostics believed in a divine redeemer who would bring the knowledge of the true self. Some identified that redeemer with Jesus; others did not. Those who did talk of "Christ" were not thinking of the Jewish King but of a sort of spirit who had "emanated" from "the divine absolute." Some believed Jesus was the Christ but only appeared to have a flesh-and-blood body during his time on earth. (They thought matter was too corrupt for a pure spirit being to take on.) Others said the Christ-spirit descended upon Jesus at his baptism and departed just before his death.

Evidently some people with views like these joined the Christian communities around Ephesus and provoked strife. They eventually withdrew in anger when they failed to persuade the majority, but the believers were upset and asking questions: What's the truth about Jesus and "the Christ"? How can you tell a real child of God from a fake one? How can I tell if I'm really a child of God? John's first letter answers those questions.

Truth, Obedience, Love

John's style in 1 John seems repetitive to readers accustomed to step-by-step logic. He writes in a spiral, cycling deeper and deeper through the same basic ideas from every angle. The ideas of knowledge and confidence recur over and over as John emphasizes what believers know and how they can be confident that they know it. John himself was confident that his readers really did have a relationship with God, and he didn't want them to worry about it. But he also didn't want them to be led astray by people who claimed they needed something different.

There are three basic tests, John told his readers, to know who really are children of God. First, genuine children of God walk in the light of moral truth. They're not sinless—maybe they lapse into selfish behavior regularly—but they're at war with the self-centered side of their nature. They're seeking every possible strengthening of the Holy Spirit and making every choice they can for right over wrong. They don't tell themselves their behavior doesn't matter just because they've been "saved." And when they catch themselves doing wrong, they're quick to admit it to God and fervent in asking God to change them. They want to be like God, who is the perfection of goodness. Obeying God is a joy to them, not a teeth-gritting duty. They're glad when God shines a spotlight on the areas where they tend to lie to themselves. And they don't gloss over their actions with excuses. They regularly take a hard look at their lives and call the slime what it is.

Second, real children of God love the rest of the family. "Love each other" was Jesus' paramount command, so people who want to obey God will make this instruction a priority. Jealousy, hatred and indifference will be fading traits in people who have God active in their lives. And love is not mere sentiment—it's deeds like taking care of brothers and sisters with material needs and laying down one's very life for them. "Dear children," John said, "let us not love with words or speech but with actions and in truth" (1 John 3:18).

Third, people who truly know God hang on to the certainty that Jesus is the Christ who was born, lived and died with a physical human body. John stresses that he himself actually heard, saw and touched the eternal one who came from God. Anyone who bends the truth about Jesus to make him less than fully God and fully human doesn't really know God at all, for one can't not know the Father without knowing the Son.

Believing the truth about Jesus, obeying his commands and loving other believers were for John the three interwoven strands of belonging to God. One could not obey without believing, and to obey and to love were aspects of each other.

John had just one final request: "Dear children, keep yourselves from idols" (1 John 5:21). Or, as he put it earlier, "do not love the world" (1 John 2:15). John was not telling people to hold their pagan neighbors in contempt. He was warning against the temptation that plagues the most seasoned believer: desiring something in the world's system more than God. It might be a person's longing to feel really important through the work they do, or a yearning for a spouse who will truly cherish them. It might be the desire for possessions, power, comfort, security or praise. Such desires can be good and God-honoring when put in perspective, but they become idols and addictions when a person pursues one of them as though it will give life. John's solution: Stop believing your life depends on any of those things. Pursue God with that unquenchable longing, for he alone gives life.

HOSPITALITY

Love and truth figure prominently in John's first letter as key features of life with God. In his next two letters he shows how to apply them in a balanced way to two practical situations.

The Romans knew that a prosperous, united empire needed a way for people to travel safely. So they invested a lot of money and effort in building roads and guarding them from bandits. The stone highways were smooth and wide enough for soldiers to get to trouble spots quickly. And while robbers and wild animals were not eliminated in lonely areas, they were curbed enough to let civilians travel with some security.

And civilians did travel. Not only merchants and government officials, but tourists, pilgrims, magicians, priests of every cult and teachers of every imaginable doctrine walked or rode from Syria to Spain and back again. A teacher of grammar or philosophy would arrive in a town and try to attract paying students among the sons of local families. Religious missionaries sought adoration (and money) for their deities and doctrines. Among all these the ambassadors of Jesus Christ traveled, doing their best to stand out from the competition as messengers of truth.

There were inns every twenty-two miles or so along the Roman roads, but we've already seen that they were no place for respectable folk. Most people tried to stay with friends of friends when they traveled. And because the spread of the gospel depended on apostolic teams, hospitality was considered a key expression of Christlike love. Paul often stayed with converts when he visited a town. Likewise, he asked believers to house messengers and teachers and to help them with provisions for the next leg of their journeys (Romans 15:23-24; 16:1-2; Titus 3:12-13).

But when it became known that believers would feed and house anyone who claimed to be a teacher of the gospel, unscrupulous people began to take advantage. The Didache, a manual for Syrian communities, gave guidelines for hospitality: an apostle may stay up to two days and may receive only provisions, not money, upon leaving, a person who wants to stay longer must work and so on. John's communities around Ephesus were having similar problems, and he wrote 2 and 3 John to address them.

LOVE AND TRUTH

Second John was sent "to the lady chosen by God and to her children" (2 John 1). In the name of love, this lady was welcoming into her home some of the false teachers John combatted in his first letter. John affirmed the importance of loving other believers, but, he said, love ceases to be love when it loses sight of truth. To give aid and a forum to teachers who distort the gospel is to do harm to real believers. If you really want to show love for the people of God, he said, reject visitors who teach falsehood about Jesus.

John's third letter was addressed to a friend named Gaius, whose hospitality reflected both love and truth. The letter reached Gaius by an emissary named Demetrius, whom John was sending to Gaius's community. John asked Gaius to offer Demetrius the same hospitality he had shown to John's earlier emissaries. Third John is basically a letter of introduction letting Gaius know that Demetrius represented John. With so many impostors around, it was a good idea to send genuine emissaries with letters.

John was especially concerned because a leader in Gaius's community—one "Diotrephes, who loves to be first"—had told the community to have nothing to do with John and his messengers. Diotrephes's doctrine may have been pure, but his arrogant, controlling attitude was far from the love and truth John expected. John warned Gaius that Diotrephes might try to have Gaius expelled from the community for housing a friend of John's, but Gaius was not to worry. John hoped to arrive in person soon to face Diotrephes.

Both of these little letters are snapshots of the kinds of tensions that arise as soon as the people of God gather in community. It's easy to become frustrated when pettiness poisons intimacy. It would be nice to think that becoming God's children would immediately make men and women the loving people they should be. But it doesn't. John's response was not to throw up his hands in disgust, but to hang in with the Father's stubborn family and urge them on to maturity. His approach required strong doses of both love and truth.

These eight letters—passionate and practical, devoted to the truth about Christ and a true way to live—give us just a glimpse into the vibrant communities of the kingdom that were spreading across the empire by the time the people who had known Jesus face to face were growing old.

Questions for Reflection and Discussion

1. Why do so many of these letters talk about how a Christian deals with suffering?

2. How is faith more than just mental assent to some facts about Jesus?

3. What are some of the themes of the false teaching that Paul, Peter, Jude and John all fought against?

37

THE VIEW FROM HEAVEN

Revelation

For a while after Nero's death in A.D. 68, persecution of believers had been a small-scale affair—a brawl here, a little job discrimination there, malicious gossip nearly everywhere. The main thorns in the community's side were self-proclaimed teachers of divine truth.

But in the second half of Emperor Domitian's reign (A.D. 81-96), Ephesus and the other wealthy cities of western Asia Minor became more and more serious about worshiping the emperor as a god. They were competing with each other for the money that came with Domitian's favor, and any group that resisted the ever more elaborate titles and rites could downgrade a city's chances of receiving financial investment. Roman poets had always sung extravagant praises of their emperors, but Domitian seriously expected to be addressed as "our lord and god." It became law that anyone holding public office or testifying in court—effectively almost everyone—must offer a pinch of incense to the emperor's guardian spirit and declare "Caesar is lord." People who refused to worship the emperor in this way might lose their jobs, their homes, even their lives.

For decades the slogan of God's people had been "Jesus is Lord." The gospel asserted that Jesus was King of the world and would come back soon to claim his domain. But the years had passed and there was no sign of him. Arrogant teachers were a cancer within the communities, and claiming allegiance to Christ was growing more and more dangerous. Was it worth it? Was God really in control of events on earth?

Around A.D. 95, a series of visions came to a man named John in the Roman penal colony on the island of Patmos, off the coast of Asia Minor. John was there either as a prisoner or as chaplain to the increasing scores of believers exiled there. We don't know if this John was the apostle John or someone else with that common name. The apostle never used his own name in his gospel or his letters, but instead called himself "the elder" or "the disciple whom Jesus loved," while the John of Revelation gives his own name. What we do know is that this John was Jewish and a prophet.

One Sunday while praying, he received this series of visions with a single message: Yes, I am still in control. John wrote a letter to the churches of seven cities in Asia Minor, urging them to stand firm in the face of the attacks assailing them. That letter, the book of Revelation, recounts John's glimpse into the spiritual realm.

Seven Communities

When the resurrected Lord appeared to John glowing with divine fire, John fainted, just as more than one prophet had done before him. Jesus picked him up and identified himself in terms calculated to shake John's wavering comrades to attention: "Do not be afraid." (John was no doubt trembling with terror.) "I am the First and the Last. I am the Living One; I was dead, and now look, I am alive for ever and ever! And I hold the keys of death and Hades" (Revelation 1:17-18).

Jesus dictated brief notes to each of the seven churches. Each memo offered praise, criticism or both; counsel; and a promise "to the one who is victorious." The messages were blunt.

For instance, the Ephesian church was doing well at rejecting falsehood, but in the process had hardened into a tight, loveless orthodoxy. Jesus warned them that if they didn't regain their youthful passion for God, their group would soon shrivel and fade out of existence.

Believers in Smyrna were being denounced to the authorities by Jews who considered their beliefs blasphemy. Jesus reminded them of his own death and resurrection and urged them to face martyrdom with confidence.

The imperial governor resided in Pergamum, the province's political capital. He held the "right of the sword" to execute whomever he willed. But Jesus told the community in Pergamum that he held the sword that mattered. He commended them for not flinching under persecution but rebuked them for tolerating certain members who still dabbled in paganism.

Some Thyatirans wanted to believe it was okay to share in the pagan practices that were so much a part of trade guilds in their town. It was tough to do business and avoid idolatry, and a so-called prophetess was winning fans by offering an easier way. Jesus praised the Thyatirans' love, faith, service and perseverance but warned them not to tolerate compromise with debauchery and idolatry.

Jesus had harsh words for the community in Sardis: "You have a reputation of being alive, but you are dead" (Revelation 3:1). A glitzy public image meant nothing without the dynamic group life that came from active love.

Jesus had nothing but tender encouragement for the little embattled group in Philadelphia. But his message to wealthy Laodicea pulled no punches. The community there deemed itself rich, but Jesus called it "wretched, pitiful, poor, blind and naked." The city took pride in its banks, its industry in black textiles and its famous eye ointment. Jesus counseled the Laodiceans to get gold, white robes and eye salve from him. Material comfort had made the Laodiceans lazy and self-satisfied. They had no passion for Jesus because they didn't feel any great need for him. Jesus loved them too much to leave them in their complacency. He bared his heart to them, urging them to open their hearts to him before it was too late.

VISIONS

After recording these jarring memos, John was treated to a tour of heaven. He saw the Father enthroned, blazing like the fire of a thousand gems. Four bizarre angelic beings sang ceaseless praise, and twenty-four "elders" added their song to the Creator. A slain but living Lamb appeared and received a scroll. The worshipers sang a new song to the Lamb, because he was worthy to open the scroll and disclose its contents.

What did it all mean? John's readers would have had much less trouble than we at deciphering it, since apocalypse was a familiar type of literature at that time. The second half of the book of Daniel is apocalypse, and other Jewish apocalypses were written after Daniel. In an apocalypse, a heavenly visitor unveiled secrets of the unseen world through symbolic visions. The meaning of many symbols (numbers, certain objects) was fairly standard among apocalypses, somewhat like the symbolism of political cartoons today.

We are often forced to guess at the meaning of specific bits of John's visions. The gist of this one seems to be that by his death as a sacrifice for sin, Jesus won the right to bring the contents of the scroll—perhaps a contract declaring God's plan for the fulfillment of history—into effect.

John watched as the myriad inhabitants of heaven exulted that Jesus was bringing about the climax of history. But as Jesus broke each of the scroll's seven seals, the inhabitants of earth were not so ecstatic. Conquest, bloodshed, war, famine and death accompanied the breaking of the first four seals. With the fifth, the souls of martyrs cried to be avenged. When the sixth broke, cataclysm swept the earth and sky and all humankind cringed in terror of the Lamb. Angels marked the people of God who remained on earth to protect them from the rending of land and sea—and a multitude sang praises to God from heaven. Jesus broke the seventh seal, and heaven hushed.

Then followed a cycle in which seven angels blew seven trumpets. A third of the land was burned, a third of the sea turned bloody, a third of the fresh water became poisonous, a third of the sky's light was darkened, a plague of demonic locusts rose from the abyss to plague men, and a third of earth's population died. One might have thought that such calamity would humble the surviving humans, but it did not. They clung stubbornly to their worship of the snake and his deeds: murder, theft, witchcraft, debauchery. Partial destruction achieved nothing. One trumpet remained. An angel appeared and swore that the martyrs would wait no longer for justice. Then John saw Jerusalem with its temple rebuilt but harassed by pagans for three and a half years, while two witnesses stood against the persecution. The witnesses were martyred but raised from death, and an earthquake ravaged Jerusalem, bringing survivors to their

STORY OF STORIES

knees before God. The seventh angel sounded his trumpet, and a song burst forth in heaven proclaiming the coming of God's kingdom.

Next John saw war on earth between a woman and a dragon—the children of Eve and the children of the snake—and war in heaven between God's angels and the dragon's. He saw a beast with the dragon's power to attack God's people, and another with snakish power to delude unbelievers with false religion. The persecution was terrible, but more terrible still was the bloodshed of those who fell before God's angels.

Seven angels struck the earth with seven horrific plagues. Babylon, symbolizing the great whore city of the earth, fell amid mourning and mocking. But the chorus of heaven raised another song: the whore is dead, long live the Bride of the Lamb, the people of God. The wedding feast of the kingdom was at hand.

Jesus appeared as a white horseman leading the armies of heaven against his foes. The dragon and his human servants were crushed, and the martyrs came to life to reign with Christ for a thousand years. Then came a final battle and the dragon's final defeat, and then all humanity faced judgment before the throne of their rightful King. Those who were found guilty of treason were destroyed; those found to be loyal subjects were welcomed to the kingdom.

Finally John saw the kingdom itself in symbols woven from throughout the Old Testament. A voice proclaimed,

> Look! God's dwelling place is now among the people, and he will dwell with them. They will be his people, and God himself will be with them and be their God. "He will wipe every tear from their eyes. There will be no more death" or mourning or crying or pain, for the old order of things has passed away. (Revelation 21:3-4)

To read John's visions is to be overwhelmed by color, sound, weird creatures and strange events. One can study the specifics for clues to the future, or one can stand back to behold the tapestry. Whatever the details, the essence is clear: God's people can expect terrible suffering as the dragon escalates the war in the final days of his fury. But they must cling to hope, confident despite everything that God will triumph in the end. Beyond martyrdom lies a kingdom that fulfills every longing of the prophets. In Eden God visited his children, but that intimacy was brief. In the wilderness he dwelt with his people in a tent that could be approached only with blood sacrifice. For thirty years he lived among his people in a human body that became the ultimate sacrifice. But one day he will dwell with them as never before.

John identified himself as "I, John, your brother and companion in the suffering and kingdom and patient endurance that are ours in Jesus" (Revelation 1:9). Those words summarized for John the believer's life. Suffering now. The glorious kingdom just on the horizon. And therefore, patient endurance.

> *In Eden God visited his children, but that intimacy was brief. In the wilderness he dwelt with his people in a tent that could be approached only with blood sacrifice. For thirty years he lived among his people in a human body that became the ultimate sacrifice. But one day he will dwell with them as never before.*

"I am coming soon!" Jesus promises three times in the last chapter of Revelation. Two thousand years later, his people still wait. Yet, John wrote, those who can look past the anguish of today and trust their God for the joy of tomorrow are genuinely blessed: "Let the one who is thirsty come; and let the one who wishes take the free gift of the water of life" (Revelation 22:17).

And we say, along with John, "Amen. Come, Lord Jesus."

Questions for Reflection and Discussion

1. What was the original historical situation that Revelation addressed?

2. How would you summarize the main themes of Revelation?

3. How is this book a fitting conclusion to the story of the Bible?

LEADER'S GUIDE

PART ONE: A PROMISE OF DELIVERANCE

The first section of God's story tells how he creates a people to love, how they persistently refuse to trust and obey him and how he sets in motion a plan to redeem them from the consequences of their refusal. Central to that plan is a promise, and many of the questions at the ends of the chapters help readers trace the promise as it is handed down from generation to generation. The promised son of Eve becomes a son of Abraham and later a son of Judah. Another theme of these early chapters is how Yahweh uses various means—life experiences, one-time commands, laws, worship rituals—to show people who he is and who they are meant to be.

Below are some questions that deal with the section as a whole. You may also want to discuss some of the questions at the end of each chapter. You can choose among questions that focus on facts and analysis, those that ask you to look at your own lives and those that call for creative response. Don't feel you need to cover all of the questions.

1. The Bible's main story line is about Yahweh, his loving pursuit of a people and his promise to one day send a son of Eve to defeat the snake and redeem his people. Where does each of the following fit into that story?
    - Cain
    - Noah
    - Abraham and Sarah

- Jacob
- Joseph
- Judah
- Moses
- the law Yahweh gave to Israel

2. Was there anything that surprised or especially moved you in this part of the story? If so, what was it?

3. What role does faith play in these early episodes of the story?

4. What role does obedience play?

5. What's your impression of Yahweh from this part of the story? How would you describe him? What draws you to him or pushes you away? (You might look at Exodus 34:6-7.)

6. Throughout history, people have told this story in myriad ways. If you like, hunt through the Internet for artwork, songs or poems that respond to characters or elements of this part of the story. (For example, there are paintings and poems of Adam and Eve, of Abraham offering Isaac as a sacrifice, of Moses.) Talk about what you think of the way those artists have portrayed the story.

7. If you like to write or create art, consider creating your own response to this part of the story and sharing it with the group next time. Or if something in the next section of the story grabs you as you're reading and you want to write or make something, you can bring that to your next group meeting.

8. Respond to God in prayer. Have three group members read aloud Deuteronomy 6:4-7, Deuteronomy 30:19-20 and finally Genesis 3:15. Then let people pray as they are led.

PART TWO: THE RISE AND FALL OF ISRAEL

Note: Part Two is the longest and most complex part of the story. If you prefer, you can spread it over two group meetings: chapters 9 through 13 and chapters 14 through 18. You would go from Joshua to Elisha in one meeting, and then the writing prophets and the fall of Israel and Judah in the next meeting.

This is the most complex part of the story, and the most tragic. It begins with the Israelites newly formed as a nation and just entering the Promised Land. It follows the nation's political and moral ups and downs until it is destroyed as a nation state and the people are driven out of the Promised Land.

Group members may not follow all of the political intrigue and remember every king. Focus on (1) the main people and events, (2) what happens to the promise in each episode and (3) what we can learn about Yahweh. It's not necessary to cover every question. Feel free to select questions from the ends of the chapters that you think your group will enjoy discussing.

1. What were some of the thoughts and emotions that went through your mind as you read this part of the story?

2. Look at the timeline in the back of the book. What were the key events in this part of story? What were the high points? The low points?

3. Select two or three kings or queens who especially interest you. What is most memorable about their lives?

4. What jobs did the miracle-working prophets fulfill? What jobs did the writing prophets fulfill? What about the other prophets, such as Nathan?

5. Which of the prophets would you least like to be? Why?

6. What do we know about the promised son of Eve at the beginning of this part of the story? What do we know about him at the end of this part? What has happened to the promise now that Judah is destroyed?

7. What impression of Yahweh do you get from this part of the story? What does he say or do that draws you toward him? What, if anything, does he say or do that scares or puzzles you? What do you think of the proverb "The fear of Yahweh is the beginning of wisdom"?

8. Poetry plays a huge role in this part of the story: the Psalms for worship, the Song of Songs, the poetic messages of the prophets, the Lamentations. What do poetry and song do that prose can't?

9. Give everyone a moment to find a portion of a psalm, prophecy or lamentation that says something they would like to say to God. Then have a time of prayer in which people can simply read their passage or pray in their own words about what it says.

Note: If you run out of time and want to continue this discussion without adding an additional group meeting, part three is much shorter, so you could take some time in your next meeting.

PART THREE: EXILE AND RETURN

In this part of the story the people of Judah become Jews, subjects of one pagan empire after another. They deal with exile and subordination in various ways. You can supplement the questions below with those at the ends of each chapter.

1. Choose one of the characters in this part of the story. What did that person contribute to the task of keeping the promise on track even though God's people were scattered? What do you admire about that person?

2. In what ways is your situation in your culture like the situation of the Jews in Persia? What similar character qualities and ways of thinking does it call for?

3. Yahweh fulfilled his promise to restore his people to Judah, but life was hard for them. How did that affect their faith? What attitude do you think they should have had toward Yahweh?

4. Why do you suppose Yahweh didn't enable his people to be politically independent when he restored them to their land?

5. Given the state of the royal line of David in this part of the story, what has become of the promise about the son of David?

6. The Pharisees formed their attitude toward God's law as they reflected on the horrible things their people had been through because of disobeying God. To what extent does their stance on the law make sense to you in light of that? If you think they should have responded differently, describe how.

7. What were the pros and cons of retreating to the desert and waiting

for God to act, as the Essenes and Qumran sect did?

8. Have someone read aloud Isaiah 62:6-7. What are the things you think God's people today should pray for with this degree of commitment? Make a list, and then take time to pray for those things.

PART FOUR: THE COMING OF THE KING

At last the promise is fulfilled—in a way that nobody expects. God becomes human. He lives as Adam should have lived, as the nation of Israel was meant to live. He demonstrates how a citizen of God's kingdom should live, how the law of Moses should be understood, what the drama of the sacrificial system was meant to convey. The whole of the ritual law has always pointed toward him, and he fulfills it. The whole of the moral law has always aimed toward character like his, and he fulfills it. The writing prophets foresaw him, and he fulfills their words. The miracle-working prophets Elijah and Elisha foreshadowed him, and he does greater works. He does what God has been doing from the beginning: he embodies holiness, he offers truth married to love, he pays the terrible price of human folly. He triumphs.

Much, much more could be said about the birth, life, death and resurrection of Jesus than what these chapters cover. Focus your discussion on who Jesus is and how he fulfills what has gone before. Draw connections. Help people see the big picture. As always, select among the questions at the ends of the chapters.

1. Who was Jesus to you when you were about ten years old? (Maybe he played a big role in your life, or maybe he wasn't part of the culture you grew up in, or maybe you had some limited impressions of him.)

2. Which part of Jesus' story is currently most prominent in your mind: his entry into the world as a human, his teaching and ministry to people, his death or his resurrection from death?

3. Make a list of ways Jesus fulfilled earlier parts of the story. Try to remember as many as possible. (For instance, what was said in Genesis about the son of Eve? How does Jesus fulfill God's promise to Abraham? How did the manna in the wilderness point toward Jesus?)

4. What is surprising about the way God fulfilled his promise?

5. How would you describe Jesus from the way he lived, including the way he faced his death?

6. The kingdom of God is "the realm in which what God wants done is done without resistance." What does this mean? (For instance, does the kingdom exist mainly in our hearts? Or does it exist mainly almost everywhere except most human hearts?)

7. Jesus invites us to choose: Renounce your resistance to what God wants done. Choose God's kingdom voluntarily. Where are you in relation to this choice? What are the hard parts? The appealing parts?

8. In what ways does Jesus agree with Old Testament teaching about holiness? In what ways does he deal with holiness differently from the way the Pharisees did?

9. Why did Jesus' enemies hate him?

10. Why did Jesus allow himself to be crucified?

11. How has God always paid the cost of our wrongdoing?

12. Why does it matter to us whether Jesus really did rise from the dead, alive with a body?

13. A tremendous amount of visual art, sculpture, music and poetry has been created in response to the story of Jesus. Share some of your favorites with the group.

14. When Jesus taught his followers to pray, one of the central issues he wanted them to pray for was for the Father's kingdom to come in its fullness, for the Father's will to be done on earth (Matthew 6:9-10). Pray for the kingdom. Tell God what you think about his kingdom, the things about it that you long for, the things you've resisted, and the ways you want to stop resisting it. Ask for his will to be done in your personal lives and the wider world.

PART FIVE: MESSENGERS TO THE NATIONS

Up to now, much of the story has focused on the descendants of Jacob-Israel, the Jews. But the nations—Gentiles, or non-Jews—have always been in view. God promised Abraham that through him all the nations would be blessed. The law of Moses was supposed to get the attention of the nations, Solomon's temple was supposed to become a house of prayer for all nations, Israel was supposed to be a light to the nations. God sent Elijah to a widow outside Israel, and through Elisha God healed Naaman the Syrian. Daniel and his friends lived as God's servants among the Persians. But Israel as a whole fell short in its role among the nations, and when "the desire of all nations" came, most Jews decided he wasn't the Messiah they wanted.

So in this part of the story, we see messengers take the gospel first to their fellow Jews but then increasingly to the nations. This transition was possible because of the way people like Paul and Barnabas thought through the gospel and how it should be lived and communicated.

1. How do you generally relate to customs and traditions? Do you tend to like living by longstanding traditions? Do you tend to be suspicious of traditions? Indifferent to traditions?

2. Who were the Hebraists and the Hellenists? How were the differences between them important in shaping the church in Jerusalem?

3. What impression of these men do you get from your reading?
   - Peter
   - Stephen
   - Philip
   - Barnabas
   - Paul

4. Consider the story of the Jews as the Bible tells it: the law God gave them through Moses, their history in the Promised Land, the prophets' promises that God would judge them for failing to obey his commands, their exile, their struggles after the exile as subjects of one Gentile empire after another. After all this, why was it reasonable for Jews who believed in Christ to assume that obedience to the law of Moses was still important?

5. Again, consider the story of the Jews. Why was their attitude toward Gentiles not surprising?

6. Why was it important that Peter was the first to treat Gentiles as Christ-followers without requiring them to convert to Judaism?

7. What do you think would have happened to the movement if Paul had not insisted that Christ-plus-Moses was not the gospel?

8. Among the Christians you're familiar with, what are some of the optional ideas and practices that tend to get treated as essential to the faith? (For example, are there any non-essentials that have acquired the status of "Real Christians believe _____" or "Good Christians do _____" or "Good Christians don't _____"?)

9. Christianity has now been around for two thousand years. What is the value of knowing and being rooted in that long tradition? What are the pros and cons of reinventing the practice of the faith in each generation and each culture?

10. What is noteworthy in Paul's strategy for planting and cultivating churches?

11. What is hope? How is hope amidst tragedy different from minimizing tragedy? What gives Christians hope? What signs of a lack of hope do you see in secular culture today?

12. The first believers in cities like Philippi and Thessalonica were God's representatives in hostile neighborhoods. It wasn't easy, but they understood that their mission was to live godly lives while maintaining involvement with their unbelieving coworkers and neighbors. Ask God to help you do this. Tell him the challenges you face. Pray for individual nonbelievers around you. Pray for one another.

PART SIX: LETTERS TO THE CHURCHES

As the Bible comes to a close, the story of God has become the story of Jesus. It has also become our story. Paul, Peter, John and other leaders have a lot to say about what the story means for their generation and for us.

In fact, the story isn't over. Each of us has a role to play as we look forward to the final chapter, Jesus' triumphant return. Even as we become aware that unseen spiritual beings are engaged in the cosmic drama with us, the writers of these letters insist that practical, down-to-earth living is central to our role.

The questions at the ends of the chapters deal with issues in the specific books. You may choose to dig into some of those in addition to using this time to look back at the story as a whole.

1. How has God's story intersected with your story during the past week? When have you had an opportunity to participate in his story?

2. What is faith? How has faith been a theme throughout God's story?

3. What is righteousness? How has righteousness been a theme throughout God's story?

4. How has dealing with suffering been a theme? How should we deal with suffering? Why?

5. What will the end of the story be like? How should that affect the way we live now?

6. How has your view of God grown since you began this study of God's story?

7. What will you take away from this look at God's story?

8. Worship is one of the themes of Revelation, and the book includes a number of poetic passages that have been set to music for worship. Below are some of those passages. Do you know any songs based on them? If so, you could sing them together or play recordings of them. Or choose one or more of these passages to read aloud and use as springboards for your group's prayer time.

  - Revelation 4:8
  - Revelation 5:9-10
  - Revelation 5:12-13
  - Revelation 7:10, 12
  - Revelation 7:15-17
  - Revelation 12:10-12
  - Revelation 15:3-4
  - Revelation 19:1-8

Timeline. Dates are approximate, based on the *NIV Study Bible.*

2100 BC	2000	1900	1800	1700	1600	1500

•Joseph

•Jacob's family settles in Egypt 1876

•Moses

900 BC	800	700	600

KINGS OF ISRAEL
◄Jeroboam I 930-909   •Jeroboam II 793-753
•Baasha 908-886
   •Omri 885-874   •Menahem 752-742
     •Ahab 874-853   •Pekah 752-732
       •Joram 852-841
         •Jehu 841-814   •Hoshea   732-722

KINGS OF JUDAH
◄Rehoboam I 930-913   •Azariah (Uzziah) 792-740
•Asa 910-869   •Josiah 640-609
                                    •Jotham 750-735
   •Jehoshaphat 872-848
     •Jehoram 853-841   •Ahaz 735-715
       •Athaliah 841-835
         •Joash 835-796   •Hezekiah 715-686
                                              •Manasseh 697-642

PROPHETS
                                • Jonah 785-775
   •Elijah 875-848   •Jeremiah 626-585

                                  •Amos 760-750
       •Elisha 848-797
                                    •Hosea 750-715

                                      •Isaiah 740-681

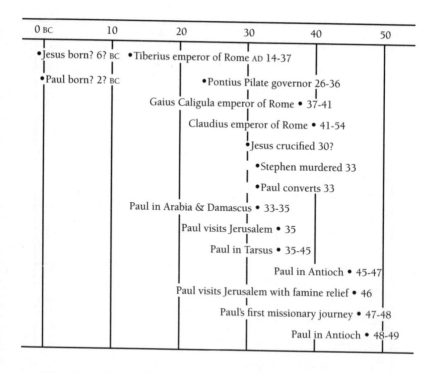

600 BC	500	400	300

◄Assyria destroys Israel 722 BC   •Esther becomes queen of Persia 479
 •Babylonian captivity 605-538   •Ezra leads another return 458
 •Babylonia takes first captives to exile, incl. Daniel 605
   •Babylonia takes second captives to exile, incl. Ezekiel 597
    •Jerusalem falls to Babylon 586   •Nehemiah arrives in Jerusalem 446
      •Cyrus lets Jews return to Judah 538
       •Persian period 538-323
         •Second temple completed 516

0 BC	10	20	30	40	50

•Jesus born? 6? BC   •Tiberius emperor of Rome AD 14-37

•Paul born? 2? BC
                        •Pontius Pilate governor 26-36
            Gaius Caligula emperor of Rome • 37-41
                  Claudius emperor of Rome • 41-54
                         •Jesus crucified 30?
                            •Stephen murdered 33
                            •Paul converts 33
          Paul in Arabia & Damascus • 33-35
              Paul visits Jerusalem • 35
               Paul in Tarsus • 35-45
                              Paul in Antioch • 45-47
          Paul visits Jerusalem with famine relief • 46
              Paul's first missionary journey • 47-48
                      Paul in Antioch • 48-49

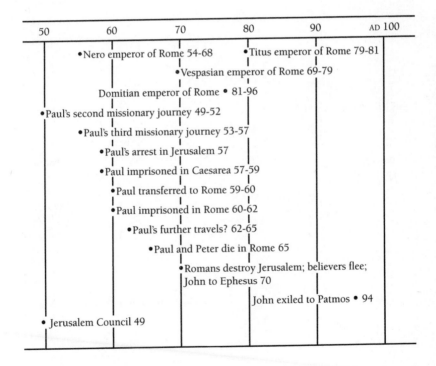

300 BC   200   100   BC 0

•Alexander the great conquers Persia, beginning of Greek empire 323 BC

•Antiochus Epiphanes desecrates Jewish Temple, as in Daniel's vision 167-164

•Romans conquer Judea • 63

•Herod the Great king of Judea 37-4 BC

Augustus Caesar first emperor of Roman Empire • 27-14 BC

50   60   70   80   90   AD 100

•Nero emperor of Rome 54-68   •Titus emperor of Rome 79-81

•Vespasian emperor of Rome 69-79

Domitian emperor of Rome • 81-96

•Paul's second missionary journey 49-52

•Paul's third missionary journey 53-57

•Paul's arrest in Jerusalem 57

•Paul imprisoned in Caesarea 57-59

•Paul transferred to Rome 59-60

•Paul imprisoned in Rome 60-62

•Paul's further travels? 62-65

•Paul and Peter die in Rome 65

•Romans destroy Jerusalem; believers flee; John to Ephesus 70

John exiled to Patmos • 94

• Jerusalem Council 49

Map: The Middle East, 2000-100 B.C.

Map: Palestine, 2000-100 B.C.

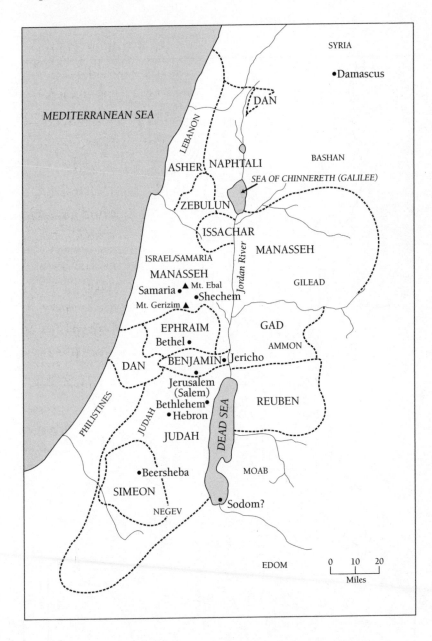

350

Map: The Roman Empire

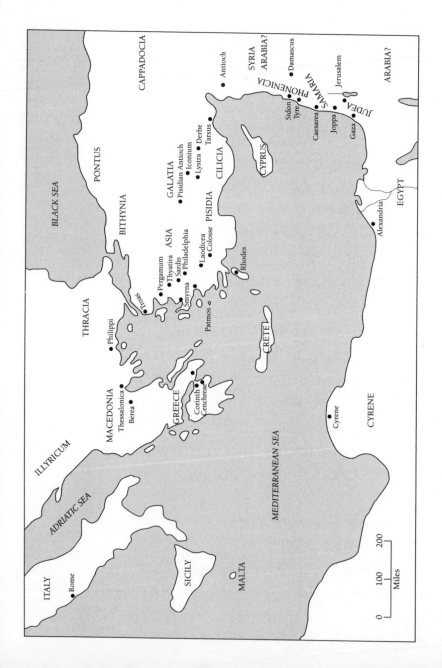

Map: Palestine Under the Romans

Map: The Middle East Today

NOTES

Page 15   *Genesis* is a Greek word: While Moses wrote in Hebrew, his works are known today by titles that come from an early Greek translation of the Bible.

Page 16   According to tradition: Our general practice in this book will be to follow traditional beliefs about the authors of the biblical books, because explaining the scholarly debate surrounding the authorship of some books would require a long detour from our story.

Page 27   The covenants: The two big divisions of the Bible are the Old Testament and the New Testament. In modern English, a "testament" is a document that declares what people want to do with their property when they die. But in the Bible it is an old English rendering of the Hebrew word for "covenant." So the two divisions of the Bible are the Old Covenant and the New Covenant. The Old Testament could correctly be called the "Books of the First Covenant"—books about the agreement between God and a certain nation of humans. Because the humans found it impossible to live up to their commitments in that covenant, God promised to make a new one. The New Testament records how God made that new covenant and what life is like under that agreement between God and people.

Page 38   So Jacob-Israel: The man Israel became the founding father of a nation by the same name. It was common practice in the Middle East for tribes or nations to be named after a noteworthy patriarch. Jacob's brother Esau, nicknamed Edom ("red"), gave his name to a nation southeast of Israel. Two nations east of Israel, Ammon and Moab, were named after great-grandnephews of Abraham.

Page 49   "Sea of Reeds": This was probably one of the large freshwater lakes between the Gulf of Suez and the Mediterranean Sea. The Hebrew name Yam Suph, "Sea of Reeds," included what we now call the Red Sea, the gulfs of Suez and Aqabah, and these lakes. Greek translators rendered Yam Suph as "Red Sea," and some modern commentators think the Israelites crossed that large saltwater body. But the Hebrew name in Exodus could mean one of the gulfs or lakes, and most scholars lean toward the latter.

Page 97   Allowing an evil spirit: It seems that while psychological problems can come from chemical imbalance, responses to childhood trauma and other causes, evil spirits can also be involved. Yahweh lets them attack people who give them permission by choosing to reject him. If people want to serve darkness, he lets them reap the results in hopes that they will come to their senses.

Page 105   Our current book of Psalms: Scholars debate whether the label "of David" in the headings of the psalms always means David wrote the psalm, or whether it sometimes means the psalm was dedicated to him. Also, the headings of the individual psalms were written according to later tradition, well after the original psalm was written, so they're not considered part of inspired Scripture. In this chapter we've treated the traditional headings as accurate, but it's the psalms themselves that really matter.

Page 110   A collection of wedding songs: Some scholars think one of Solomon's court poets composed the Song of Songs for one of Solomon's weddings. Others see it as a collection of poems gathered together and dedicated to Solomon. Others think he wrote it himself. As noted above, our general practice in this book is to follow traditional understandings about the authors of books. There is wide room for disagreement about authorship when a book doesn't say who wrote it. The Song says it belongs to Solomon, but that could equally mean a dedication. Likewise, Ecclesiastes alludes to Solomon, but it doesn't clearly claim him as author.

Page 199   Darius's son Xerxes: Other Bible versions translate this name as "Ahasuerus." Xerxes and Ahasuerus are the Greek and Latinized Hebrew forms of this king's Persian name.

Page 282   The Corinthians entirely misunderstood: There seem to have been more people recognized as apostles than just Paul and the Twelve. Paul includes Apollos with himself and Peter in 1 Corinthians 3:1–4:13, where he speaks of "us apostles" (1 Corinthians 4:9). Barnabas, Epaphroditus, Silas and Timothy also receive the title (Acts 14:1-4; Philippians 2:25—translated "messenger"; 1 Thessalonians 1:1; 2:6-7). Then there were those Paul called "super-apostles" or "false apostles" (2 Corinthians 11:5, 13), whom the Corinthians considered apostles but who were not sent from God. The term may have had a fluid meaning; the Twelve certainly held an authority in the international community that Epaphroditus or Timothy did not.

Subject Index

Scripture Index